THE REVIEW *of* CONTEMPORARY FICTION

FLANN O'BRIEN: CENTENARY ESSAYS

FALL 2011 | VOL. XXXI, NO. 3

EDITOR

JOHN O'BRIEN

ASSOCIATE EDITORS

MARTIN RIKER

IRVING MALIN

GUEST EDITORS

NEIL MURPHY

KEITH HOPPER

MANAGING EDITOR

JEREMY M. DAVIES

BOOK REVIEW EDITOR

JEFFREY ZUCKERMAN

EDITORIAL ASSISTANTS

AARON KERNER

JEFFREY ZUCKERMAN

PRODUCTION

LAURA ADAMCZYK

PROOFREADERS

MADELEINE HAMLIN

AARON KERNER

EOIN RAFFERTY

REVIEW OF CONTEMPORARY FICTION
Fall 2011
Vol. XXXI, No. 3

The *Review of Contemporary Fiction* is published three times each year (March, August, November). Subscription prices are as follows:

Single volume (three issues):
Individuals: $17.00 U.S.; $22.60 Canada; $32.60 all other countries
Institutions: $26.00 U.S.; $31.60 Canada; $41.60 all other countries

ISSN: 0276-0045
ISBN: 978-1-56478-646-3

Partially funded by the University of Illinois at Urbana-Champaign and by a grant from the Illinois Arts Council, a state agency.

Indexed in *Humanities International Complete, International Bibliography of Periodical Literature, International Bibliography of Book Reviews, MLA Bibliography,* and *Book Review Index.* Abstracted in *Abstracts of English Studies.*

The *Review of Contemporary Fiction* is also available on 16mm microfilm, 35mm microfilm, and 105mm microfiche from University Microfilms International, 300 North Zeeb Road, Ann Arbor, MI 48106-1346.

Address all correspondence to:
Review of Contemporary Fiction
University of Illinois
1805 S. Wright Street, MC-011
Champaign, IL 61820

www.dalkeyarchive.com

THE REVIEW OF CONTEMPORARY FICTION

BACK ISSUES AVAILABLE

Back issues are still available for the following numbers of the
Review of Contemporary Fiction ($8 each unless otherwise noted):

William Eastlake / Aidan Higgins
William S. Burroughs ($15)
Camilo José Cela
Chandler Brossard
Samuel Beckett
Claude Ollier / Carlos Fuentes
Joseph McElroy
John Barth / David Markson
Donald Barthelme / Toby Olson
William H. Gass / Manuel Puig
José Donoso / Jerome Charyn
William T. Vollmann / Susan Daitch /
    David Foster Wallace ($15)
Angela Carter / Tadeusz Konwicki
Stanley Elkin / Alasdair Gray
Brigid Brophy / Robert Creeley /
    Osman Lins
Edmund White / Samuel R. Delany
Mario Vargas Llosa / Josef Škvorecký
Wilson Harris / Alan Burns
Raymond Queneau / Carole Maso
Curtis White / Milorad Pavić
Edward Sanders
Writers on Writing: The Best of The *Review of Con-
    temporary Fiction*
Bradford Morrow
Henry Green / James Kelman / Ariel Dorfman
David Antin

Janice Galloway / Thomas Bernhard / Robert
    Steiner / Elizabeth Bowen
Gilbert Sorrentino / William Gaddis /
    Mary Caponegro / Margery Latimer
Italo Calvino / Ursule Molinaro /
    B. S. Johnson
Louis Zukofsky / Nicholas Mosley /
    Coleman Dowell
Casebook Study of Gilbert
    Sorrentino's *Imaginative Qualities of Actual
    Things*
Rick Moody / Ann Quin /
    Silas Flannery
Diane Williams / Aidan Higgins /
    Patricia Eakins
Douglas Glover / Blaise Cendrars /
    Severo Sarduy
Robert Creeley / Louis-Ferdinand Céline /
    Janet Frame
William H. Gass
Gert Jonke / Kazuo Ishiguro /
    Emily Holmes Coleman
William H. Gass / Robert Lowry /
    Ross Feld
Flann O'Brien / Guy Davenport / Aldous
    Huxley
Steven Millhauser
William Eastlake / Julieta Campos /
    Jane Bowles

NOVELIST AS CRITIC: Essays by Garrett, Barth, Sorrentino, Wallace, Ollier, Brooke-Rose, Creeley, Mathews, Kelly, Abbott, West, McCourt, McGonigle, and McCarthy

NEW FINNISH FICTION: Fiction by Eskelinen, Jäntti, Kontio, Krohn, Paltto, Sairanen, Selo, Siekkinen, Sund, and Valkeapää

NEW ITALIAN FICTION: Interviews and fiction by Malerba, Tabucchi, Zanotto, Ferrucci, Busi, Corti, Rasy, Cherchi, Balduino, Ceresa, Capriolo, Carrera, Valesio, and Gramigna

NEW DANISH FICTION: Fiction by Brøgger, Høeg, Andersen, Grøndahl, Holst, Jensen, Thorup, Michael, Sibast, Ryum, Lynggaard, Grønfeldt, Willumsen, and Holm

NEW LATVIAN FICTION: Fiction by Ikstena, Bankovskis, Berelis, Kolmanis, Ziedonis, and others

THE FUTURE OF FICTION: Essays by Birkerts, Caponegro, Franzen, Galloway, Maso, Morrow, Vollmann, White, and others ($15)

NEW JAPANESE FICTION: Interviews and fiction by Ohara, Shimada, Shono, Takahashi, Tsutsui, McCaffery, Gregory, Kotani, Tatsumi, Koshikawa, and others

NEW CUBAN FICTION: Fiction by Ponte, Mejides, Aguilar, Bahr, Curbelo, Plasencia, Serova, and others

SPECIAL FICTION ISSUE: JUAN EMAR: Fiction and illustrations by Juan Emar, translated by Daniel Borzutzky

NEW AUSTRALIAN FICTION: Fiction by Murnane, Tsiolkas, Falconer, Wilding, Bird, Yu, and others

NEW CATALAN FICTION: Fiction by Rodoreda, Espriu, Ibarz, Monsó, Serra, Moliner, Serés, and others

NEW WRITING ON WRITING: Essays by Gail Scott, William H. Gass, Gert Jonke, Nicholas Delbanco, and others

GEORGES PEREC ISSUE: Essays by Perec, Harry Mathews, David Bellos, Marcel Bénabou, and others

SPECIAL FICTION ISSUE: ; OR THE WHALE: Radically abridged *Moby-Dick*, edited by Damion Searls

WRITING FROM POSTCOMMUNIST ROMANIA: Fiction and essays by Andrei Codrescu, Dumitru Tsepeneag, Mircea Cartarescu, and others

SLOVAK FICTION: Fiction by Johanides, Juráňová, Kapitáňová, Karvaš, Kompaníková, and others

EDITIONS P.O.L NUMBER: Tributes and excerpts by Marie Darrieussecq, Jacques Jouet, René Belletto, and Leslie Kaplan

THE FAILURE ISSUE: Edited by Joshua Cohen; fiction and essays by Gilbert Sorrentino, Keith Gessen, Richard Kostelanetz, Gary Indiana, Eileen Myles, William Gaddis, Helen DeWitt, and others

GILBERT SORRENTINO AND *MULLIGAN STEW*: Edited by Stefanie Sobelle; essays and fiction by Jonathan Lethem, Ammiel Alcalay, Jeffrey Frank, Gerald Howard, and others

Individuals receive a 10% discount on orders of one issue and a
20% discount on orders of two or more issues. To place an order,
use the form on the last page of this issue.

CONTENTS

THE REVIEW *of* CONTEMPORARY FICTION

EDITORS' INTRODUCTION: A(NOTHER) BASH IN THE TUNNEL

In 1951 the Dublin literary magazine *Envoy* devoted a special issue to its patron saint and presiding deity, James Joyce. In a magnificently rambunctious editorial entitled "A Bash in the Tunnel," guest editor Brian Nolan—aka Brian O'Nolan (or Ó Nualláin), aka Flann O'Brien, aka Myles na gCopaleen (or na Gopaleen)—sketched a rather cantankerous portrait of Joyce as an egotistical iconoclast: "James Joyce was an artist. He has said so himself. His was a case of Ars gratia Artist [art for the artist's sake]."[1] After mischievously comparing Joyce to Satan—"both were very proud, both had a fall"—Nolan relates an apocryphal tale told to him by an archetypal pub bore. The central conceit of this shaggy-dog story involves a man stealing a bottle of whiskey from a train's buffet car and secretly drinking it, alone, in the toilet of an empty carriage: "surely there you have the Irish artist," remarks Nolan, "resentfully drinking somebody else's whiskey, being whisked hither and thither by anonymous shunters, keeping fastidiously the while on the outer face of his door the simple word, ENGAGED? I think the image fits Joyce."

This elaborate and abstruse metaphor introduces more sober reflections, including the perceived relationship between comedy and religion in Joyce's writings: "Humour, the handmaid of sorrow and fear, creeps out endlessly in all Joyce's works . . . With laughs he palliates the sense of doom that is the heritage of the Irish Catholic." More than this, Nolan sees Irish Catholicism as being central to Joyce's worldview (although it could be argued that this particular vision of Catholicism says more about Nolan than it does about Joyce):

> It seems to me that Joyce emerges, through curtains of salacity and blasphemy, as a truly fear-shaken Irish Catholic, rebelling not so much against the Church but against its near-schism Irish eccentricities, its pretence that there is only one Commandment, the vulgarity of its edifices, the shallowness and stupidity of many of its ministers. His revolt, noble in itself, carried him away. He could not see the tree for the woods. But I think he meant well. We all do, anyway.

Although he admires Joyce intensely, Nolan remains skeptical of what he sees as Joyce's tyrannical notion of authorship: "Joyce spent a lifetime establishing himself as a character in fiction . . . Beginning with importing real characters into his books, he achieves the magnificent inversion of making them legendary and fictional. It is quite preposterous." Moreover, Nolan is suspicious of what he regards as Joyce's elitism and inaccessibility, especially in the "home-made chaosistry" of *Finnegans Wake* (1939).[2] Ultimately, Nolan concludes his broadside with a barbed (but still valid) comment about the hermeneutics of the literary-academic complex which have canonised Joyce at the expense of the "ordinary" reader: "Perhaps the true fascination of Joyce lies in his secretiveness, his ambiguity (his polyguity perhaps?) his leg-pulling, his dishonesties, his technical skill, his attraction for Americans. His works are a garden in which some of us may play."

Throughout his career, Brian O'Nolan—who was born a century ago this year—engaged critically and creatively with Joyce's legacy, both in his novels and in his long-running "Cruiskeen Lawn" column in the *Irish Times*. In retrospect, this Joycean auto-da-fé did O'Nolan no favours; in 1939, Seán Ó Faoláin complained that Flann O'Brien's debut novel, *At Swim-Two-Birds*, had "a general odour of spilt Joyce all over it,"[3] and this notion of O'Brien as a kind of diluted Joyce has dogged his critical and academic reception ever since. Ironically, Joyce himself declared O'Brien to be "a real writer, with the true comic spirit," but when Samuel Beckett met O'Nolan in Dublin and passed on the Master's praise, O'Nolan reportedly snarled: "Joyce, that refurbisher of skivvies' stories!"[4]

O'Brien's publisher, Longmans, had originally accepted *At Swim-Two-Birds* on the strength of a wildly enthusiastic report from its reader, the novelist Graham Greene, who compared it to *Tristram Shandy* and *Ulysses*: "I read it with continual excitement, amusement and the kind of glee one experiences when people smash china on the stage."[5] However, the first edition sold only 244 copies before Longmans' London warehouse was destroyed during the Blitz, and *At Swim-Two-Birds* sank into obscurity for over twenty years. As Myles na gCopaleen later claimed, Hitler "loathed it so much that he started World War II in order to torpedo it. In a grim irony that is not without charm, the book survived the war while Hitler did not."[6]

O'Brien's second novel, *The Third Policeman*, was completed in 1940. In its opening pages, a nameless narrator confesses that he has murdered an old man in order to get the money to publish a book on an eccentric philosopher, de Selby. As a consequence of his actions the narrator is transported to a hellish parallel universe populated by killers and madmen, and patrolled by three sinister policemen. It is at once an existential whodunit, an absurdist science fiction, a postcolonial allegory, and a dark Menippean satire. In its philosophical scope and comic vision it is arguably funnier than Joyce and bleaker than Beckett, and is now considered one of the first—and finest—examples of postmodernist literature. It was immediately rejected by O'Nolan's publishers, who wrote: "We realise the author's ability but think that he should become less fantastic and in this novel he is more so."[7] Disheartened and embarrassed, O'Nolan pretended to have lost the manuscript, and *The Third Policeman* remained unpublished until 1967, a year after his death.

His third novel, *An Béal Bocht*—from the Irish phrase "putting on the poor mouth," meaning to exaggerate one's own misery—was written in Irish, and first appeared in 1941. O'Nolan refused to render it into English, insisting that the intertextual playfulness of the work made it untranslatable. Linguistically accomplished and brutally funny, *An Béal Bocht* is both a celebration of the Irish language and a ritual slaying of sacred national cows. As O'Nolan wrote in a letter to Seán O'Casey (who had lavishly praised the book), "it is an honest attempt to get under the skin of a certain type of 'Gael,' which I find the most nauseating phenomenon in Europe. I mean the baby-brained dawnburst brigade who are ignorant of everything, including the Irish language itself."[8]

By 1941, O'Nolan had written three of the most innovative novels in the Irish canon, yet had received very little public acclaim: *At Swim-Two-Birds* was still out of print; *The Third Policeman* remained unpublished; and *An Béal Bocht*, by virtue of its Gaelic mode, was marginalized as inaccessible (it was eventually translated as *The Poor Mouth* in 1973). This lack of exposure, along with his deepening alcoholism, would adversely affect the quality of O'Nolan's later novels, *The Hard Life* (1961) and *The Dalkey Archive* (1964), which most Flanneurs regard as inferior stuff.

In *A Colder Eye* (1983), the critic Hugh Kenner summed up the traditional view of O'Nolan's literary career: "Was it the drink was his ruin, or was it the column? For ruin is the word. So much promise has seldom accomplished so little."[9] Whatever about the drink affecting his work—although that too may be open to question—this myth of underachievement is certainly worth debunking; in fact, while Flann O'Brien floundered, his alter-ego, Myles na gCopaleen, flourished.

Myles na gCopaleen's satirical column in the *Irish Times*, "Cruiskeen Lawn" ("full jug"), appeared several times a week, virtually without interruption, from 1940 to 1966. Of the seven anthologies of Mylesiana currently available (the best of which is *The Best of Myles*), none of them fully capture the anarchic spirit of the enterprise (Myles frequently transgressed the boundaries of his own column in order to comment on neighbouring items). As the modern successor to Jonathan Swift, Myles's comic anecdotes are invariably underpinned by his acid deconstructions of the established order. Over its twenty-six-year history, his column became a collective monologue of what he called the "Plain People of Ireland": a mosaic portrait of everyday madness in the Irish Free State. Some critics now regard it as his magnum opus.

In 1943, *Time* magazine published a profile of O'Nolan entitled "Éire's Columnist." Elusive as ever, O'Nolan compounded the myth of the author by fabricating a fake biography for himself. Although Myles later dismissed it as a "superb heap of twaddle that would deceive nobody of ten years of age,"[10] the profile (by Stanford Lee Cooper) does convey the subversive energy of his writings:

> Erudite, ironic, he devotes many a column to the hilarious, systematic destruction of literary cliché, to parodies of Éire's leprechaun literature and the red-taped verbiage of Government service, to absurd home-economics hints. He is an unsparing, beloved critic of devotees of Irish, who overuse Éire's national tongue; a subtler critic of the clerics who are not unaware of his innuendo.[11]

Brian O'Nolan died of cancer on 1 April 1966. In recent years, he has gradually been acknowledged as a writer of genuine international importance. With academic conferences being held as far afield as Singapore and Vienna in 2011 to mark his centenary, and with several new scholarly publications already in the pipeline, the traditional view of O'Nolan as a "lesser Joyce" seems set to change. O'Nolan's works are a garden in which all of us may play.

In this special centenary issue of the *Review of Contemporary Fiction*—devoted, appropriately enough, to the patron saint and presiding deity of Dalkey Archive Press—it is heartening to see so many new and established scholars picking up the gauntlet thrown down by "A Bash in the Tunnel" some sixty years ago. Although the essays in this collection are autonomous in themselves, and employ a diverse range of critical methods and cultural contexts, there are certainly some recurring themes and patterns. (Whether or not this constitutes a paradigm shift in O'Nolan studies, we leave that for others to judge.)

First, although James Joyce is mentioned sporadically, there are none of the paralysing comparisons of old, and O'Nolan finally seems to be emerging from the murky Joycean shadows. (In truth, that particular anxiety of influence was as much a paper dragon constructed by critics as it was a fictional golem created by O'Nolan.)

Second, and related to this, is the issue of comparative analysis, and this current volume usefully compares O'Nolan to writers outside of the Irish tradition—Dante, Nabokov, Calvino, Alfred Jarry, Graham Greene, etc.—as well as to less well known Irish writers such as Tomás Ó Criomhthain and Sheridan Le Fanu.

Third, this more internationalist approach—reflected in the cultural backgrounds of the contributors themselves—brings with it an openness to new (or neglected) modes of thinking, which are less dependent on "Theory" (as it used to be known), and more indebted to classical and contemporary philosophy, aesthetics, philology, and even theology.

Fourth, this broad church of opinion actively tackles the significance of the Catholic church in O'Nolan's writings. On this scheme, O'Nolan is still a postmodernist and a Menippean satirist, but as he said of Joyce in "A Bash in the Tunnel," "all true blasphemers must be believers."

Fifth, this new critical dispensation allows for a new and productive engagement with the increasingly hoary debates about modernism and postmodernism, which have tended to dominate much recent O'Nolan criticism. While postmodernism—and other hyphenated variations of the word—is still a presence here, it is not the primary critical frame it once was in the 1990s. Although the issues that have characterised the postmodern debate—meaning (or the lack thereof), epistemological collapse, narrative instability, self-consciousness, etc.—remain in play, they do seem to be finding their purchase within wider philosophical frameworks.

Sixth, and finally, the essays in this current volume—which cover most of O'Nolan's major writings—have as their textual focus *The Third Policeman* rather than *At Swim-Two-Birds*. If the high point of self-conscious, game-playing metafiction has passed, perhaps it is inevitable that *The Third Policeman* now takes centre stage; brilliant as it is, *At Swim-Two-Birds* has tended to distract readers and critics from the more subtle and nuanced complexities of O'Nolan's "lost" masterpiece.

The opening essay in this collection, "The Hidden Narrator" (first published in 1995), is from a writer increasingly regarded in some critical quarters (including our own) as the direct descendant of Joyce, Beckett, and O'Brien.[12] Aidan Higgins recalls a bizarre encounter with O'Nolan in the early 1960s, and this Mylesian anecdote gives way to a more serious meditation on a writer who had effectively refined himself out of existence: "Myles surrounded himself with fantasy . . . and the face he saw observing him in the mirror was no longer his own; he could go anywhere, do anything; camouflaged within his pseudonyms he had become invisible."

Following on from this discussion of identity and invisibility, Thierry Robin considers the "paradoxical energy and inventiveness" that Flann O'Brien "devoted to the illustration of that formal void" in his fiction. Drawing on the contemporary French philosopher Clément Rosset, Robin demonstrates how "O'Brien explores the infinite 'idiocy' of the universe," particularly in *The Third Policeman*. As Robin concludes, "O'Brien's corrosive prose and its postmodern quality amply illustrate the paradoxes of our times, the permanent quest for a local particular identity and the simultaneous craving for universal answers echoing cosmic conundrums or . . . void."

Robert Lumsden continues this theme of voidance in *The Third Policeman* using the tools of classical rhetoric to illuminate "a cannily told story." Lumsden's close reading is informed by a number of fertile philosophical concepts, including Parmenides' ideas on "the nature of being and its relation to not-being," Nietzschean recurrence, and the Freudian uncanny. As the author admits, "To set Parmenides and Flann O'Brien alongside each other is to seek for a consanguinity of perception, not lines of influence," but the evocation of classical philosophy is apt and revealing.

Carlos Villar Flor takes a more theological approach to the existential themes identified in *At Swim-Two-Birds* and *The Third Policeman*. Utilizing the emergent field of "Christian Literary Theory," Flor examines some of the theoretical and practical gaps between competing views of O'Brien as a postmodernist and as a Catholic writer. His close reading is governed by a radical reconfiguration of several literary concepts, including "the implied author" and, in a witty coinage, "the implied censor." As Flor concludes, O'Brien remains a postmodernist who "just happens to be a Thomist."

Jennika Baines also considers the importance of Catholic faith and revelation in O'Brien's writings, especially in *The Third Policeman*. Drawing on Catholic writers and theologians—Augustine, Loisy, Cardinal Newman, Graham Greene—she makes a strong case for O'Brien as a Catholic writer, without ever being reductive or moralising: "While it is reductive to read *The Third Policeman* as any sort of morality tale or Catholic allegory, the novel does confront, albeit in an ultimately devout way, some of the incomprehensible facts of Catholic faith, mysteries and revelations."

Maciej Ruczaj offers a somewhat different interpretation of *The Third Policeman*, one which considers the possibility that it *is* a "morality tale" of sorts. Ruczaj proposes that "a reading of O'Brien's novel centred on the theme of the netherworld and realized by means of an analogy with Dante's *Commedia* makes it possible to resolve the inherent paradox between the heteroglossic poetics of the novel and the dimension of the 'morality tale' at the heart of the text."

Anthony Adams, in "Butter-Spades, Footnotes, and Omnium," adopts a different set of intertextual priorities, and considers *The Third Policeman* in terms of Alfred Jarry's 'Pataphysics. Nonetheless, even within this new paradigm, crime and punishment remain constant themes: "*The Third Policeman* presents a curiously confusing hell in which inventiveness and verbosity pose greater dangers than any corporal punishment." For Adams, the synthesis of 'Pataphysics and metafiction in *The Third Policeman* "creates a world whose most uncanny quality is also a diversion: the key that would unlock this set of boxes is itself another box."

Joseph Brooker extends the European contextualisation of O'Brien by considering how much Nabokov's *Pale Fire* resembles O'Brien's work. While much of the focus is on *The Third Policeman* ("Anon is to de Selby as Kinbote is to Shade, the 'beloved old conjurer' whose last work he obsessively annotates"), Brooker also broadens the discussion to include other works by O'Brien. His discussion of English as a second language in the work of both Nabokov and O'Brien is particularly informative: "Both were writers whom history had strung across languages, and hence made them more watchful . . . Both are at once peculiarly at home in [English] . . . and peculiarly detached from it."

W. Michelle Wang also detects a resonance with the European novelistic tradition by reading O'Brien's first novel in the context of Italo Calvino's concepts of lightness and weight, and focuses on "how structural lightness is created in *At Swim-Two-Birds* through the subtraction of weight from its characters and narrative structure." Wang's comments on the way that the "semi-porosity [of characters] gives them the license to drift between narrative levels in flagrant transgressions of the ontological worlds they are supposed to inhabit" are convincing, and they extend a recurring interest in O'Brien's complex narratology in this issue of the *RCF*.

Neil Murphy similarly positions O'Brien's early fiction within a broad European fictional tradition, extending from Sterne and Diderot to Nabokov, Calvino, and Kundera, arguing that the relative failure of O'Brien's *The Hard Life* can be explained by its abandonment of the distinctive aesthetic characteristics that were central to the success of the earlier novels. He argues that *The Hard Life*, as a satire, is poorly executed and that it deviates "from the world of sublime invention and daring imaginative risks that we find in the first three novels" and fails to provide "the self-containment, the inner cohesion that the most successful storyworlds offer."

Val Nolan, alternatively, switches the focus back to an Irish context by assessing a hybrid blend of Irish fantasy and science fiction in *The Third Policeman* and *The Dalkey Archive*. The focus of Nolan's essay is largely on O'Brien's "portrayal of the confrontation between the rational and the irrational, a conflict characteristic of much of the Irish fantasy tradition." The essay considers the influence of Gothic fabulist Sheridan Le Fanu, and this gives substance to the subsequent discussion of the figure of de Selby, one of those "fantastical 'leisured bachelors'" so common to the Gothic genre.

Brian Ó Conchubhair offers a close analysis of O'Brien's Gaelic novel, *An Béal Bocht* (*The Poor Mouth*), by painstakingly considering the marginalia in Brian Ó Nualláin's personal copy of Tomás Ó Criomhthain's *An tOileánach*, which serves to reposition *An Béal Bocht* as a postmodernist text. This original approach uses archival material that both emphasises the author's Irishness and manages to build a theoretical bridge between O'Brien's Irish-language novel and the postmodern frame most frequently used to define *At Swim-Two-Birds* and *The Third Policeman*.

Flore Coulouma's discussion of "Cruiskeen Lawn" in terms of Bakhtin's dialogic imagination makes a good case for considering the newspaper column to be a major part of the author's canon. The author's consideration of Myles na gCopaleen's *diglossia*—"the complementary use of two languages or dialects within one speech community, based on the opposition between official and vernacular languages"—offers critical insight into the complex language issues inherent in the author's bilingualism.

Amy Nejezchleb, similarly, focuses on a text that has received little or no critical response, the unfinished novel *Slattery's Sago Saga*. Reading it in a socio-historical context, she illustrates how it represents a significant departure for O'Nolan who here re-trained his satirical guns on American Modernization, and Ireland's connection to it: "*Slattery's Sago Saga* is an effort to recast painful historical events in both America and Ireland through rhetorical tactics that Brian O'Nolan polished over the decades. Complicating the novel's execution is O'Nolan's uncertainty as to whether he should write in the mode of Flann O'Brien or Myles na gCopaleen—that is, as a novelist experimenting with formal devices or as a satirical commentator on national events."

The diverse nature of these distinctive perspectives eventually gives way to a series of patterns and threads of significance, many of which speak of the critical expansion in O'Nolan scholarship in recent years. Since Anne Clissmann's pioneering work in the mid-1970s, more than twenty additional book-length studies of O'Nolan's work, as well as hundreds of book chapters and articles, have been published. In this special centenary issue the international profile of O'Nolan studies is also apparent, both in terms of the literary and philosophical traditions that he is situated in, and the range of critical perspectives that are trained on his work. And, while several of the essays remind us of the importance of the Irish context, they simultaneously situate it beside postmodernism, the dialogic imagination, Irish-American history, and speculations about O'Nolan's position in the atomic age.

While one must, of course, resist the temptation to assert too emphatically the critical significance of a single gathering of essays, it does appear that the individual essays in this special issue together signify a distinct movement towards an internationalisation of critical context, and a deepening of the philosophical frames that are used to open up new lines of commentary and evaluation. That Flann O'Brien is no longer primarily seen as a poor man's Joyce or Beckett, and has been rightly re-contextualised in a range of different scholarly discourses, is cause for much optimism. So too is the fact that these essays are written both by established O'Nolan scholars and by a whole new generation of younger scholars, indicating that the author's best work retains a strong and increasing relevance for literary studies. Furthermore, they are drawn from many geographical regions, ranging from Ireland, Britain, and the United States (the traditional centres of O'Nolan criticism), to a range of continental European countries including the Czech Republic, Spain, France, and Italy, with several contributors hailing from Asia and Australia. On his one-hundredth birthday, it is fitting that O'Nolan's true critical context is beginning to declare itself.

Neil Murphy & Keith Hopper
Sligo-Kerry-Oxford-Singapore, 2011

NOTES

1   Brian Nolan, "A Bash in the Tunnel: An Editorial Note," *Envoy* 5.17 (April 1951), James Joyce special issue: 5–11, repr. Flann O'Brien, *Stories and Plays* (1973; London: Grafton, 1991), 199–208. An online version of this essay is available on the Dalkey Archive Press website: <http://www.dalkeyarchive.com/book/?GCOI=15647100273550& fa=customcontent&extrasfile=A126232F-B0D0-B086-B60AEA9B32ABDFDD.html>.

2   Elsewhere, commenting on *Finnegans Wake*, Myles wrote: "Joyce has been reported as saying that he asked of his readers nothing but that they should devote their lives to reading his works. Such a method of spending a lifetime would be likely to endow the party concerned with quite a unique psychic apparatus of his own. I cannot recommend it." See Myles na Gopaleen, "Finnegan," *The Hair of the Dogma: A Further Selection from "Cruiskeen Lawn,"* ed. Kevin O'Nolan (London: Grafton, 1987), 154.

3   Seán Ó Faoláin, *John O'London's Weekly*, quoted in Anthony Cronin, *No Laughing Matter: The Life and Times of Flann O'Brien* (London: Grafton, 1989), 92.

4   Aidan Higgins, "The Hidden Narrator," *Asylum Arts Review* 1.1 (Autumn 1995): 2–7. A variation of this article appeared under the title "The Faceless Creator," *The Recorder: The Journal of the American Irish Historical Society* 8.1 (Spring 1995): 30–35.

5   Graham Greene, Reader's Report on *At Swim-Two-Birds* for Longmans Green Ltd., later quoted as blurb on the original Longmans jacket of *At Swim-Two-Birds* (1939), repr. *Alive-Alive O!: Flann O'Brien's At Swim-Two-Birds*, ed. Rüdiger Imhof (Dublin: Wolfhound, 1985), 41.

6   Myles na Gopaleen, "Cruiskeen Lawn," *Irish Times* (4 February 1965), quoted in Anne Clissmann, *Flann O'Brien: A Critical Introduction to his Writings* (Dublin: Gill & Macmillan, 1975), 78.

7   Patience Ross of A.M. Heath & Co. (11 March 1940), quoted in *A Flann O'Brien Reader*, ed. Stephen Jones (New York: Viking Press, 1978), 31.

8   Brian O'Nolan, letter to Seán O'Casey (13 April 1942), "A Sheaf of Letters," ed. Robert Hogan and Gordon Henderson, *The Journal of Irish Literature* 3.1 (January 1974), ed. Anne Clissmann and David Powell, Flann O'Brien special issue (California: Proscenium): 75.

9   Hugh Kenner, "The Mocker," *A Colder Eye: The Modern Irish Writers* (New York: Knopf, 1983), 255.

10   Myles na Gopaleen, "Cruiskeen Lawn," *Irish Times* (13 April 1960).

11   Stanford Lee Cooper, "Éire's Columnist: An Interview with Brian O'Nolan," *Time Magazine* (23 August 1943): 90.

12   See Neil Murphy, Introduction, *Aidan Higgins: The Fragility of Form: Critical Essays and Observations*, ed. Murphy (Dalkey Archive Press, 2010), 13–20; and Keith Hopper, "Rory Rides Again," *Times Literary Supplement* (2 April 2010): 3–4. Online version: 'Aidan Higgins, The Writer's Writer' (31 March 2010): <http://entertainment.timesonline.co.uk/tol/arts_and_entertainment/the_tls/article7082554.ece>.

AIDAN HIGGINS

The Hidden Narrator

Paper read at Irish Writers' Centre,
19 Parnell Square, Dublin,
on 2nd March 1995.

Around this time of year twenty-nine years ago Flann O'Brien, that phantom figure, had taken to his bed, afflicted with all manner of ailments, and was sinking into his last decline. On April Fool's Day, 1966, he passed away, appropriately enough.

I met Myles once; and this evening here thought I might give you some account of that . . . you can hardly call it "a meeting."

* * *

It fell to my lot once to read a paper at UCD.

After the reading a lady of surpassing beauty with cornflower-blue eyes sailed up to say, "I liked your line *Only ghosts see the wind.*"

What I had in fact written was "Only goats see the wind." A thought lifted from *The Worm Forgives the Plough*, a title which John Stewart Collis had pilfered from William Blake.

When wild goats had the run of the place we may assume that their perceptions of the surroundings qua surroundings were sharper than those of the domestic variety that came later. Their innate knowledge of upwind and downwind were strategies for survival; at every moment of their existence they knew where they stood, as goats; so they soon learnt to "read" the wind. This useful knowledge has atrophied in us humans; we have no such firm ground to stand on. "Ill half seen" was Beckett's knacky formulation.

And wasn't it Collis who had overheard Yeats humming poetry to himself in a bluebell wood above in Coole Park? The thin, nervy, edgy voice flitting up and down the emotional scale had reminded him of another voice. But where had he heard it? In Munich? *Ja!* Herr Hitler captivating the Bavarian ladies in a Munich drawing room.

When the Dictator addressed immense crowds he flew off the handle; it was his way of controlling them. But was the power emanating from the podium or from the people? This spellbinding orator knew how to wind them up, get them on their feet. Goering and Goebbels were bludgeon and rapier, cosh and hypodermic; Dr Goebbels sounded as charged-up as Jim Jones the madman of Guyana, distraught with power, who in turn was oily as Bob Guccione the odious coxcomb of *Penthouse*, purveyor of wet dreams.

Who spake of the void endlessly generative, of the dark varnish of public moralising? Nietzsche?

Gore Vidal and Paul Bowles (*The Sheltering Sky, Let It Come Down*) were indifferent novelists who had independently agreed that the novel was on its last legs and would be quite dead at last in spite of all within their separate lifetimes, and possibly extinct by the middle of the coming century, the very noisy oncoming one.

Readers (a quiet breed) would become extinct. The few remaining would know each other by whispering titles, as Freemasons exchange secret hand-signals. Readers of serious literature would have become a secret confraternity, lending out dog-eared and annotated copies of Martin Buber and Søren Kierkegaard.

Certainly the rapid onrushing manner in which children are quickly weaned on software and CDs in the nursery, the TV screen (always glowing, howling) replacing Nanny and Granny, with hardcore porn available at adolescence, confirms the worst fears of Huxley and Orwell, neither of whom, in their worst imaginings, could have imagined Desert Storm.

The kids of the next century are in for a hammering, a pasting, a Kursk tank battle on the air and ground, miles high, miles deep, for the hearts and minds of innocents. The kids demand their kicks and turn-ons. They'll get it, pressed down and running over.

Pictures are easy.

The flickering images on the screen are idle and arbitrary as the antics of a bored baboon caged in the zoo and idly playing with straw, dying of boredom. It's a discontinued tale that they, the viewers, gape at, an occupation fit for idle baboons and simpletons, which our great-grandchildren will have become with Sky Sports and Murdoch's morons numbed in millions, passive dupes.

But where will the readers be?

By AD 2045 both Paul Bowles and Gore Vidal will have paid their debt to nature. It is disputable whether either ever wrote a novel, properly speaking. They were just airing prejudices, posturing, stalling. The writing of a novel is a mysterious process, an inspired form of daydreaming. It is not what Saul Bellow calls "cosying up" to the reader, to which Mr Updike (for example) is very prone.

Flann O'Brien certainly wrote two novels, before he began airing prejudices in two other polemical works full of pawky jokes and flatulence.

When I first began to be published some thirty-five years ago by John Calder in London, Irish writers were thin underfoot and rarely seen around. They tended to be self-effacing if not exactly invisible. Nothing much was stirring on the home front. Both *More Pricks Than Kicks* and *Murphy* were out of print, as was Flann O'Brien in two languages, and *The Third Policeman* lost. We had to make do with Austin Clarke and *Men Withering*.

At the old Abbey, the very seat of infection, amid the creaking of ancient corsets and the spent smell of stale porter, *The Rugged Path* ran forever, to be succeeded by fare no less stodgy, *The Righteous Are Bold*. While over the way, at the Metropole, an American tear-jerker movie, *The Best Years of Our Lives*, was breaking all records and all hearts.

The Bovril sign still flamed above College Green.

Frank O'Connor, Francis Stuart, and Francis MacManus, the doughty penmen of the past, had a faded look about them, sere as withered leaves or the sepia heroes of old celluloid, Gene Autry and Tom Mix forever riding off into the sunset. Young Beckett aged twenty-seven had just contemptuously dismissed our entire poetic tradition, rigid as an apostolic succession: "Antiquarians and others, the former in the majority."

The relative obscurity of those poor pen-pushers of yore was in striking contrast to the extreme visibility of the pushy pen persons of today who come into prominence from one Booker or Whitbread prize to the next.

Each new generation of writers loathes the generation immediately in front and the generation immediately behind; and I should know, with seven titles out of print or remaindered, having come through three such baptisms of fire. The self-effacing Señor Borges wrote somewhere that he would like nothing better than, under an assumed name, to publish a merciless tirade against himself, his entire oeuvre.

"B. Traven" was an elusive fellow with several identities at his disposal; all different, none known, all fake. Nor was that his "real" name; he kept that secret and died unknown.

What remains constant is the intractable nature of the given material. In a prose draft or *aide-mèmoire* to his poem "Coole Park, 1929," Yeats wrote, for his eyes alone: "Each man more than himself through whom an unknown life speaks." And later: "I am a crowd, I am a lonely man, I am nothing."[1]

The diplomatic garden gnome Harold Nicolson noted in his diary that every family had its secret sayings, picked up from reading and set circulating within the closed family circle; a coda or little language known only to initiates. He was of course thinking of privilege, *his* privilege, the Nicolson and Sackville-West tenure, the God-given rights of upper class English to appreciate Earl Grey tea at four in the afternoon, served up in thin china tea-service; as they would appreciate the novels of Jane Austen, each thin and tasteful as well-sliced cucumber sandwiches. Lobster and cutlets in aspic were for the gentry. *Don Giovanni* at Sandler's Wells: "For as long as Wimpole Street remains, civilisation is secure," qua *Flush*.

Earl Grey tea served up punctually at four in the afternoon with muffins constituted their notion of high art, an art that became them; hence the huffiness and stuffiness of Bloomsbury.

Punctuality begat propriety which begat politeness which in turn begat order which begat good manners which is largely a question of obeying one's best—as opposed to one's worst promptings; above all following good sound common sense, for those lovers of the finer amenities. Art for the Woolfs and the Nicolsons and the Sackville-Wests was largely an affair of good manners. Something to be enjoyed with one's equals (Mrs Dalloway and Lily Briscoe and those twittery debs in *The Waves* of whom I can only recall Rhoda). Art concerned itself with good breeding and good taste, equals to equals on the croquet lawn and tennis court.

Virginia Woolf mocks Septimus Smith, the suicide clerk who impales himself on railings, for being unlucky enough to have been born Septimus Smith, thus born to inevitable set-backs (a common clerk, a nothing much), even though it was she herself who had named him thus in the novel *Mrs Dalloway*.

Yeats's own even more hierarchical notion of the common man, your average bloke, the chap on the top deck of the Clapham omnibus, was "Jones of Twickenham." For Yeats the unthinkable would be Dagenham. No. 7 Eccles Street was more than a bad address; it was an unthinkable place. Yet Joyce mocks Bloom by giving us an inventory not only of Bloom's worldly possessions but the sad inventory of his dreams. Dreams of *more* possessions for the little home which Bloom dearly loves, Joyce implying that Bloom has no taste.

Now if the unthinkable occurred and the Nicolsons or the Woolfs were cordially invited to tea with the Joyces, they would have been dismayed to find a non-fictional squalor as bad as the fictional squalor they so deplored, with no guarantee that Jim's terrible old man (all too real) would remain reasonably sober.

Virginia Woolf had dismissed James Joyce as a low-bred fellow and to this day English critics as sound and level-headed as Sir Victor Pritchett have entertained certain reservations about the unappealing sordidness of *Ulysses*, sordidness being the natural terrain of low-bred fellows.

The sound and stinks of Bloom at stool or the spectacle of Bloom abed, lying upside down in order to ardently kiss Molly's bum, for that close intimacy is foisted upon us readers, must have been deeply offensive to the finer sensibilities of Mrs Woolf.

The idea of the Blooms being invited to tea with Virginia and Leonard in Sussex or with Vita and Harold at Sissinghurst is too ludicrous to contemplate.

Like the infamous rubric above the gate of the death-camp, over Sissinghurst flew a banner with the bold device "C P O J D W T K !" which decoded read: Certain People One Just Doesn't Wish To Know.

Virginia Woolf was herself smothered in good taste; indeed she probably died of it. Behind Mr Dalloway one detects the willowy form of Mrs Miniver.

During the last widow-making war, which (some would wish to aver) had nothing to do with us, our Emergency, Miss Elizabeth Bowen of Bowen's Court was co-opted into British intelligence to act as a sort of unpaid lady spy operating in Dublin and Cork, planted as a mole in Mitchelstown. She was briefed by Harold Nicolson of the Foreign Service, told to keep her ear to the ground and report back to him. She mentions this in a chatty indiscreet letter to her false friend Virginia, so it cannot have been very serious spying.

Writing is in any case a form of spying, and can even be an exalted form of spying and betrayal (step forward Monsieur Genet). Behind any text of any value lurks the sub-text.

Our family had adopted certain catch-phrases from *At Swim-Two-Birds*, Flann O'Brien's (real name Brian O'Nolan) great comic work, about which I'd like to talk.

As part of its secrecy, a monstrous practical joke, the entire stock of Longman's first edition went up in flames early in the London Blitz, along with Beckett's first novel, *Murphy*.

At Swim has a strong sadistic streak amid deft touches of vernacular lunacy, insouciant as the death-wish that runs, or dances, through the work of Synge. The torture scenes in *At Swim* and the cold-blooded account of the murder of old Mathers in the first page of *The Third Policeman* must remind us that our ancient progenitors (Joyce's "horde of jerkined dwarfs"), the daddies of us all, were a rapacious lot and liked to play skittles with human skulls. Philosopher egoarch Ussher used to argue that we Irish are a deeply conservative race; but I wouldn't be so sure.

And we had our own spy amongst us.

Nobody knew what he looked like and he operated under a number of pseudonyms, working certain pubs off the fashionable areas, processing his information from his office in the Scotch House back to HQ at 31 Westmoreland Street, to be published twice or thrice a week in smooth, learned Gaelic in a column in the *Irish Times* that was so much Double Dutch to editor Smyllie, most of the subs, and ninety-nine per cent of the readership.

The Plain People of Ireland were a match for Joyce's Citizen, when it came to chauvinism and bigotry.

Myles surrounded himself with fantasy, for which potent spirits (distilled) would be fuel, preservative and afterglow. With five half ones aboard, the Swords Road began to resemble nothing on earth, and the face he saw observing him in the mirror was no longer his own; he could go anywhere, do anything; camouflaged within his pseudonyms he had become invisible.

He even contrived to make himself persona non grata on our freshly established television network. The great hygienic leveller and homogenising Irish Washing Machine that was to create a living saint from material as saccharin as Gay Byrne could not even begin to swallow such an intractable subject as Flann O'Brien or Myles na gCopaleen or however he (Brian Ó Nualláin) preferred to be known.

I had the honour to appear with him on an early arts programme with Ben Kiely, Tony Cronin, and the publisher Allen Figgis. The plan was to get your man sober into the studio and endeavour to keep him that way by dosing him with nothing stronger than Vartry water. They didn't know their man, slippery as an eel.

In strolled he with Big Ben (scarcely a good augury for sobriety). Ben, as the Pope O'Mahony before him, was strong on Irish genealogies and family trees and had already discovered that he and Myles were kinsmen and bloodbrothers, the Mookse and the Gripes close as arse and shirt-tail, Omagh and Tyrone; were, verily, forty-second cousins, twice removed.

Myles sat himself down at the round table and as if by magic a ball of malt appeared out of one cuff. In no time at all he had the table and in less time than it takes to tell he had wound himself up into a fury and begun to launch into a diatribe against "them"—the shower of bastards or present set of bastards, the gurriers, bogmen, turnip-snaggers, chancers, upstarts, mountebanks or persons of inferior education who had the country in the state it was in, and was on the point of naming names when a message on yellow paper was swiftly conveyed to the Anchorman and the proceedings brought to an abrupt close before charges were preferred and libel writs began to fly.

Television sets were few in those far-off halcyon days when Lemass "led on" and my mother was upstairs in a Ranelagh flat with a Protestant neighbour who had TV, sitting on the edge of her seat, on tenterhooks at the prospect of seeing her lad on television with the famous Flann O'Brien, whose face and form were unknown even in his own adopted city. If anybody saw him shuffling along Clifton Avenue they wouldn't have know who it was; it might have been anybody.

But RTE, the national grid, in its wisdom quickly substituted *The Dubliners* in raucous mid-gig for the arts programme which had been going out live and unrehearsed until Myles put the kibosh on it; and there was the bold Ronnie Drew bearded to the eyeballs, belting out "The Rattle a da Thompson Gun," which greatly astonished my ma.

She watched this heavily bearded rascally fellow rasping out this sorry subversive stuff, turned to the good neighbour (a Miss Turner) to whisper: "And I never knew Aidan played the guitar."

Meanwhile in the studio Myles had turned to me, I not having appeared on camera or uttered a single word good, bad, or indifferent in the course of a very long thirty minutes of what I believe is called Prime Time, in Tube speak, and inquired how had it "gone down," evidently under the impression that I was one of the sound-engineers.

"Grand," I said. "It went down grand."

We were then told we could disperse.

Consternation in the control box!

Myles, a ruffianly muffler wound about his neck, was backing down the corridor, lighting up a fag. When politely asked where his cheque could be sent to, he replied that he could accept no remuneration. His German publisher retained all subsidiary rights and he (Myles) "shouldn't be here at all." Mad Sweeny was persona non grata everywhere and had no pot to piss in. I later received, through the post, a small cheque for my non-participation and a covering letter of apology from the Producer, Jack White.

We repaired, as the saying goes, to McDaid's, the ruin of many. For Myles I ordered up a double Jameson and set it down before him. When civilly asked whom he had to thank for this bounty I replied as civilly, "Another admirer of *At Swim-Two-Birds*," not aware of how much he detested the novel, or its fame. He felt about it rather as Yeats felt about "The Lake Isle of Innisfree," or as Beckett felt about *Murphy*: he *abominated* it.

As I sat by him I was not aware of being in the presence of a sharp observer, for his glance tended to stray about; I had the impression of a shadowy presence, a spirit collapsing inward (with many a sigh); the oblique gray hooded eyes, evasive, guarded, and secret, scarcely saw me. He was an intensely indrawn man. Behan, occasionally astute, said you had to look twice to make sure he was there at all.

Anecdotalists and alcoholics prefer not to catch your eye. Myles's attention was fixed on someone else out there, far removed from me. The dehydrated tongue shot in and out lizardlike, moistening the thin lips, two front teeth prominent, ball of malt atremble in hand. He threw me an evasive look and spoke out of the corner of his mouth.

"You ought to be ashamed, and you a Christian Brothers' boy."

I had been transformed, thrice, into other beings viz.,

Ronnie Drew, Lord of Fleadh,

an RTE sound-engineer, and now the broth of

a Christian Brothers' boy.

The revival of *AS2B* by MacGibbon & Kee in 1960 and its progress through ten printings as a Penguin Modern Classic had something of the marvellous about it, though its success continued to puzzle and sorely vex the author for as long as he lived. He had instructed Tim O'Keeffe, his new publisher, that no jacket photo was to appear and absolutely no biographical details for this second edition. When a photo in dim profile did appear with one of the many reviews, Myles repudiated it; it wasn't him.

Few knew him by sight.

It added a spice of the subversive to the mischievous nature of the column, "Cruiskeen Lawn" (The Full Measure? The Brimming Jorum??) appearing now in cultured Gaelic, now in lordly English, with woodcuts purporting to be the author's own; one depicting a horse and carriage being driven smartly through an Act of Parliament conveniently suspended across the roadway. No mast-head image afforded any clue as to the identity of the author who claimed to write editorials on the progress of the war now raging in Russia. He was said to live in high style at Santry Great Hall with a titled da, Sir Myles na gCopaleen. The column had a secret following, as with the cultured Gaelic-speakers who could follow *An Béal Bocht*. Its true circulation must have greatly exceeded the actual print-run. Odd people read it in out-of-the-way places. Old Martin O'Donnell sniggered over the masterly Gaelic in an ingle on In-ishere; I knew two hash-house cooks in Texas who independently devoured *At Swim* for it had made that remote place—Dublin circa 1942—close and familiar. I knew a Welshman who landed a job in what was Radio Rhodesia by reciting *A Pint of Plain Is Your Only Man* for the audition. And Borges reviewed it favourably in Spanish for a women's publication in Buenos Aires soon after it came out.

When out of print its fame had spread. Copies were lent around. Under-graduate Philip Larkin discovered it and he lent it to Kingsley Amis who lent it to John Wain, an improbable trio of admirers. It inspires affection perhaps be-cause *you cannot imagine the author;* it came out like spontaneous combustion. Dylan Thomas thought it would make a fine present for a dirty boozy sister.

Shabby thought-wracked Stephan Dedalus with his Italian-sounding name is an idealised version of the even shabbier young Joyce, as lawyer Gavin Stevens is an idealised version of William Faulkner (formerly Falkner) or as Malcolm Lowry can be vaguely discerned behind the preposterously disguised Sigbjorn Wilderness or William Plantagenet, that redoubtable trio of crashing bores in false beards.

Lowry was Plantagenet as much as he was Kennish Drumgold Cosnahan, Ethon Llewlyn the fake Welshman, or the equally fake Manxman Roderick McGregor Fairhaven (Lowry was never very good at inventing names). He was all his own heroes rolled into one and was himself his own half-brother (preposterous "Hugh") of the deeply absurd novel *Under the Volcano.*

All was posturing, manifestations of an alcohol-induced self-aggrandisement, a puffing up of the old alter ego, the one with pretensions (head-staggers?). But where is the author of *At Swim-Two-Birds,* tell me that? Strangely absented; the fellow who disowned his own book is nowhere to be seen, refined out of all existence.

I was told that a photo of him did exist, taken at a golf outing of the Dublin Diplomatic Corps, which hung in the bar of Delgany Golf Club, of which I was once a member. The French representative Monsieur Goor was in it, as was Bertie Smyllie the pipe-puffing monstrously fat editor of the *Irish Times,* with his no less corpulent obituary writer Eamonn Lynch; with some IT staffers lolling on the grass, presumably Golf and Political correspondents, and Myles.

I found it.

The group might have been a Ralph Steadman illustration for one of the unpublished or forgotten novels, a lost novel with himself a character in it. Not the narrator, no; a walk-on character such as Pisser Burke.

I identified him in the back row.

Just the head and shoulders, chubby face shadowed by the brim of a black homburg; a dark-visaged, small-sized, portly savant with what appeared to me a *mensur* scar athwart one podgy cheek, lending credence to the rumour spread about in the famous *Time* magazine interview, where he had laid claim to be the illegitimate offspring of a Cologne basket-weaver. I forget to whom he attributed paternity; his own feelings about his own da being well disguised.

The life of language is in speech.

The O'Nolan family had two languages at their disposal. Those bilingual Ó Nualláins of Strabane had smooth Tyrone in the home, and didn't approve of *At Swim-Two-Birds,* which seemed to hold the family up to derision. As with Mahatma Gandhi shrivelled up on the pyre, the Gandhi family couldn't make head or tail of him. Myles was rather an enigma to his brothers and sisters, (some of whom ended in a nunnery) as no doubt he would have been for his father, had he lived. The novel was a far cry from weepy Mother Machree and the cuddly yokels beloved of Somerville and Ross. I myself could never stomach that great anthropomorphic lie about Mother-Eire-our-mother-dear spread about like slurry by O'Flaherty.

Even if Joyce himself had praised it, Beckett had absolutely refused to open it, from a sense of loyalty to the Master whom the young whippersnapper, aspirant to great things, had somewhat impertinently dismissed (to Sam's face) as "that refurbisher of skivvies' stories." A sally that might have gone down well in the Palace or the Pearl Bar but failed to amuse Beckett.

The severe features of the great reductionist glares out from a poster on the cylindrical sides of a Berliner Litfassäule hard by Europa Centre, advertising NICHT ICH . . . Nicht Ich . . . Nicht ich . . . Nicht ich . . . Not I Not I Not I.

NOTE

1   Immigrant extraordinaire and fastidious sourpuss V. S. Naipaul, triply exiled, superstitiuously refused to number the pages of his early fictions; could not even bring himself to affix the name of the author to his books (a colleague wrote it or typed it in, V. S. Naipaul); on all official forms his occupation was given as "a broadcaster." He was the genie in his own bottle.

THIERRY ROBIN

Representation as a Hollow Form, or the Paradoxical Magic of Idiocy and Skepticism in Flann O'Brien's Works

> "... the beauty of reading a page of de Selby is that it leads one inescapably to the happy conviction that one is not, of all nincompoops, the greatest." (O'Brien, *The Third Policeman* 92)

As James Joyce was reported to say, O'Brien is definitely "a real writer with the true comic spirit." This is all the more savoury if one bears in mind the equivocal relationship O'Brien had with the famous exile. Yet it would be restrictive to think O'Brien is *only* a comic writer. Of course his works can be described as "funny," but then the whole contradictory semantic scope of the adjective has to be taken into account and explained, to prove relevant to his writings. For not only is his literary output amusing but also strange and then, more often than not, outlandish. Undoubtedly, one of the key motifs developed in O'Brien's works is that of the absolute singularity—not to say quirkiness—of reality and hence, the hollowness of all attempts at its representation, be it performed at a scientific, literary, social, historical or purely linguistic level. Beyond O'Brien's postmodern deep awareness of the limits of language as a tool to account for this original intrinsic singularity, what is striking is the unabated paradoxical energy and inventiveness he devoted to the illustration of that formal void or cul-de-sac best epitomized in his masterpiece *The Third Policeman* and de Selby's nonsensical theories purporting to explain real phenomena or banal things ranging from nightfall to houses and roads.

The contemporary French philosopher Clément Rosset's apposite analysis of reality and knowledge proves profitable to shed light on these matters, for he actually posits the same fundamental ambivalent uneasiness that characterizes hubristic—and often comical—attempts to grope for the essence of reality. Quoting from Ernst Mach who saw the world as "a unilateral entity," Rosset goes even further, asserting that "reality in general is made of singular objects, which are, as an indeterminate set, unidentifiable" (Rosset, *L'Objet singulier* 22). He adds that "objects, which are by essence indescribable, are all the more evocative of reality since their description is difficult to achieve."[1] The adjective he uses to describe reality may initially baffle unprepared readers; it is "idiotic," or "*idiot*" in French, an ambiguous concept I intend to develop in this essay. One cannot help but think of MacCruiskeen's ineffably delirious inventions on reading these lines.[2]

In this essay, my contention is precisely to show how relevant this concept of *idiocy* pertaining to reality unexpectedly proves to be with respect to O'Brien, a postmodern writer fully aware of the illusionistic and limited aspects of all fictions and representations. To do so, I will explore language, the notion of individuality, and history, be the latter defined as typically Irish or as a general field of research in humanities. I will also endeavor to assess the value of O'Brien's skepticism, which alternates between a bright postmodern hypercritical relativistic canon, as in *The Third Policeman,* and a conservative "malcontent mode"—for instance typified by acrimonious pieces on James Joyce[3] or his trifling diatribes lashing at Cork University's chairman Alfred O'Rahilly[4] or the Irish Electricity Supply Board.[5]

Consistently, the epistemology developed in O'Brien's novels is eminently disastrous. *At Swim-Two-Birds* describes novels, tongue-in-cheek, for what they are or should be: "a self-evident sham" (19). De Selby in *The Third Policeman* is the great gravedigger of science, philosophy and theology, probably apophatically the greatest of "nincompoops." His extensive manuscripts are said to be illegible (145), and "the commentators, it is to be feared, have not succeeded in extracting from the vast store-house of his writings any consistent, cohesive or comprehensive corpus of spiritual belief and praxis" (144). The periphrastic irony pervading these statements is simply admirable. As for *The Poor Mouth,* it is probably the most comical novel ever published on the frail and aberrant nature of any given national tongue, though the Irish language comes out of this excruciatingly funny novel as not even superior to porcine squeals, especially after chapter three. Paradoxically and conversely it is one of the most vivid, cogent, invigorating examples of literature in Gaelic. This is the O'Brien paradox, namely that vast fields of human knowledge and activity are simultaneously satirized, deconstructed—for satire implies deconstruction—and criticized, shown as futile, incomprehensible while concurrently rendered fascinating, puzzling, and thought-provoking. This double movement also unexpectedly foreshadows the Beckettian dilemma as regards artistic creation and vanity at large thus summed up in *The Three Dialogues* in 1949:[6] "The expression that there is nothing to express, nothing with which to express, nothing from which to express, no power to express, no desire to express, together with the obligation to express." O'Brien precisely inhabits that poetic and epistemological gap between reality and art, fact and fiction, silence and blather, facts and obscure scientific discourse. He indefatigably explores the stupendous domains of the human predicament, that is the boundless stupor and amazement deriving from the absurd condition humbly mortal mankind is afflicted with.

Against this dark forbidding backdrop of final silence, O'Brien explores the infinite "idiocy" of the universe, and the actual "paranoid" processes requested to make sense of precisely senseless occurrences. To do so, one should appreciate the whole polysemy or potential range of meanings characterizing the concept of "idiocy." Originally, the word *idiot*, which comes from ancient Greek *idios*, "one's own, pertaining to oneself, private,"[7] was used disparagingly in ancient Athens to refer to one who declined to take part in public or political life. A strong association between individual singularity and idiocy ensues from these common origins.

The concept of "idiosyncrasy" illustrates the same self-centered, egocentric streak. According to Clément Rosset, in his essay entitled *Reality A Treatise on Idiocy*,[8] reality is precisely what cannot ever be duplicated. What stems from this statement is that something real is doomed to be singular, unique; representation and copy, which are mere metonymical, superficial constructs, are not to be confused with the original reality and engender in turn new singular entities. Therefore reality, and this of course applies to historical reality too, is "idiotic" so to speak, so hermetically unique though multifarious, peculiar, unfathomable, and undecidable in its origins and causes as well as in its finality and goals, that it does not make obvious sense, except perhaps through the ideological prism of retrospective reconstruction. As the French saying goes, wisdom always comes late: *on est toujours sage après l'événement.*

I used the analogy "paranoid processes to make sense," because, quite aptly, paranoia is usually described in clinical terms as excessive, delusional, untamed, proliferating knowledge.[9] Paranoid patients usually think they know more about reality than actual circumstances entitle them to, and consequently lose track of it. Paranoia is a pathology characterized by an extreme propensity to see intentions and purposes (especially negative ones) everywhere. As a matter of fact, hallucinations loom large in our corpus: they are mentioned in the epigraph in *The Third Policeman*: "Human existence being an hallucination containing in itself the secondary hallucinations of day and night . . . it ill becomes any man of sense to be concerned at the illusory approach of the supreme hallucination known as death" (3). Later, the reader also finds out that "a journey is a hallucination" (50). In Myles na gCopaleen's column, the "facts of experience" are described as a "grim corpus of hallucinations" (O'Brien, *Further Cuttings from Cruiskeen Lawn*, 98). "Hard-to-believe hallucinations" are also evoked at the end of *At Swim-Two-Birds* (238).

In his works, O'Brien carefully follows the same half-idiotic, half-lunatic pattern in his descriptions of diegetic reality. Descriptions and situations, which initially purport to provide the reader with a sensible insight into the mystery of things, deliberately turn out to be derisive and shallow, especially and more delightfully so if they initially aimed to convey some sense of "intelligence"—that is, literally displaying that uncanny capability of reading (cf. Latin "legere") between (cf. "inter") the metaphorical lines of a situation or story, collecting relevant data amongst chaos.[10] The equation made between knowledge and illusion is reinforced by a strange empty rhetoric made of repetition and mirror games. *The Third Policeman* is literally littered with odd though little-enlightening statements or phrasings such as "Omnium is the essential inherent interior essence which is hidden inside the root of the kernel of everything" (110), "inside the interior of my inner head" (103), "we are going where we are going" (78), "I must now go to where I am going" (104), "informative information" (77), "happenings could happen" (91), "extraneous externalities" (91), "... how certain the sureness of certainty is" (87).

Redundancy, pleonastic reasoning, tautology, ironic apophasis, to name but a few instances of the recurring rhetoric displayed by O'Brien, inform *The Third Policeman*, along with fractal-like hypodiegetic stories and objects illustrating the *matryoshka* principle and the impossibility to delve into the essence and signification of things. *Surface* is a very apt concept in O'Brien's writings, which often look like loops where the beginning and the end coincide. All his works point in the same direction, building a coherent aesthetics of eventual absence (of absolute meaning, of a rational subject, of psychological depth). In *The Third Policeman*, the police barracks looks false and unconvincing, Sergeant Pluck's head sounds hollow like a watering can when tapped with a finger. Even the narrator ends up suffering from the same vertiginous syndrome: "How can I know why I think my thoughts?" he asks (117). And he goes so far as to think of himself as an endless series of self-contained, receding entities that is "A body with another body inside it in turn, thousands of such bodies within each other like the skins of an onion, receding to some unimaginable ultimatum" (118). The subject as a stable, reliable, autonomous concept is made impossible. As Keith Hopper says (*Portrait* 264), O'Brien uses anti-Cartesianism as a starting point in his novel. Descartes' cogito is called into question. "I" may think but this does not bring about any valid knowledge about being in general or "my" being in particular. Ihab Hassan's table of differences between modernism and postmodernism can be put to profit to show that *The Third Policeman* is clearly a peculiar postmodern work bespeaking play, antiform, chance, deconstruction, antithesis, absence, dispersal, intertext, rhetoric, metonymy, combination, rhizome, surface, etc., as opposed to symbolism, purpose, hierarchy, totalization, synthesis, presence, depth, etc.

Figures and symbols of order—including that of the author—are carefully deconstructed and criticized. In O'Brien's short story "Two in One," Kelly's and Murphy's (that is, the employer's and the employee's) lives seem to be eventually interchangeable as if devoid of any intrinsically unquestionable—I was about to say further than skin-deep—identity. Fundamentally, in his writings, O'Brien explores the faults in logic and language. "Two in One" is a powerful investigation into the superficial dimension of the social self. In a postmodern fashion, the surface is the limit. So-called truth can only be glimpsed through a rhizomatic approach as described, for instance, by Gilles Deleuze. The final outcome of the short story atomizes all ideas of causality and control as regards the unfolding of events. Murphy, a taxidermist, thought he could kill and get rid of his boss Kelly, but eventually realizes he has become undistinguishable from him, only because he has donned his corpse's skin. The conclusion simply blurs the usual hierarchy and chronology of cause and effect: the murderer becomes the murdered victim and vice versa (326). The same happens to Noman who is *ab ovo* both murdered and a murderer in *The Third Policeman*. Clément Rosset resolves and sheds light on this seemingly paradoxical reasoning by analyzing the radically amphibological dimension of the very concept of *identity*:

> The thought of identity reunites and confuses the two opposite meanings of sameness and otherness, simultaneously and contradictorily referring to what is unequalled and to what equals something else. In a word, it is therefore impossible to conceive sameness without simultaneously implying the exact opposite . . . (*L'Objet* 20, my translation)

Amphibology implies that the same word or sentence may simultaneously refer to diverse, not to say conflicting, meanings. Adequately enough "identity" both refers to what is radically unique and cannot be copied and simultaneously to what is equal or identical, thus positing two opposite interpretations: that of absolute singularity and that of pure replication through identification. Singularity and sameness are eventually conveyed through the same word.

In *At Swim-Two-Birds*, diegetic levels also overlap and intertwine in an undecidable manner. As for the conclusion on the last page of *The Dalkey Archive*, it can be summed up by quoting "What had happened, after all? Nothing much" (203). This coherent aesthetics reveals the same patterns based on circularity, a rhizomatic perception of events refusing the hierarchy of depth, linguistic reflexiveness, aporetic idiosyncrasy: concepts thoroughly analyzed by thinkers such as Gilles Deleuze, Clément Rosset, or even Jacques Derrida.

Yet again ambivalently, O'Brien's prose both thoroughly debunks authority while conversely reasserting potentially skeptical and consequently conservative values, be they patriarchal, cryptically religious or aesthetically traditional. For if reality is impenetrable, and history a repetitious illusion, no progress is worth advocating or fighting for. In *The Third Policeman*, the end more or less repeats the beginning. *At Swim-Two-Birds*, as a talented original and farcical parody of avant-garde writing, also constitutes a clear, implicit indictment of over-sophisticated, gratuitous transgressions that (Joycean) modernism may be problematically, though complacently, rife with. Even *The Poor Mouth*, in its comical, repetitive palimpsestic dimension, points towards the same critical questioning of representation, be it national, literary, individual, or from a postcolonial or a deconstructive vantage point.

Crucially, language in *The Third Policeman* is anything but crystal-clear. It is often presented as unintelligible noise, from the narrator's father's voice, which sounds like a drone, in which the separate bits of words cannot be made out (8), to Old Mathers' final words, whose meaning oscillates between "I do not care for celery" and "I left my glasses in the scullery" (16). Language is so obscure that even when the phonemes seem to be accurately articulated they do not make sense. When John Divney talks about social justice, the narrator immediately concludes that he does not "properly understand the term" (15). In other words, the characters' ability to understand what is said or what is going on seems to be extremely tenuous. That lack of intelligence, or comprehension, fuels the *idiotic* representational agenda skillfully elaborated by O'Brien. Thus the narrator lacks understanding at all levels. He is constantly faced with a reality so strange, so unique, so singular, so abstruse that he cannot hope to describe what surrounds him through language, as when Noman happens to be trying to recover his loot—a black box—in Old Mathers' house. The situation is said to be indescribably subtle, yet momentous, ineffable. In other words again, the narrator remains dumbfounded. And of course later when *Noman*, that is the nameless narrator, starts speaking again, the process is seen as the production of gibberish, meaningless sounds, mechanical utterances: "suddenly I began to talk. Words spilled out of me as if they were produced by machinery. My voice, tremulous at first, grew hard and loud and filled the room . . . I am sure that most of it was meaningless . . ." (26). The reader delightedly spots many details reminiscent of a transhistorical brand of idiocy pointing towards the same Shakespearean "tale told by an idiot, full of sound and fury" (*Macbeth* 5.5.26–27). Beyond the negative isotopy which is apt to describe the hellish surroundings in which Noman evolves—ninety-one negative semantic units are to be found from page 53 to page 59 in the book,[11] which clearly reminds the reader that this is a novel of crime and retribution set in hell—what is striking is the astounding, unique strangeness[12] of the setting. Noman thus declares: "My surroundings had a strangeness of a peculiar kind, entirely separate from the mere strangeness of a country where one has never been before" (41). So much so that the narrator often finds it difficult to describe looks that are "too tricky for description" (49) in the same movement theorized by Jean-François Lyotard, who posits that postmodern literature is particularly concerned with presenting the unpresentable.[13] Incidentally, *The Third Policeman* concentrates postmodern traits and parables to an astounding degree for a book which was written some decades before postmodernity was thoroughly and problematically established by a constellation of thinkers. For instance, MacCruiskeen's inventions all revolve around the same representational aporias; his spear "is so thin that maybe it does not exist at all" (68–9), his series of matryoshka-like chests ends with a chest which is so tiny that it "probably does not exist at all" (113). In any case it is "nearly too nice . . . to talk about it," "it is unmentionable" (70). MacCruiskeen's magnifying glass also "magnifies to invisibility" (136). Similarly, the colour of the card inside the box which drove policeman Fox crazy is simply "not one of the colours a man carries inside his head" (154). In a Derridean way, it is "different," not to say "différant." Reality is so profuse, complex, *singular*, that it escapes perception and comprehension.

Characteristically human understanding in the novel generally seems to be of little avail to make sense of the words uttered or "shouted" by the quantum light mangle devised by MacCruiskeen. Grotesquely, the cryptic messages emanating from wrung light could be any of the following: "Change for Tinahely and Shillelagh!"; "Two to one the field!"; "Mind the step!"; "Finish him off!"; "Don't press so hard!"; "Second favourites always win"; "Two bananas a penny"; or something else entirely (110). Language is so uncertain, polysemous, that it becomes meaningless. Metaphorically, the reader is forced to acknowledge the perplexing nature of the signs or facts, which usually prompt scientific discourse. This idea of linguistics leading to nonsense because of the saturation of conflicting meanings or undecidable sounds is also at the core of *The Poor Mouth*, where it is stated that "good Gaelic is difficult but that the best Gaelic of all is well-nigh unintelligible" (44).

Yet again, paradoxically, O'Brien does manage to create an authentically Irish brand of postmodernism, which may sound like pure contradiction. But the way the Irish identity is presented is so carefully deconstructed, just as clichés on Irishness are, that the seemingly oxymoronic concept of "Irish postmodernism" seems justified.

Caustically, what O'Brien states is that the illusion of sense, beauty, and superiority are usually derived from total obscurity or idiotic blather, not to say—satirically—from brutal snorts and grunts, reminding one of Antoine Culioli's apothegm that comprehension is but an exception in general misunderstanding. Idiocy, nonsense, and insanity converge in the same direction. In *The Third Policeman*, de Selby, the "idiot savant," defines a house as "'a large coffin,' 'a warren,' and 'a box'" (22). In *The Best of Myles*, a collection of some of his best columns, O'Brien also describes Gaelic as a language so rich, so polysemous that it is incompatible with common sense. His target then turns out to be Father Dineen, the famous Irish lexicographer (1860–1934), whom he regards as a funny figure who worsened the hermetic nature of Gaelic by the finicky definitions collected in his dictionary. O'Brien, as a postmodern satirist, stretches this polysemy till it reaches hilarious nonsense, idiotic blather, of which here is an astounding example:

> *Cur,* g. *curtha* and cuirthe, m.—act of putting, sending, sowing, raining, discussing, burying, vomiting, hammering into the ground, throwing through the air, rejecting, shooting, the setting or clamp in a rick of turf, selling, addressing, the crown of cast-iron buttons which have been made bright by contact with cliff-faces, the stench

of congealing badger's suet, the luminance of glue-lice, a noise made in an empty house by an unauthorized person, a heron's boil, a leprechaun's denture, a sheep-biscuit, the act of inflating hare's offal with a bicycle pump, a leak in a spirit level, the whine of a sewage farm windmill, a corncrake's clapper, the scum on the eye of a senile ram, a dustman's dumpling, a beetle's faggot, the act of loading every rift with ore, a dumbman's curse, a blasket, a "kur," a fiddler's occupational disease, a fairy godmother's father, a hawk's vertigo, the art of predicting past events, a wooden coat, a custard-mincer, a blue-bottle's "farm," a gravy flask, a timber-mine, a toy craw, a porridge-mill, a fair-day donnybrook with nothing barred, a stoat's stomach-pump, a broken—

But what is the use? One could go on and on without reaching anywhere in particular. *(The Best of Myles* 278–279)

This hilarious semantic proliferation is outlandishly erratic and aptly prophesies in an extreme manner Derridean dissemination. What O'Brien does simultaneously is typically postmodern; by satirizing the neverending cycle of meaning production, he simultaneously deconstructs the very possibility to build sense univocally, calling the reader's attention onto the conflicting, annoyingly though inexorably centrifugal forces inherent to language and communication. The paradoxical outcome of this critical process operated by O'Brien is precisely the promotion of digression, of freakish associations—"a stoat's stomach-pump"—and bizarre combinations—"a wooden coat"—leading to slightly perturbing though joyful nonsense. What is finally asserted is twofold: the bizarre nature of reality, its ineffable, *idiotic* dimension, and the ensuing fractal nature of language forever missing its multiple referential targets. "But what is the use? One could go on and on without reaching anywhere in particular" (279).

The discourse on Ireland in O'Brien's works is treated with the same ambivalence. If Ireland is eminently recognizable as the setting for O'Brien's stories, it is simultaneously defamiliarized and described as strange. Most of the time it is even equated with a place which can only initiate puzzlement, incomprehension, amazement. Seamus Deane's interpretation of this radical Irish strangeness may prove apt. As a matter of fact, I think that any reader will agree with him when he declares in *Strange Country* that

> When a story is so fragmented that it cannot provide a climactic moment from which a "Whig interpretation" can be derived, there is no normalizing narrative procedure available. Or, there is none apparently available. In Irish discourse, the compensatory stratagem for this is the generation of a narrative of strangeness, the story or stories of a country that is in a condition that cannot be represented at all or that still has to be represented. (145–146)

And the leitmotif of strangeness is clear right from the start in *The Third Policeman* with the nameless narrator's father who repeats that Ireland is "a queer country" (7). Indeed queerness—with all its polysemous and retrospectively potentially homoerotic ramifications (think of the improbable Divney-Noman couple) I will not have time to dwell upon—makes up a postmodern mantra in the book. Thus the narrator and his father are "all happy enough in a queer separate way" (8). The same narrator—who at that stage is still alive so that strangeness cannot be caused by death or the anti-logic prevailing in hell—is sent to "a strange school" (8). The friendship developed between John Divney and Noman is also said to be "a queer one" (13). Old Mathers is also "a queer mean man" (18). In short, one could quote Noman who simply says in an atmosphere imbued with eeriness: "I was clearly in a strange country" (41). And Noman is of course reduced to his unintelligent condition, as shown in the following quotes: "'Very wonderful,' I said, 'but I do not understand you'" (68), "I did not understand his meaning, but I said that I agreed with him" (82), "Your talk . . . is surely the handiwork of wisdom because not one word of it do I understand" (84). The same insistence on strangeness and its correlative—that is, an apparent lack of intelligence of circumstances—seems to preside over Bonaparte O'Coonassa's story in *The Poor Mouth*: "My father never expected me because he was a quiet fellow and did not understand very accurately the ways of life" (13). The narrator's mother similarly states, when addressing the Old Fellow: "Any word and nearly every sound out of you are sweet to me, said she, but truly I don't understand what you're saying" (16). The Gaelic population seems to be plagued with that lack of wisdom or understanding, precisely understandable, in reversible postcolonial victimized terms. Hence even at the end of the story, Bonaparte repeats: "I never understood a single item of all that happened around me nor one word of the conversation nor my interrogation" (122). The same idiotic pattern looms large at the end of *The Dalkey Archive* with the narrator stating of Mick: "This speech of his own, as he heard it, sounded *strange* and pathetic . . . He was upset, and felt *a fool*" (202). Mick's girlfriend Mary insists on the same idea, saying to Mick: "You're just *a bloody fool*," to which statement Mick replies: "But *the bloody fool* you're going to marry?" (203) In the finale in the same book, this summary is also quite revealing: "What had happened, after all? Nothing much. They had *stupidly* lost each other, but only for a matter of hours" (203, emphases mine).

In *At Swim-Two-Birds*, the same emphasis on singularity is tangible right from the epigraph, which states that obviously "all the characters represented in this book, including the first person singular, are entirely fictitious and bear no relation to any person living or dead." And the thematic issue, already mentioned, of random foolishness, is clear at the end of the novel:

> But which of us can hope to probe with questioning finger the dim thoughts that flit in a fool's head? One man will think he has a glass bottom and will fear to sit in case of breakage. In other respects he will be a man of great intellectual force and will accompany one in a mental ramble throughout the labyrinths of mathematics or philosophy so long as he is allowed to remain standing throughout the disputations. (238)

Idiocy, in both its acceptations, incidentally opens and closes the book. The reader will doubtlessly notice that singularity is associated with all efforts at representation: "the mental ramble throughout the labyrinths of mathematics or philosophy." Coleridge's whole concept of the "willing suspension of disbelief" is also affected in what looks like a metafictional parody in *The Third Policeman*: "Apparently there is no limit, Joe remarked. Anything can be said in this place and will have to be true and will have to be believed" (86).

Of course, this "place" is precisely both hell and the book the "willingly gullible" reader is holding in his hands. *The Hard Life*, which is subtitled "an exegesis of squalor," in addition to being a dreary and critical presentation of a provincial Ireland, also focuses on the lack of understanding that plagues most human beings, as the narrator's brother Manus clearly summarizes in his lavish letter:

> Every day you meet people going around with two heads. They are completely puzzled by life, they understand practically nothing and are certain of only one thing—that they are going to die. I am not going to go so far as to contradict them in that but I believe I can suggest to them a few good ways of filling up the interval. (112)

Death, puzzlement, foolishness, incomprehension, and Pascalian diversion seem to pervade all the works by O'Brien. The main thread which runs through his writings deals with the gaps, faults, loopholes, chasms, and traps that separate reality and its desultory, fragmentary, unreliable doubles or attempted representations. Reestablishing the radical strangeness of reality and being, O'Brien questions the possibility of actual creation and also the stability of knowledge. By deconstructing all representations and discourses, he emphasizes antagonistic dimensions of language. This leads either to an ethos of transgression, quite in keeping with the postmodern reading of his works, or to a skeptical philosophy that reasserts the two arch-traditional poles of human experience, namely laughter and terror as analyzed by Clément Rosset (*L'Objet* 37), incidentally illustrating the ageless dialectics opposing comedy and tragedy.

The reader who follows Noman's and Bonaparte O'Coonassa's or even Mick's or Dermot Trellis's adventures oscillates between two codes of interpretation, that of infinite cruelty or that of exquisite idiocy. The same applies to the ulterior motives lying in O'Brien's subtext.

A careful reader cannot miss the fact that Noman discovered de Selby on the seventh of March (9), which is the day Thomas Aquinas died (in 1274). What is more, Policeman Fox happens to disappear on the twenty-third of June (154), which is the day Giambattista Vico was born (in 1668). The same cunning reader will certainly apply his mathematical abilities to the totaling of years—that is thirty-three—lived by the narrator when he is about to die (19). The all too predictable results of these exceedingly knowing operations will invariably oscillate between yet another cryptically obsessive attack on an exile called Joyce and his alleged inspirers, a series of unlikely yet possible co-incidences, or the timeworn continuation of a biblical parable on knowledge and sin: "it was for de Selby I committed my first serious sin" (9). In any case, the demanding, though self-centered, not to say idiotic, task of reading—as defined by Rosset—can never be innocent after reading O'Brien. It also flamboyantly illustrates metalepsis in Genette's narratological sense, and the blurring of boundaries between worlds. O'Brien's corrosive prose and its post-modern quality amply illustrate the paradoxes of our times, the permanent quest for a local particular identity and the simultaneous enduring craving for universal answers echoing cosmic conundrums or . . . void.

NOTES

1   Rosset, *L'Objet singulier* [*The Singular Object*] 22. My translation.

2   Chapters 5 and 6 in *The Third Policeman* contain various bizarre sets of objects devised by Policeman MacCruiskeen, an endless series of chests, an infinite spear, a light mangle, etc.

3   See "A Bash in the Tunnel," *Envoy*, vol. 5, no. 17 (May 1951). Repr. *Stories and Plays* (London: Paladin, 1986), 169–75.

4   See Myles's column in *The Irish Times* in April and May 1951. Repr. in *Further Cuttings from Cruiskeen Lawn*, 158–173. O'Rahilly is called a "thooleramawn," a "gawskogue," etc.

5   On the trivial controversy between O'Brien and the ESB, read Anthony Cronin's de-tailed biography: *No Laughing Matter, The Life and Times of Flann O'Brien*, 238–239.

6   These were initially published in the review *transition* 49 in 1949. They consist mainly of Beckett's views on art and more specifically three different painters' works.

7   Read Clément Rosset's essays *Le Réel Traité de l'idiotie*, or *Le Réel et son double* or even *Le Démon de la tautologie*.

8   That is my translation from the French *Le Réel Traité de l'idiotie*.

9   To know more about the semantic and clinical fluctuations in the apprehension of the concept of paranoia, one may refer to Aubrey Lewis, "Paranoia and paranoid: a historical perspective," in *The Journal of Psychological Medicine*.

10   The word *intelligent* is thought to come from these two Latin roots.

11

Negative semantic units	NO	NOT	UN-	DIS- DIF-	IM-/IN-/ IR-	NEVER	NONE NULL-
No. of occur- rences	28	19	19	8	12	3	2

12   If isotopy in semiotics according to Greimas can be defined through the repetition of the same semantic trait or unit, then *The Third Policeman* is rife with the isotopy of queerness, puzzling and strangeness. For instance, the adjective queer is repeated p. 7, 8, 30, 46, 47, 59, 69 (2 occurrences), 71, 80, 110, 115, 117, 161, 171 etc. Strange can be found p. 9, 37, 54, 74, 123, 162, 163 (2 occurrences), 202 etc. But the landscape in the book is also said to be "eerie," "unusual," "surprising," "recondite," "obscure," "astonishing," "peculiar," "mysterious," "enigmatic," etc.

13   Lyotard's initial definition of postmodernism stems from his criticism of the Kantian sublime in relation to painting, but applies to art and literature in general as he asserted in *The Postmodern Explained*:

> The postmodern would be that which in the modern invokes the unpresentable in presentation itself, that which refuses the consolation of correct forms, refuses the consensus of taste permitting common experience of nostalgia for the impossible, and inquires into new presentations—not to take pleasure in them, but to better produce the feeling that there is something unpresentable. (Lyotard 15)

WORKS CITED

Beckett, Samuel. *Trois Dialogues*. Paris: Les Editions de Minuit, 1998.

Cronin, Anthony. *No Laughing Matter: The Life and Times of Flann O'Brien*. London: Grafton Books, 1989.

Deane, Seamus, *Strange Country, Modernity and Nationhood in Irish Writing since 1790*. Oxford: Clarendon Press, 1997.

Deleuze, Gilles and Félix Guattari. *A Thousand Plateaus*. Minneapolis: Univ. of Minnesota Press, 1987.

Hassan, Ihab. *The Postmodern Turn: Essays in Postmodern Theory and Culture*. Columbus: Ohio State Univ. Press, 1987.

Hopper, Keith. *Flann O'Brien: A Portrait of the Artist as a Young Post-modernist*. Cork: Cork Univ. Press, 1995.

Lewis, Aubrey. "Paranoia and Paranoid: A Historical Perspective," *The Journal of Psychological Medicine*. Cambridge: Cambridge Univ. Press, 1970. (1:1, 2–12). Print. 09

Lyotard, Jean-Francois. *The Postmodern Explained: Correspondence, 1982–1985*. Trans. Don Barry et al., eds. Julian Pefanis & Morgan. Thomas Minneapolis & London: Univ. of Minnesota Press, 1992.

na gCopaleen, Myles. *An Béal Bocht*. Dublin, An Preas Naisiunta, 1941; English trans. Patrick C. Power, *The Poor Mouth*. 1973; London: HarperCollins, 1993; Normal, Illinois: Dalkey Archive Press, 1996.

—. *The Best of Myles*. Ed. Kevin O'Nolan. 1968; London: HarperCollins, 1993; Normal, Illinois: Dalkey Archive Press, 1999.

—. *Further Cuttings from Cruiskeen Lawn*. Ed. Kevin O'Nolan. 1976; Normal, Illinois: Dalkey Archive Press, 2000.

O'Brien, Flann. *At Swim-Two-Birds*. 1939; London: Penguin Books, 1967; Normal, Illinois: Dalkey Archive Press, 1998.

—. *The Dalkey Archive*. 1964; London: HarperCollins, 1993; Normal, Illinois: Dalkey Archive Press, 1993.

—. *The Hard Life*. 1961; London: HarperCollins, 1990; Normal, Illinois: Dalkey Archive Press, 1994.

—. *Stories and Plays*. 1973; London: HarperCollins, 1991.

—. *The Third Policeman*. 1967; London: HarperCollins, 1993; Normal, Illinois: Dalkey Archive Press, 1999.

—. "Two in One." *A Flann O'Brien Reader*. Ed. Stephen Jones. New York: Viking. 1967. 321–326.

Rosset, Clément. *Le Démon de la tautologie*. Paris: Gallimard, 1997.

—. *L'Objet singulier*. Paris: Les Editions de Minuit, 1979.

—. *Le Réel Traité de l'idiotie*. Paris: les Editions de Minuit, 1977.

—. *Le Réel et son double*. Paris: Gallimard, 1984.

ROBERT LUMSDEN

Voidence in *The Third Policeman*

"... thinking defies its own finitude, as if fascinated by its own excessiveness."
Jean-François Lyotard, *Lessons on the Analytic of the Sublime*

On the matter of a missing bicycle Sergeant Pluck advises Mr. Gilhaney: "... put your hands in under [the bush's] underneath and start feeling promiscuously the way you can ascertain factually if there is anything there in addition to its own nothing" (O'Brien 80). Pluck doesn't say: *start feeling about and that way you can ascertain*, but: *start feeling the way you can.* His injunction rides a hypothetical whose possibility the sentence also eliminates: *this is the way it would feel to ascertain the bicycle, if you could ascertain it.* (But you won't be able to.) The bits and pieces of bicycle which are found initially—a bell, a lamp—are a mockery of completeness. That he pronounces the (very) partial first retrieval "satisfactory" confirms the Sergeant's suggestion concerning the bicycle's essential nature, brought back whole or not (in due course it is recovered). It has no existence, except as the nothing it is.

The search for the token bicycle occurs in one of several simulated landscapes, especially those described in chapters three and six (40–3, 80–3, 88–9) where "Mother" Nature's blandishments, despite the narrator's initial passing sense of being "on the right track" (42), prove as disturbing as a pre-Raphaelite elaboration, a gesture of disclosure as the sign of something not disclosed. Such passages set out the narrator's state of being, though not his state of mind. He considers himself bound for his desire's destination which is, he supposes, happily complicit with his destiny.

That this landscape seems at first to chime with de Selby's characterization of the friendly road that "will always be discernible for its own self and . . .

lead you safely out of the tangled town" (38) makes its turn towards imitation the more unsettling when it comes. Apprehension is insinuated, settles, pervades.

The realization breaks upon us before it reaches the narrator: the world he perceives cannot be real, for a quietly devastating reason: it is too pleasant to be convincing. The beautiful degrades to prettiness. *Pilgrim's Progress* becomes *Pleasantville*. But O'Brien operates with something even deeper than disquiet at a hyper-articulated perfection; he strikes at desire itself. For if the beautiful is less than it seems at first sight to be, desire that takes the beautiful as a value sufficient in itself is compromised. There is a negative feedback from sense impression to affective predisposition which colours it distinctly. An infection of response passes from perception to whatever inclines us to arrange hierarchies of preference:

> My surroundings had a strangeness of a peculiar kind, entirely separate from the mere strangeness of a country where one had never been before. Everything seemed almost too pleasant, too perfect, too finely made. Each thing the eye could see was unmistakeable and unambiguous, incapable of merging with any other thing or being confused with it. The colour of the bogs was beautiful and the greenness of the green fields supernal. Trees were arranged here and there with far-from-usual consideration for the fastidious eye. (O'Brien 39)

Subsequently, this landscape is revisited in a number of passages apart from the one the narrator enters with Sergeant Pluck in chapter six, and on each occasion plenitude reviewed is charged with a kind of sparkling vacuity. In the perspective of this novel, to see life steadily is to see it flawed. An idea of nature is mocked, and with that, something more: the perceiver's very sense of himself as a coherent individual begins to weaken:

> Something strange then happened to me suddenly. The road before me was turning gently to the left and as I approached the bend my heart began to behave irregularly and an unaccountable excitement took complete possession of me. There was nothing to see and no change of

any kind had come upon the scene to explain what was taking place within me. I continued walking with wild eyes. (O'Brien 52)

The narrator next approaches a house—the police station—which "astonish[es]" him in seeming both dimensionless and inhabited, "as if it were painted like an advertisement on a board" (52). When the house is revisited near the denouement of the story (198–9), part of its presentation is a verbatim recapitulation of the narrator's earlier description, suggesting a version of the Nietzschean recurrence with the significant addition that the narrator is joined by the just-deceased John Divney, and the surrounding landscape undermines his powers of comprehension even more thoroughly than it had previously:

> It seemed ordinary enough at close quarters except that it was very white and still. It was momentous and frightening; the whole morning and the whole world seemed to have no purpose at all save to frame it and give it some magnitude and position so that I could find it with my simple senses and pretend to myself that I understood it. (O'Brien 198–9)

Parmenides

Though it should be conceded that no discursive critical framing is likely to prove adequate to a cannily told story, certainly not to this story, and that setting Parmenides and Flann O'Brien alongside each other should be done to look for lines of connection and disconnection rather than influence, the exercise does highlight enough of what might not otherwise have been apparent to make the imposition worthwhile. What becomes immediately clear is a fundamental point of departure from Parmenides in the novelist's text.

Philosophers of mind, being largely bound by the ratiocinative and discursive methods they favour, typically fall short of offering an experience of the "other" of language in describing it. Flann O'Brien's ability to place his reader in the midst of an experience of the unspecifiable, to put him or her affectively in the mix of the subject he presents, stands in sharp contrast even to such relatively recent of the metaphysical schools as the British idealists of the late nineteenth and early twentieth century. Even such fellow travellers as John M. E. McTaggart in his demonstration that our grasp of time is self-contradictory, and F. H. Bradley, the litterateur's logician who took T. S. Eliot's attention for a while, cannot help but hold at a ruminative distance that sense of estrangement in the ordinary they set out to define.

The contrast between the experience of reading Parmenides and Flann O'Brien on the infinite is even more marked than it is with more recent metaphysicians, perhaps because, standing as he does at or near the beginning of ontological enquiry in the Western tradition, the outlines of Parmenides' thought are more summary than those who have tended to give themselves to the enticements of elaboration.

It is a curiosity about Parmenides that his work belies its reputation for striking little flares of mystical *éclaircissement* in his reader. To the contrary, a number of passages show him shrinking from all possibility of discursive close encounter with the beyond of language in any of its forms, and especially the possibility of rendering non-being in accounts of it, the very territory Flann O'Brien readily occupies in *The Third Policeman*. Here is perhaps the clearest of such passages:

> Come then, I shall tell you, and you pay attention to the account when you have heard it, which are the only ways of inquiry that can be conceived; the one [says]: "exists" and "it is not possible not to exist," it is the way of persuasion (for persuasion follows upon truth); the other [says]: "exists-not": and "not to exist is necessary," this I point out to you is a path wholly unknowable. For you could not know that which does not exist (because it is impossible) nor could you express it. (Tarán 32)

The author who stands behind the narrator of the novel knows as well as does the philosopher the intractability of not-being to language. Even so, he chooses not only to speak of the matter, but to try to convey it. The difference between the two metaphysicians—how little O'Brien would have liked the word; fair game for a paragraph in a Parnassian *Cruiskeen Lawn*—is that the novelist is able to create an enduring feeling of the unspeakable, which the philosopher can only discuss. The fictional sense sticks, as philosophic discourse might not. But that is the edge (some) fiction has over (much) philosophy: it is of its nature to strike at affective responses more deeply than the languages contrived to explain them. O'Brien's text in this respect may be considered as a type of contra-Parmenides insofar as pressing against denotation is its principle means of creating a sense of experiencing not-being as both a paralysis and a tangible galvanizing interruption of ordinary life. We might at this point begin to think of the intelligence of the book as a thing apart, not only to distance Flann O'Brien's from the narrator's opinions, but to underscore this persistent crumbling of the authority implied in any report or description offered in this text, however apparently straightforward.[1]

It is because *The Third Policeman* speaks so convincingly of the untrustworthiness of ordinary appearances that its references to eternity are uncommonly persuasive, however much, or little, we manage to mean by that word. A familiar house proves depthless yet contains what appear to be actual people. An unexceptional thicket in a picture postcard countryside hides an elevator to a hellish eternity. Boxes contain smaller boxes to a point beyond invisibility. When so many impossibilities are woven matter-of-factly into a relishable entertainment, can not-being be so hard to swallow?

But there is a price to pay for entering fairyland. The question of assent at its most fundamental is raised at every turn of the road or shift of attention:

> I decided in some crooked way that the best thing to do was to believe what my eyes were looking at rather than to place my trust in memory. (O'Brien 26)

> I am becoming afraid occasionally to look at some things in case they would have to be believed. (O'Brien 82)

His senses unable to provide explanation of the abnormal, and reason proving consistently incapable of offering an understanding of the inherently puzzling, the narrator's only recourse seems to lie with his instinctual sense. But throughout *The Third Policeman* the instinctual is closely associated with the uncanny, which is not only unpredictable, but always potentially, and sometimes actually, terrifying.

The "astonishing piece of nullity" (101) at the heart of the narrative, the swerve from nihilism which keeps the book on the right side of whimsy, is often approached by way of a "rap" between a funnyman (Sergeant Pluck, in the quotation just given) and the narrator himself who is a "negative nullity neutralized and indeed rendered void" (102), not only in being measured against the death prepared for him by Pluck, but by everything, without exception, that happens to him away from Pluck's hangman's eye. The nurture-scape of the book has at its heart a tick that depletes speculation as surely and furtively as the invisible worm in "The Sick Rose" does celebration, and the novel in crowding both narrator and reader with wildly useless information feeds its appetite. Very soon, the expectation is well established in reader and narrator alike that the next piece of information is unlikely to do anything more than augment the mounting sense of irresolution that pervades the narrative. As Pluck might have put the matter, the bucolic traipse has become a plunge into cosmologic incomprehensibility rendered in prose of extraordinary exactness. The spirit of de Selby's footnotes has leaked into the text proper; a hyper-material enlightenment madness is brought to revelation's threshold by beguilement.

There is no nihilism in what the narrator proposes for himself in the larger part of his journey, however. The book's central, wicked, joke is that he continues to imagine himself a survivor as his world within and without falls steadily apart, projecting himself, albeit intermittently shaken, as one who expects to be brought, around the next turn in the road, to the box of useless wonders at the end of the rainbow.

The least of the novel's attempts to establish this "nullity" is by means of an apophatic exhaustion of names,[2] but the method frustrates reason more than it challenges feeling. It has too much of the treatise about it, as though a page were torn from a neo-Platonist's *Summa* and grafted onto the twentieth century text. The figure of Policeman Fox is a better throw at reassuring substantiation, with his "massive rearing of wide strengthy flesh, his domination and his unimpeachable reality" (180), but unfortunately for the narrator's desire for homecoming in his inherited world, Fox's reliability is compromised when he swaps the head on his shoulders for Divney's, and also by Fox leading him into Old Mathers' house, whose distressing distortions the über-Policeman treats as entirely normal. Neither of these measures has the purchase of Flann O'Brien's use of the uncanny, nor of his deployment of reference, whose anchorage in the objective is often as uncertain as it is boldly proclaimed.

The Uncanny, Avoidance and Voidance

According to Sigmund Freud, the appearance of the uncanny marks the partial return of repressed material, which the subject is trying, not altogether successfully, to refuse entry into consciousness.[3]

The narrator's spectacularly porous memory extends most tellingly from the Freudian point of view to his attempts to ignore, not Old Mathers' murder, but the sense of criminal responsibility that should naturally attach to it. Even more significantly, in addition to claiming not to know his own name, the narrator has "forgotten" his death, the circumstances of which are implied, though not disclosed (from the reader's point of view) near the beginning of chapter two.[4] Not until the novel's conclusion, after the reaction to him of John Divney, and his surprise at the appearance of the aged Pegeen Meers, does the narrator begin to recognize that his condition is in some fashion deathly, though not even at this point does he allow himself to admit what should be obvious: that as the living view such matters, he is, beyond all dispute and peradventure, deceased.

This is a repression so great that it holds even against the evidence of his co-conspirator perceiving him as a ghost. Although the narrator goes along with Divney's explicit claim that he is dead, there is constraint, resistance, signalled in the flat tone of his report:

> [Divney] told me to keep away. He said I was not there. He said I was dead. He said that what he had put under the boards in the big house was not the black box but a mine, a bomb. It had gone up

when I touched it. He had watched the bursting of it from where I had left him. The house was blown to bits. I was dead. He screamed to me to keep away. I was dead for sixteen years. (O'Brien 197)

Two factors converge to bring the sense of the uncanny to a pitch: the narrator's denial of death, especially his own, and, as Freud predicts, the charging of repressed material with uncanniness, which occurs at the precise point that reality and imagination become interchangeable in experience:

> ... an uncanny effect is often and easily produced when the distinction between imagination and reality is effaced, as when something that we have hitherto regarded as imaginary appears before us in reality, or when a symbol takes over the full functions of the thing it resembles. (Freud 244)

The distinction between the imaginary and what can be said with confidence to be real is of course a major theme of the book. But Freud's comment applies more particularly in this final merging of the police station or house as symbolic of the abnormal uncanny and the (fictional) substantiation of that presence. Similarly, in the book's final paragraph, John Divney is suddenly "there," fully present in the narrative rather than distanced as an object of the narrator's account of him. It isn't that Divney and the police house become more real, not even fictionally speaking, than they were the moment prior to Divney's death. Rather, these grounding opposites of perception show the very names they go by as insufficient to what we might be compelled to make of them. This, Freud tells us, is the proper setting and ambience of the uncanny.

A fictionalised reality substitutes for a sense of the real which the novel shows to be illusionary. Or the other way around. It doesn't matter, because the difference in *The Third Policeman* between these polar opposites of our waking state is only representational, the line between phantasmic and concrete not as fast as we suppose it to be when our minds are not meddled with by such iconoclastic slices of similitude as Flann O'Brien's book. In this fundamental matter, Freud might have said, had he been more postmodernist than eighteenth-century scientist, all fictional texts are uncanny. (For this, much thanks; had Freud chosen a less well-trodden path we would not have his account of the uncanny by which to illuminate such novels.)

Deixis[5]

Not even the uncanny is as useful in bringing intimations of the unknowable to bear in pursuit of "oppressive" mind-meddling as Flann O'Brien's sport with grammar and reference.

The gap that keeps opening in *The Third Policeman* between anaphoric and cataphoric reference (anaphoric: a phrase that draws meaning from other references within a text; cataphoric: a meaning yet to be identified within the text) continually denies the reader grounding within the text or even beyond it. That this displacement is done humorously should not take attention from the fact that it *is*, continually, done; that it is a powerful strategy which undermines the confidence we prefer to maintain that something said, if we but follow the thread of it diligently, will lead in due course to an object-thing whose substantial existence can be trusted.

Here are three typical examples of deictic shift, and the defensive laughter it compels. In the first, Sergeant Pluck is quizzing the narrator; in the second, the narrator declares tactically insincere sympathy with MacCruiskeen. In the third, Sergeant Pluck provides a thumbnail sketch of MacCruiskeen's character:

> "What is your pronoun?" he inquired.
> "I have no pronoun," I answered, hoping I knew his meaning.
> "What is your cog?"
> "My cog?"
> "Your surnoun?"
> "I have not got that either." (56)

> "Such work must be very hard on the eyes," I said, determined to pretend that everybody was an ordinary person like myself. (74)

"He is a comical man," said the Sergeant, "a walking emporium, you'd think he was on wires and worked with steam." (76)

In the first excerpt, pronominal reference is assailed where it seems most secure. Undermining the pronoun as a referential lynchpin has been foreshadowed early in the plot business with the narrator's ignorance about his name, but here O'Brien moves against nominalism altogether in mocking first person identity openly, the nearest we can come in a written text, as in existential encounters, to the security of ostensive definition. In the same stroke, a bridge is made with the central figure of the absurd, the wondrous trans-corporeal bicycle, so that grammar and lexis converge in the narrator's inability to lay claim to anything— of the categories on offer—that might be said to be essentially himself.

In the second excerpt, the phrase *such work* is anaphoric because Mac-Cruiskeen's business with the ultimately invisible sequence of boxes has been described—"explained"—at some length previously. Because that earlier description has been ridiculous, this later reference to it is void of sensible meaning. Seemingly anaphoric, the phrase awaits—and waits—substantiation. The comedic-earthy, so often a solace in uncertainty, remains suspended. A similar consideration holds, more subtly, of "eyes" in the phrase *[it] must be very hard on the eyes*, since eyes capable of working with invisible objects cannot be eyes in any sense we can find for the word. The term is referred, (apparently) anaphorically, to the figure of MacCruiskeen whose previous appearance might be expected to anchor this extra-logical sense, but what MacCruiskeen has been shown doing with boxes makes him an unconvincing agent of a new order of seeing. The two phrases throw hooks back into anaphoric reference, but the text is glacial to them; they find no purchase in reference.

Of the third passage, the reader wonders which of the three descriptions accurately represents MacCruiskeen, given that the terms divide into two groups, the first of which refers to human characteristics, and the second to a machine which only appears human.[6] And wonder is what we have and what we are left with. Neither intra-textual referencing, nor referencing by contextual knowledge, nor travelling in hope of the shaft of light from above, will be sufficient to rationalise this MacCruiskeen.

Such "descriptions" wear away assurance that the formal quality of statement and its semantics are square with each other at the point of delivering information, and this matters, greatly, because such categories represent compartments of experience with which we feel comfortable, inscribed in grammar and in mind. Representation in *The Third Policeman* is continually unsettling at this fundamental, pre-verbal, level.

There is no deictic *origo* in *The Third Policeman*. But it is not sufficient to say that about the book and no more, since alongside the evacuation of common sense from reference there is a growing feeling that the language of the novel itself coincides with the substance of the objects and events it reports; that the language of the book overlaps exactly with the absurdities and the instances of non-being it describes so that it wears the appearance of a sort of plenitude, finally. The *Third Policeman* is strangely filled with the impossible to talk about, in talking about it.

Reference without foundation and laughter at the brilliance of it, but not comfortable laughter, if we are aware of what Flann O'Brien is doing in this great book. There is no resting place for us in comedy, once we see that he is busy about what Parmenides thought inconceivable, which is to offer a convincing account of something that in good reason can only be experienced unmediated, if at all; to persuade his reader of what it would be to stand on the edge of the unutterable and see a little beyond it; if that were possible.

NOTES

1   This "intelligence of the text" cannot be O'Brien/O'Nolan because the originator of the impressions and opinions of the book and *in potentia* of numberless others cannot be represented by aggregate or by a line drawn through them. (This might be called the "bard is myriad-minded" argument for the freedom of the text.) The speaker-narrator of the novel is also unlikely to be one with its author because the text often stands in a superior relation to him, mocking his opinions and aspirations. There seems to be another narrator—call it N1—antecedent to the first-person reporter, and, on that account alone, a surplus of meaning impossible to ascribe either simply to the concept

narrator, or to Flann O'Brien or to Brian O'Nolan in any of the versions we might settle around those names. In this case it makes best sense to think of the text as a hovering of meaning between or among origins rather than a settling upon any one of them.

2   Pluck reports, of MacCruiskeen's mantelpiece box: "MacCruiskeen says it is not smooth and not rough, not gritty and not velvety. It would be a mistake to think it is a cold feel like steel and another mistake to think it blankety" (O'Brien 156). The method, of god-seeking by god-voidance, which has become associated in western metaphysics with the neo-Platonic Christian theologian pseudo-Dionysus, is redeemed by O'Brien's side-stepping of obvious choices suggested by the previous items in a sequence. In this quotation, for instance, "blankety" saves the sentence from bravura performance.

3   ". . . for this uncanny is in reality nothing new or alien, but something which is familiar and old-established in the mind and which has become alienated from it only through the process of repression" (Freud 241).

4   ". . . Most likely our fear still implies the old belief that the dead man becomes the enemy of the survivor and seeks to carry him off to share his new life with him" (Freud 242). In the last few lines of the novel, it is Divney who is "carried off" by the narrator, not the narrator who is taken by an always about to be specified imminent invasion, which is what he has feared.

5   "Pronouns, whose shifting reference relates to participants in the speech act, and demonstratives, whose shifting reference relates to spatial location . . . (are) 'deictic', effectively 'pointing' at some person or thing" (Dixon 189).

6   Commenting on this passage from Jaentsch, Keith Hopper sees the uncanny as being generally at work in most of the characterization of *The Third Policeman* (Hopper 99). While this is certainly a valid and evocative reading, in my view much of the effectiveness of the uncanny in the book depends on the suddenness of its intrusion into the lives of characters previously established as comically exaggerated, 'flesh-and-blood' presences. This is not only true of MacCruiskeen in the passage cited, but also of the unnamed narrator in the first dozen or so pages of the book, where the circumstances of his engagement with Divney, in particular, are given a realist presentation. The business between them in its early stages has an undertow of the sinister about it, but it is not yet uncanny, in my view. Hopper's description of the general application

of uncanniness applies, I think, more to the presentation of landscape in The *Third Policeman* than to O'Brien's characterization.

WORKS CITED

Dixon, R. M. W. *Basic Linguistic Theory 2.* Oxford: Oxford Univ. Press, 2010.

Freud, Sigmund. *The Complete Psychological Works Volume XVII (1917–19): An Infantile Neurosis and Other Works.* Translated and edited by James Strachey in collaboration with Anna Freud, assisted by Alix Strachey and Alan Tyson. London: The Hogarth Press, 1955.

Hopper, Keith. *Flann O'Brien: A Portrait of the Artist as a Young Post-Modernist.* 2nd edition. Cork: Cork Univ. Press, 2009.

O'Brien, Flann. *The Third Policeman.* London: HarperCollins, 2007; Normal, Illinois: Dalkey Archive Press, 1999.

Tarán, Leonardo. *Parmenides: A Text with Translation, Commentary, and Critical Essays.* Princeton, New Jersey: Princeton Univ. Press, 1965.

CARLOS VILLAR FLOR

Flann O'Brien: A Postmodernist Who Happens to Be a Thomist

There has been ample critical debate about the propriety of including Flann O'Brien among the portents or forerunners of postmodernist (either with or without a hyphen) writing. Keith Hopper places him among the "Holy Trinity" of Irish writers who, by the start of the Second World War, produced emblematic works marking "the moment when high modernism drifted, almost imperceptibly, into post-modernism: Joyce's *Finnegans Wake* (1939), Beckett's *Murphy* (1938), and Flann O'Brien's *At Swim-Two-Birds* (1939)" (Hopper, "The Dismemberment," 120). Since a comprehensive definition of postmodernist literature is rather inaccessible, whatever claims are made for O'Brien's inclusion must examine his compliance with the various notions associated with this contemporary sensibility. Certainly many of such are easy to find in O'Brien's early oeuvre: irony, playfulness, parody, pastiche, pun, metafiction, intertextuality, *poioumenon* . . . But some other ingredients of postmodernity, perhaps closer to the Derridean deconstructive relativism, may admit some further, possibly vigorous, discussion. A common attitude among postmodernist authors, which distances them from the modernist search for meaning in a fragmented world, is the abandonment of any pretence of undertaking this search, which for them is pointless and often the object of a playful parody. Or in the words of Snipp-Walmsley, "postmodernism attacks the ideas of a stable, autonomous being and the possibility of grounding our knowledge in certainty and truth" (408). Critics such as Thomas Shea imply that O'Brien's subversion of conventional narrative structure and rendering of collapsing discourses entail an ultimate lack of meaning and its resulting "desperately squalid void" (Shea 142). But such an approach may not be easily compatible with the sense of purpose of a Christian outlook and its perspective of the ultimate realities of existence.

Although modern literary theory teaches us that biographical input should not be decisive for criticism, some credit may be given to O'Brien's major biographer, Anthony Cronin, who had contact with the writer over twenty years, when he affirms that the author remained a practising Catholic, and never rejected the Christian faith in which he was brought up. Cronin even goes as far as stating that he "was a medieval Thomist in his attitude to many things including scientific speculation and discovery. For the Thomist all the great questions have been settled and the purpose of existence is clear. There is only one good, the salvation of the individual soul; and only one final catastrophe, damnation" (Cronin 104). Far from attempting to evaluate the degree of personal commitment to his faith, my aim here is to determine if the implied author of O'Brien's early fiction (following Seymour Chatman's 1990 revision of the traditional concept proposed by Booth in 1961, that is, the productivity of the meaning of a given text such as given by the real reader) reveals a sense of purpose and an assumption of the ultimate realities of life conceived from a Christian perspective. My attention will focus on O'Brien's early novels, *At Swim-Two-Birds* and *The Third Policeman,* which hold considerable critical unanimity as regards their stature as O'Brien's masterpieces and early examples of an experimental writing arguably akin to postmodernism. Even if we may find in both novels some essential postmodernist traits such as "ambiguity, discontinuity, heterodoxy, pluralism, randomness, revolt, perversion, deformation" (Hassan 94), the implied author's (alleged) understanding of a world ruled by a divine providence must make a substantial difference to the major postmodern tenets.

It is true that not every critic places O'Brien primarily on the postmodern shelf. Joshua D. Esty, for example, considers it more "appropriate to evaluate O'Brien's aesthetic anew in postcolonial rather than postmodern terms" (Esty 41). Neil R. Davison, in turn, feels inclined to deny O'Brien the benefit of the (postmodern) doubt precisely because he sees the author as "a product of parochial Irish Catholicism," displaying a characteristic "somatophobia" and male repression projected onto the female, "which in turn serves to image, contain, and defeat sexual appetite, psychoanalytic investigation, incestuous desire, fear of female power, and, indeed, subversion of patriarchal authority." He prefers using postmodern-feminist theory to expose all these tendencies and finds this method "much more valuable than once again addressing its 'indeterminacy' as a key to its status as a Postmodern piece" (Davison 32). Davidson's own radical theory draws his analysis to some simplifications and commonplaces, but it seems obvious that whatever orthodoxy, especially religious, is a serious hitch for any application for inclusion in the postmodern canon. Cronin insists that O'Brien and his circle did not reject the central concerns of a Christian outlook, but were mostly irked at "the Catholic triumphalism, the pious philistinism, the Puritan morality" of the new Irish state (Cronin 48).[1] It is true that many Irish late twentieth-century writers apparently regard their Catholic upbringing as marked by repression, fear, and superstition, stressing issues of censorship, sexual restraint, and sense of guilt. Characters in the works of Edna O'Brien, John McGahern, Lee Dunne, Frank McCourt, Maeve Kelly, or Julia O'Faolain, to mention but a few, must struggle against the social pressure of middle-class respectability in order to find true freedom and self-realisation. Fewer writers, on the contrary, acknowledge the imaginative possibilities that such education may have entailed for their literary vocation. In the words of Hilary Mantel, to be brought up as a Catholic "is to learn by the age of four, or to be told, that this world is not simply as we perceive it, but that beyond the literal truths, the material truths, there are metaphors and metaphysical truths" (Galván 31). It is hard to imagine what would have become of Joyce without his Jesuitical instruction, and Flann O'Brien, who was ever aware of the literary ascendancy of his beloved/hated master, acknowledged the strong influence of Irish Catholicism in Joyce's sense of humour, and indirectly his own, in the well-known article "A Bash in the Tunnel":

> Humour, the handmaid of sorrow and fear, creeps out endlessly in all Joyce's works. He uses the thing . . . to attenuate the fear of those who have belief and who genuinely think that they will be in hell or in heaven shortly, and possibly very shortly. With laughs he palli-

ates the sense of doom that is the heritage of the Irish Catholic. True humour needs this background urgency. ("Stories" 175)

While further pursuing the inevitable Joyce/O'Brien comparison, Bernard Benstock denies any deliberate religious commitment on the part of the latter:

crediting O'Nolan with being a Catholic writer is as exact as crediting Joyce. Both have Catholic backgrounds and are immersed in Catholicism, but what must be considered are O'Nolan's religious attitudes, and as a Catholic novelist he betrays none. In fact, a ball of malt or a pint of plain porter take on the proportions of a creed in the Flann O'Brien books. (Benstock 62)

Certainly, O'Brien's work is not committedly Catholic in the fashion of Flannery O'Connor's stories, Evelyn Waugh's *Brideshead Revisited*, or Graham Greene's *The Power and the Glory*—although Greene famously claimed that he was not a Catholic writer, but a writer who happened to be a Catholic—but some credit must be given to Davison when he affirms that O'Brien held "fast to his own strongly-held Catholic assumptions even while lampooning them" (Davison 33).

Recent attempts have been made to develop a literary method of analysis that might be termed "Christian poetics" or "Christian Literary Theory," "a theory of the nature and function of fictional texts found valuable, which is derived from those fundamental doctrines of the Catholic faith shared by the major Protestant and the Orthodox confessions" (Ferretter 4). Although perhaps already too immature in its methodological developments, Ferretter's proposal offers a valuable revision of some of the most insightful approaches of critics and theologians such as Jasper, Wright, Edwards, Fiddes, Detweiler, or Ledbetter, and their major contributions provide new angles for discussion of literary texts. Ferretter argues that a Christian critic, like any other critic, interprets literature in terms of a structure of pre-understandings deriving from his acceptance of the claims of a given tradition (an "interpretive community" in Stanley Fish's terms), which in this case amounts to the theology and faith of his Church. This acceptance is not a blind, immovable assertion, but is based on a rational judgement, and "it is through precisely this process of judgement that [the critic] can also reject those claims which he judges to be ideological, or in any other way false" (183). Accordingly, Ferretter establishes some specific methods that the Christian critic might employ, in dia-logue with others shared by the community of academic literary criticism to which he belongs. This model is eminently reader-oriented, as one of its aims is to enhance the ethical value of literature by making the reader "test precisely the structure of norms in whose terms he interprets against those projected by the text," thus developing and even changing "the beliefs about himself and the world which he held as he began to read" (188). Given the dialogic nature and the reader-orientation of Christian Literary Theory (henceforth CLT), the contributions of several authorised readers will be brought in for the sake of illustrating the major points, though the dimensions of the present paper do not allow for more than a mere outline and a few tentative exemplifications derived from O'Brien's early novels.

One of the consequences of Ferreter's dialogic model is that it shares common aims with some of the previous, well-grounded ideological theories such as Psychoanalysis or Marxism, and in accordance with the latter, CLT "should analyse the social and economic relations which can be shown to be of rel-evance to a given text, and judge them in the light of Biblical social ethics" (186). One influential factor of the social context when O'Brien's early novels were written is the awareness of censorship (what could be denominated "the implied censor," stretching Chatman's terms).[2] Censorship, evidently, is not a specific product of Catholicism, but introducing this aspect under a CLT framework poses some interesting difficulties: on the one hand, censorship was justified by the Irish civil/religious authorities of that time as supposedly based on considerations taken "in the light of Biblical social ethics." Similar pre-judgements, however, are contemplated in Ferreter's model as "subject to critique and even reformulation" (190). Certainly, Flann O'Brien seems to have been aware of the implications of writing in his time and country when he wished that *The Hard Life* would be banned in Ireland, in the childish belief that "nearly every professional Irish author had a book banned" (Cronin 214). In the composition of his first novel, however, O'Brien seems to have been extremely careful to avoid any unorthodox elements, sometimes resorting to skilful periphrases rendering an effect wittier than the explicit expression of the tenor. In *At Swim-Two-Birds* one of such examples is the description of the activities carried out by the College societies:

> The people who attended the College had banded themselves into many private associations, some purely cultural and some concerned with the arrangement and conduct of ball games. The cultural societies were diverse in their character and aims and measured their vitality by the number of hooligans and unprincipled persons they attracted to their deliberations. Some were devoted to English letters, some to Irish letters and some to the study and advancement of the French language. (*At Swim-Two-Birds* 45)

The word "balls," according to Hopper (*Portrait* 81), is a first indication of ambiguous sexual meaning, in its double sense either as billiard games or testicles. The concurrence of so many "hooligans and unprincipled persons" in the societies prepare the reader for the next metonymic displacement: once the reader understands the colloquial meaning of French letters as "condoms," the word-play achieves its highest comical effect. As pointed out above, the "Irish Censorship Act" included the ban on "indecent or obscene" literature. Critics such as Hopper and Davison have insisted on repressed sexuality as one dominant feature in O'Brien's writing. We have already summed up Davison's view on the consequences of O'Brien's alleged "somatophobia," but Hopper is no less critical against the omission of "formal discussion of sexuality" in O'Brien's works, which again he constantly relates to his Catholic ethos, though he admits that it is not just a product of external censorship and also that "the significant exclusions or 'silences' in his texts reveal an ideologically induced self-censorship; not just an unwillingness to speak of taboo issues" (Hopper, *Portrait* 60). This may suggest that self-restraint in sexual issues is not just an external imposition but may obey to a voluntary screening of matters judged too complex to be satisfactorily dealt with in writing. As in the previous example, this screening is imaginatively transposed by other devices; for example, the absence of women and sex in *The Third Policeman* is symbolically replaced by the idiosyncratic treatment of bicycles. In chapter 11, the narrator employs a coded language to account for his "love affair" with MacCruiskeen's female bicycle:

> I knew that I liked this bicycle more than I had ever liked any other bicycle, better even than I had liked some people with two legs. I liked her unassuming competence, her docility, the simple dignity of her quiet way. She now seemed to rest beneath my friendly eyes like a tame fowl which will crouch submissively, awaiting with out-hunched wings the caressing hand. Her saddle seemed to spread invitingly into the most enchanting of all seats while her two handle-bars, floating finely with the wild grace of alighting wings, beckoned to me to lend my mastery for free and joyful journeyings . . . How desirable her seat was, how charming the invitation of her slim encircling handle-arms, how unaccountably competent and reassuring her pump resting warmly against her rear thigh! (*The Third Policeman* 170–1)

The second and more specific analytical method proposed by Ferretter is "a kind of existential criticism, according to which the critic analyses the characteristics of the world projected by a given literary text in terms of Christian theology" (189). Perhaps the Thomistic penchant that Cronin identified in O'Brien implies the attempt to capture, often by means of the most improbable or preposterous allegories, metaphors, symbols, and other rhetorical figures, the ultimate metaphysical truths of Christianity that lie beyond the literal or material realities: the Trinitarian personality of God; the creature's rebellion against his Creator; temptation and the permanent fight between flesh and spirit; mortal sin and eternal punishment; conversion to Christianity and resistance to it; even the Eucharist.[3] For example, *At Swim-Two-Birds* features the character of Dermot Trellis, proprietor of the Red Swan Hotel, whose purpose is to write an intensely moral book exposing the dangers of all kinds of vice. According to Imhof, "Trellis is thereby brought into proximity with God when creating and calling Adam. The omniscient narrator is thus unmasked as a narratorial God of creation" (Imhof 16). But Trellis's didactic purpose is invalidated by the increasing independence gained by the characters he has created: once they achieve a high degree of free will they turn on him and write down their own revenge, a merciless torture and lawless trial against their creator. Although Trellis is not an explicit Christ-like figure,[4] the echoes of the creatures rebelling against their creator cannot escape a religious interpretation. The Pooka MacPhellimey, a devil, is the tormentor, and the cruelty of the beating reminds of some details of Christ's passion, such as Trellis's utterance that "I feel a thirst and the absence of a drink of spring water for a longer period than five minutes might well result in my death" (*At Swim-Two-Birds* 196), reminiscent of Jesus' thirsting agony as recounted in John 19:28.

The title of *At Swim-Two-Birds*, puzzling though it may sound, can also be analysed in the light of Christian symbolism in an old Irish context. Called Snámh Dá Én in Irish, this place is important for the understanding of Finn Mac Cool's role as the reciter of the Old Irish legend known as *Buile Suibhne*. In this source from which Flann O'Brien drew the story of Sweeny, Snámh-dá-én is the place where Suibhne (or Sweeny) realises the power of God and where he becomes calmer, and exclaims: "O Christ, O Christ, hear me! / O Christ, O Christ, without sin! / O Christ, O Christ, love me! / Sever me not from thy sweetness!" (qtd. in Wäppling 62). The church beside the Shannon opposite Clonmacnoise stands for "a place where cultural and religious values were for a spell coincident in a darkened Europe" (qtd. in Imhof 85), and, according to Mays, "the lay that Sweeny sang there is at the centre of the positive values in the book" (qtd. in Imhof 85).

The struggle between good and evil, and spirit versus flesh, represented by the opposition between the Good Fairy and the Pooka (no matter how ambiguous their personalities turn out to be) was significantly contemplated in the alternative title O'Brien was considering before the book's publication, *Through an Angel's Eye-Lid* (Wäppling 84). As he grew more and more worried about the novel, he moved from "Angel" to "Good Spirit" and, eventually, to "Good Fairy," because, in the words of the author, "'Fairy' corresponds more closely to 'Pooka,' and removes any suggestion of the mock-religious and establishes the thing on a mythological plane" (O'Brien to Heath, 3 October 1938, qtd. in Wäppling 85).[5]

Even on this representational or allegorical level, in his early novels O'Brien seems diffident to deal with Christian symbols explicitly. Some references to Irish religious life, such as the Christian Brothers' diatribe against alcohol (*At Swim* 21) or the preparations of the Committee Meeting chaired by the narrator's uncle (132–37) are "not so much against the Church but against its near-schism Irish eccentricities," as expressed in "A Bash in the Tunnel." Several critics, however, claim to have seen through the writer's self-contention and detect metaphysical or religious connotations in unexpected vehicles. Such is the case of Hugh Kenner, whose commentary on *The Third Policeman* not only states that the "bicycle . . . resembles the soul in the mystery of its relation to the body" (Kenner 69), but also identifies Trinitarian attributes in each of the three policemen:

> Policeman MacCruiskeen, he is a Creator: of curious boxes in infinite regress, of a mangle which wrings screams out of light, of a card of no known colour, the colour of which drives men mad.
>
> Policeman Pluck, he is the beneficent one of the trio: implacable if need be and willing to hang you if it will balance books, but also a saver of people from themselves by losing their bicycles but finding them again on petition.
>
> Policeman Fox, though, he is the great mystery: trickster, illusionist, compressor and expander of time, more than once alluded to by the others though in such bizarre terms we would place no hopes in seeing him were it not for the book's title. Christian discourse has likewise found that the Holy Spirit presents obstacles to visualisation. To painters who presented Creator and Redeemer explicitly, the dove seemed an expedient. (Kenner 69)[6]

One of the most obvious treatments of the motifs of sin and eternal punishment occurs in *The Third Policeman*, whose final revelation provides as turning point the narrator's realisation that he has been dead from the outset. This discovery modifies the reader's understanding of the character's weird adventures, which are now seen as the wanderings in hell of an unrepentant murderer. Once more, at the heart of the novel lie essential Christian motifs and that peculiar "sense of doom" that O'Brien perceived in Joyce. Indeed, Mazullo establishes significant links between both novels by O'Brien and Joyce's *Portrait*:

> in describing the pursuit and punishment of Dermot Trellis, it echoes, with its flight up and down, in an acid-reddish atmosphere, while juxtaposing Celtic and Catholic Otherworld dimensions, the physical and spiritual atrocities described in the "hell sermon," in *A Portrait of the Artist as a Young Man*. But this multi-functional fragment has another hidden aspect. It is also the generative nucleus of *The Third Policeman*, in which a new disquieting, timeless, cyclical reality is added to O'Brien's Otherworld. (Mazullo 318)

A third dimension of the suggested CLT methodology might consist in a sort of symptomatic reading in which the reader/critic may be able to find textual hints, however unconscious, of the author's search for meaning, "all these ways in which the world of a fictional or poetic text represents a better or more satisfying version of the world of the reader's experience can be understood . . . as a response to the fallen nature of that world" (Ferretter 187). This basic approach, taken mostly from Edwards (1984), could in my opinion be amplified and reversed to include "worse or less satisfying versions" without significant misdemeanour: Edwards is mostly dealing with the symptoms of a hopeful hunger for eternity, for heavenly bliss; but his approach may also account for the opposite attitude, the despair in the face of eternity that accompanies a sense of unrepentant sin. Ondrej Pilný insightfully observes, in connection with Lyotard's definition of the postmodern "conflict between nostalgia and experiment," that *The Third Policeman* can be read as an allegory of a quest for meaning and is an example of "a nostalgia for a present where perceptions and images are in accordance with concepts, a world which is 'easy to read'" (Pilný 48). But in this story the ultimate effect of the desire for interpretation and meaning is not pleasant but despairing. The narrator of *The Third Policeman* perceives the incompatibility "of a perception or image with our conceptual thinking" as ultimately distressful, and derives no joy from "inventing new rules of the game" (49).

Ferretter regards Edwards's notion of "possibility" as a major contribution to the foundations of a CLT. Following this path, Edwards develops constructive reflections on the significance of beginning and endings: "we may come to story with any version of the idea that a first beginning, if there was one, has gone deeply wrong, that universal, individual or social creation has been succeeded by Fall, and that the evil needs to be removed in a fresh start. The start of story is so fresh that it occurs in another dimension, which replaces ours in the twinkling of an opening sentence" (Edwards 73). This reflection might suggest productive ways of understanding O'Brien's narrator's claims at the start of *At Swim-Two-Birds*, that "one beginning and one ending for a book was a thing I did not agree with. A good book may have three openings entirely dissimilar and inter-related only in the prescience of the author, or for that matter one hundred times as many endings" (*At Swim-Two-Birds* 1). Certainly, if a novel should be a "self-evident sham" (19) and still retain its projection of Edwards's notion of possibility, a high number of beginnings might be thought to convey this notion more lavishly.

Edwards shows a similar interest in the significance of endings: "An ending is equally a form of salvation, substituting, for mere addition, finality and climax, and concentrating time into a shape. It may also be another kind of beginning" (74). This principle, which is meant to work with traditional narratives, can also hold water in the conscious subversions of traditional narrativity such as the circular or multiple endings, since the finality of such subversions may enhance a sense of despair or distress already referred to. Circularity is an effective way of representing the fear of eternity, and in this respect Thomas Shea has written that "the contemplation of infinity is more properly the subject of *The Third Policeman*, but the disorientation described here is carefully cultivated in *At Swim-Two-Birds*" (Shea 59). The multiple endings we find in the novel—which could have been "one hundred times as many"—prefigure the circularity implied in *The Third Policeman*, which certainly complies with Edward's proposal but in reverse, conveying an overwhelming lack of hope in the face of eternal damnation. In a similar vein, a recent insightful study of O'Brien's sense of infinity links the author with one of his earliest Hispanic admirers, Jorge Luis Borges. O'Connell argues that both writers are "characterised by a kind of transcendent perplexity, and by their shared fondness for devising metaphysical conceits and philosophical jests through which to communicate their perplexity" (234). Both stare at the universe and are possessed by awe before the "impenetrable void of infinity." O'Connell concludes that O'Brien, like Borges, is an inventor of literary labyrinths in which all sense of certainty about the universe and our place in it is lost, and in which such a loss is attended no less by exhilaration than it is by unease" (235).

This final quotation, with its confusion of uncertainty with uneasiness, returns the discussion (in a proper exercise of circularity) to our starting point, the compatibility of a postmodern sensibility with a Christian belief. Authors such as Brian Ingraffia stress their irreconcilability, when affirming that "an either/or must be proclaimed to the present age: either biblical theology or postmodern theory" (Ingraffia 241), but Ferretter's CLT does not exclude a dialogic encounter between both. He embraces Cunningham's assertion that "post-structuralist theory, despite appearing to constitute a radical critique of theology, is in fact indebted to the Christian theological tradition, insofar as the latter constitutes a culturally dominant framework in whose terms much contemporary theory is still expressed" (150), and also Cunningham's further claim that "silence, puzzle, *aporia*, blankness, stuttering, are as much part of Biblical theology, of Scriptural logocentrism, as their opposites (396). Although our previous discussion has attempted to suggest, with the aid of a novel (albeit very old) theory still under construction, that Flann O'Brien's fictional approach does not reflect the characteristic relativity or nihilism of other postmodern authors, perhaps under this perspective we may not have to opt, after all, for an exclusive label for Flann O'Brien in "either/or" terms. He may still remain, paraphrasing Greene's self-definition, a postmodernist who happens to be a Thomist.

1   Writing about his arguably most incisive novel in terms of Catholic matters, *The Dalkey Archive*, O'Brien made a point of his orthodoxy in a letter to his publisher: "There is, for instance, no intention to jeer at God or religion . . . the idea is to roast the people who seriously do so, and also to chide the Church in certain of its aspects. I seem to be wholly at one with Vatican II" (in Costello & Van de Kamp 130, for whom the novel even possesses a serious religious overtone). In this light, O'Brien even regarded Joyce as a writer emerging "through curtains of salacity and blasphemy, as a truly fear-shaken Irish Catholic, rebelling not so much against the Church but against its near-schism Irish eccentricities, its pretence that there is only one commandment, the vulgarity of its edifices, the shallowness and stupidity of many of its ministers. His revolt, noble in itself, carried him away. He could not see the tree for the woods. But I think he meant well. We all do, anyway" (O'Brien, "Stories" 174).

2   The "Censorship of Publications Act," operating in Ireland since 1929, provided for the banning of literature on the grounds of being "in general tendency indecent or obscene" (II.6), of advocating "the unnatural prevention of conception" or the "procurement of abortion or miscarriage" (II.6), or of devoting "an unduly large proportion of space to the publication of matter relating to crime" (II.7). According to Julia Carlson, censorship in Ireland was a sort of cultural paternalism emerging as a consequence of "the triumphalism that had infected Irish nationalists after the War of Independence, and the position of authority that the Irish Catholic Church had assumed in the new state" (Carlson 6).

3   With respect to echoes of the Eucharist, see Monique Gallagher's audacious comparison between the drinking rituals in *At Swim-Two-Birds* and the religious experience: "Tous les personnages s'inclinent avec respect devant le breuvage, et trouvent, en contact avec lui, les gestes d'un prêtre en train de célébrer un culte" (102, "All the characters respectfully bow to drink, and adopt, in contact with it, the demeanour of a priest celebrating a service").

4   However, Carol Taaffe analyses the textual history of the novel and produces evidence of fragments from the initial manuscript relating to the crucifixion that were deleted by O'Brien in the final version. Consistent with our claim above, Taaffe understands that O'Brien was "pragmatic in recognising that such passages would never pass the censor, though ironically their comedy is testament to a culture deeply suffused with religious imagery" (Taaffe 58).

5 He wrote to Longmans: "I am really very anxious, for reasons that have nothing to do with modesty, to have nothing that is not thoroughly orthodox in literature attributed to me" (O'Brien to Longmans, 15 January 1939, in Wäppling 85). Again Taaffe goes back to the early stages of the novel's composition and finds that originally the Pooka and the Good Fairy were "a Devil and an Angel, and their struggle over Orlick's soul firmly belong[ed] to a Christian universe of good and evil rather than to a strange corner of folk Irishry" (Taaffe 55).

6 Kenner is not claiming that O'Brien was deliberately thinking of the policemen as a representation of the Christian Trinity, and instead conjectures that if he had ever conceived of the scheme Creator-Redeemer-Mystery for them "he would have forthwith banished the book from his mind unwritten" (69). But we know that O'Brien did banish the book from publication after the only rejection by Longmans; the manuscript of *The Third Policeman* remained hidden for a quarter century and was published only posthumously in 1967.

In turn, Ondrej Pilný, apparently following a different route, comes to a similar conclusion, by rendering the translation from Irish of the second policeman's name, "Son-of-the-Little-Star" and by considering Policeman Fox, "who is not to be seen until very late in the book . . . , the 'spirit' of the mechanism of the 'parish'" (Pilný 42). But note a discrepant interpretation of the three policemen proposed by Roy L. Hunt: "the triumvirate of this particular 'force,' who make and uphold the laws and guard eternity, prove to be more akin to the guardians of purgatory than to the deity of a heavenly realm" (Hunt 65).

WORKS CITED

Benstock, Bernard. "The Three Faces of Brian Nolan." *Alive-Alive O! Flann O'Brien's At Swim-Two-Birds*. Ed. Rüdiger Imhof. Dublin: Wolfhound Press, 1985. 59–70.

Carlson, Julia. *Banned in Ireland: Censorship and the Irish Writer*. London: Routledge, 1990.

Chatman, Seymour. *Coming to Terms: The Rhetoric of Narrative in Fiction and Film*. Ithaca, NY: Cornell Univ. Press, 1990.

Clune, Anne & Tess Hurson eds. *Conjuring Complexities: Essays on Flann O'Brien*. Belfast: Queen's University Belfast, Institute of Irish Studies, 1997.

Costello, Peter & Peter Van de Kamp. *Flann O'Brien. An Illustrated Biography*. London: Bloomsbury, 1987.

Cronin, Anthony. *No Laughing Matter: The Life and Times of Flann O'Brien*. London: Grafton, 1989.

Cunningham, Valentine. *In the Reading Gaol: Postmodernity, Texts, History*. Oxford & Cambridge, MA: Blackwell, 1994.

Davison, Neil R. "'We are not a doctor for the body': Catholicism, the Female Grotesque, and Flann O'Brien's *The Hard Life*." *Literature and Psychology* 45 (1999): 31–57.

Edwards, Michael. *Towards a Christian Poetics*. London: Macmillan, 1984.

Esty, Joshua D. "Flann O'Brien's *At Swim-Two-Birds* and the Post-Post Debate." *ARIEL (A Review of International English Literature)* 26.4 (1995): 23–46.

Ferretter, Luke. *Towards a Christian Literary Theory*. London: Macmillan, 2004.

Gallagher, Monique. "'The Full Little Crock' ou la religion de l'ivresse chez Flann O'Brien." *Etudes Irlandaises* 1 (1976): 99–110.

Galván, Fernando. "On Ireland, Religion and History: A Conversation with Hilary Mantel." *The European English Messenger* 10.2 (2001): 31–38.

Hassan, Ihab. *The Postmodern Turn*. Columbus: Ohio State Univ. Press, 1987.

Hopper, Keith. *Flann O'Brien: A Portrait of the Artist as a Young Post-modernist*. Cork: Cork Univ. Press, 1995.

—. "'The Dismemberment of Orpheus': Flann O'Brien and the Censorship Code." *BELLS (Barcelona English Language and Literature Studies)* 11 (2000): 119–132.

Huber, Werner. "Flann O'Brien and the Language of the Grotesque." *Anglo-Irish and Irish Literature: Aspects of Language and Culture*. Eds. Birgit Bramsback & Martin Croghan. Uppsala: Uppsala University, 1988. 123–30.

Hunt, Roy L. "Hell Goes Round and Round: Flann O'Brien." *The Canadian Journal of Irish Studies* 14.2 (1989): 60–73.

Imhof, Rüdiger ed. *Alive-Alive O! Flann O'Brien's* At Swim-Two-Birds. Dublin: Wolfhound Press, 1985.

Ingraffia, Brian. *Postmodern Theory and Biblical Theology: Vanquishing God's Shadow*. Cambridge: Cambridge Univ. Press, 1995.

Kenner, Hugh. "The Fourth Policeman." *Conjuring Complexities: Essays on Flann O'Brien*. Eds. Anne Clune & Tess Hurson. Belfast: Queen's University Belfast, Institute of Irish Studies, 1997. 61–71.

Maher, Eamon. *Crosscurrents and Confluences. Echoes of Religion in Twentieth-Century Fiction*. Dublin: Veritas, 2000.

Mazzullo, Concetta. "Flann O'Brien's Hellish Otherworld: From *Buile Suibhne* to *The Third Policeman*." *Irish University Review* 25.2 (1995): 318–27.

O'Brien, Flann. *Stories and Plays*. 1973. London: Grafton, 1991.

—. *At Swim-Two-Birds*. 1939. Harmondsworth: Penguin, 1967; Normal, Illinois: Dalkey Archive Press, 1998.

—. *The Third Policeman*, 1967. London: Flamingo, 1993; Normal, Illinois: Dalkey Archive Press, 1999.

O'Connell, Mark. "'How to handle Eternity': Infinity and the Theories of J.W. Dunne in the Fiction of Jorge Luis Borges and Flann O'Brien's *The Third Policeman*." *Irish Studies Review* 17.2 (2009): 223–237.

Pilný, Ondrej. "Cycling Round the Bend: Interpretation and Punishment in Flann O'Brien's *The Third Policeman*." *Litteraria Pragensia* 13 (1997): 41–50.

Shea, Thomas F. *Flann O'Brien's Exorbitant Novels*. Lewisburg, P.A.: Bucknell Univ. Press, 1992.

Snipp-Walmsley, Chris. "Postmodernism." *Literary Theory and Criticism*. Ed. Patricia Waugh. Oxford: Oxford Univ. Press, 2006. 405–426.

Taaffe, Carol. *Ireland Through the Looking-Glass: Flann O'Brien, Myles na gCopaleen and Irish Cultural Debate*. Cork: Cork Univ. Press, 2008.

Wäppling, Eva. *Four Irish Legendary Figures in* At Swim-Two-Birds, Uppsala: Acta Universitatis Upsaliensis, 1984.

JENNIKA BAINES

"Un-Understandable Mystery": Catholic Faith and Revelation in *The Third Policeman*

In his 1889 textbook on logic, Father Richard F. Clarke, a Jesuit priest, explains that there are no new discoveries in the philosophy of the church, only developments of a truth that the church already possesses: "For fresh discovery means a setting aside of what exists already, and if what exists already is the perfect Truth, to set it aside is but to introduce the destructive poison of error" (Clarke 483). He goes on to argue that the Church, in her perfect wisdom, will watch as modern science proves the truths she has held all along. Philosophies will rise and fall, he argues, as the Church remains unshaken: "To her all arts and all sciences minister, but none more than the Art and Science of Logic, since the Catholic Church alone can challenge the world to point out a single inconsistency in her teaching, or a single weak point in the perfect system of Divine philosophy which God through her has given to the world" (483). St. Augustine was a key figure in developing this Catholic system of logic and explanation. Augustine held a particular fascination for Flann O'Brien, so much so that he appears "encorpified" in *The Dalkey Archive*, a novel which O'Brien wrote toward the end of his career and which contains revised excerpts of the unpublished manuscript of *The Third Policeman*, a novel he wrote as a young man. The strange scientist and philosopher de Selby also appears in both novels (though his surname is upgraded to a capital "D" in *The Dalkey Archive*). In one of the most bizarre exchanges in that most bizarre book, De Selby questions Augustine on his past. This scene strains at humor but provides interesting insight into O'Brien's quest to understand faith.

In Book III of his *Confessions*, Augustine writes of his conversion to Manichaeism, a gnostic religion founded in the third century that presented a universe divided between good and evil, light and dark. The *Catholic Encyclope-*

dia provides an extensive explanation of Manichaeism and debases its claim to provide answers to the mysteries of life:

> Manichaeism professed to be a religion of pure reason as opposed to Christian credulity; it professed to explain the origin, the composition, and the future of the universe; it had an answer for everything and despised Christianity, which was full of mysteries. It was utterly unconscious that its every answer was a mystification or a whimsical invention; in fact, it gained mastery over men's minds by the astonishing completeness, minuteness, and consistency of its assertions. (591)

In his biography of O'Brien, Anthony Cronin writes that the author was a lifelong Catholic, yet Cronin also repeatedly mentions O'Brien's Manichean leanings. Cronin writes, "If Brian O'Nolan had any doubts about the faith in which he had been born, they were, as has been said, on Manichean grounds, the Manichean attitude being to him, as to some other Catholic writers, the ultimate sophistication in belief" (105). It is easy to see why O'Brien would have been drawn, even if only on the most superficial level, to the answers offered by Manichaeism. Catholicism presented a system in which reason fits into faith, but Manichaeism presented a system in which faith fits into reason.

In *The Third Policeman*, O'Brien explores an eerie hell in which reason is perpetually thwarted by seemingly impossible facts completely disconnected from truth. The nameless narrator experiences policemen who rule the Parish with confounding maxims and reveal a series of inconceivable inventions. Light is mangled into sound. Perfect boxes contain an infinite number of identically perfect boxes. And the policemen obsessively maintain readings on the mechanical levels of a subterranean Eternity. "Attend to your daily readings and your conscience will be as clear as a clean shirt on a Sunday morning. I am a great believer in the daily readings," Sergeant Pluck tells the nameless narrator (O'Brien 346). Many critics have argued that the twisted logic and scientific impossibilities of this hell are the major source of torment for the murdering narrator. "The book is largely about the confident pretensions of Cartesian epistemology to be able to reach (and recognize) Truth, and the mysterious and inaccessible Fox serves as a personification of an equally elusive Truth," writes M. Keith Booker (48). Joseph Brooker argues that the novel is in part about the act of thinking. "It is fascinated by, and parasitic upon, logic: its wildest fancies . . . have their own kind of internal coherence" (56). The logic and pseudoscience of the text are undeniably what makes the novel so funny. But as with all of O'Brien's novels when they are at their funniest, there is always some dark truth to the humor. Part of that darkness comes from twentieth-century scientific advances that make the impossible possible. Einstein's theories about the relationship between space and time meant that science was able to understand more about the universe, but the price of this greater knowledge was the loss of the comfortable "older models" of explanation.

But for Catholics, all truths would ultimately be founded on faith in the unseen and unknowable. Cronin writes that O'Brien was a Thomist who held the orthodox view of salvation of the soul as the ultimate goal of life. Cronin writes:

> Thomistic Catholicism was the received religion of all the educational institutions he attended, including UCD, where the philosophy courses were designed to confirm that everything worth knowing was in St. Thomas Aquinas's great synthesis of Catholic doctrine and Aristotelian philosophy, the *Summa Theologica*, and that all the rest was vain speculation. (106)

The Third Policeman, with the eternal damnation of its murdering narrator, certainly upholds a Catholic system of reward and punishment. However, O'Brien also uses the novel as a creative space in which to safely explore questions about the mysteries of faith.[1] The unfathomable truths of O'Brien's faith are just as tormenting as the incomprehensible facts of science in this hell. Catholic doctrine on mysteries holds that there is powerful and significant knowledge, which is unknowable or secret. Catholic faith is founded on absolute belief in a supernatural system of truth that is not subject to human theories of proof and evidence. While rationalists would argue that belief in Catholic mysteries debases reason, Catholics would point to the difference between that which cannot be understood and that which can never be known. This is the tension that adds to the bizarrely unsettling experience of reading *The Third Policeman*. Both in concept and in metafictional medium, O'Brien is exploring the unknowable.

While it is reductive to read *The Third Policeman* as any sort of morality tale or Catholic allegory, the novel does confront, albeit in an ultimately devout way, some of the incomprehensible facts of Catholic faith, mysteries, and revelations. Here in this hell, O'Brien can express the doubts that would deviate from Catholic teaching because the text ultimately affirms the system of punishment for sins that the Catholic church holds to be true. The murdering narrator is already cast out from the kingdom promised to believers. This is what O'Brien makes reference to in a letter to William Saroyan dated February 14, 1940: "When you are writing about the world of the dead—and the damned—where none of the rules and laws (not even the law of gravity) holds good, there is any amount of scope for back-chat and funny cracks" (O'Brien, "Sheaf" 71). The rules O'Brien mentions are not only those of science and grammar, but also those of the religion of which he was a lifelong follower. David Cohen writes, "Instead of denying realism, as many Post-modernists have done, O'Brien in *The Third Policeman* uses the type of illusion associated with realism, slowly stretches the reader's suspension of disbelief as the situations grow more bizarre and then exposes the illusion and the impossibility of the narrative" (Cohen 60). Cohen is here equating the words "illusion" and "impossibility," and while this story is a self-conscious illusion, the word "impossible" needs to be qualified. Realism in the standard literary use of the term reflects, at least on one level, material reality. In this text, however, O'Brien is presenting what he would have considered to be a spiritual reality. Again, in his letter to Saroyan, O'Brien wrote, "When you get to the end of this book you realise that the hero or main character (he's a heel and a killer) has been dead throughout the book and that all the queer ghastly things which have been happening to him are happening in a sort of hell which he has earned for the killing" (O'Brien, "Sheaf" 71). In a Catholic system, unrepentant murderers will go to hell. So while the events are materially impossible, there is also a sense in which they are spiritually true. In this way, O'Brien can explore the believer and not the belief, the questions that arise within one person's mind without taking on the role of the apologist.

J.C. Whitehouse identifies a similar vein of trial and tension in other Catholic writers in the first half of the twentieth century. He writes, "In their novels, or at least in their most 'Catholic' novels, such writers were explorers, if not necessarily expounders, of their faith, illustrating the dramas and tensions of the truths of their religion seen in an existential and human context in all its confusion and messiness" (17). Significantly, O'Brien's tensions are completely external from the novel's narrator. Much of the strange anxiety of dislocation that makes the novel seem so bizarre can be traced to the machinations of an irreligious character trying to understand, and operate within, a religious world. For the nameless narrator of *The Third Policeman*, hell is not within him, but rather a place in which he finds himself. Compare this, for example, to the Catholic novels of Graham Greene, whose *The Power and the Glory* was published in the same year as O'Brien attempted to publish *The Third Policeman*.[2] In Greene's novels, religion is internalised and becomes an individual, psychological struggle. This struggle results in profoundly rich and complex characters (like the whiskey priest clinging to a faith he feels he has utterly failed) who operate in a world that is drab and dirty in comparison. For O'Brien, however, there is no such sense of the internalised struggle of faith.

References to Catholicism are frequent in the text, from MacCruiskeen contemplating putting a picture of Peter the Hermit in his magnificent box to more esoteric references to things like the idea of "social justice" or the mysteriously malevolent intent of Freemasons (O'Brien 15, 14). The narrator is aware of religion—he states at the very start of the novel that he committed his first and his greatest sins for de Selby—but there is no indication that these sins could have any real impact on his spiritual well being. The narrator's "greatest sin," of course, is his murder of Mathers so that he can steal the old man's box of money. Yet there is no remorse for the murder, no pleading for God's mercy and forgiveness after the crime is committed. Instead, the murder is more offensive to the senses than it is to God. The narrator describes Mathers' skull crumpling like an eggshell and the blood tinting the muddy water (16). When he first sees the undead Mathers, he notices the stiffness of his shoulders from digging the shallow grave, a full three years after the murder was committed.[3] The only distress the narrator feels is when he thinks he might be caught: "A chill of fright ran through me. If anybody should come, nothing in the world would save me from the gallows . . . Numb with fear I stood for a long time looking at the crumpled heap in the black coat" (17). The justice he fears is that of this world; the narrator gives no thought to that of the next.

When the narrator hears a voice inside him and comes to believe it is his soul, and that his soul is named Joe, he is surprised because "Never before had I believed or suspected that I had a soul but just then I knew I had" (25). The existence of the narrator's soul is one of the funniest and most puzzling aspects of the novel. Joe's existence implies that there is no longer a subject with one intention. The idea that Joe is of a separate mind from the narrator is evidenced on several occasions. He is able to name himself and concoct a list of names, some with elaborate backstories, for the narrator. When Inspector O'Corky arrives at the barracks to announce that Mathers was found in a ditch with his belly opened by a knife, Joe recalls the earlier threat of Martin Finnucane, "If your perplexity is an army or a dog, I will come with all the one-legged men and rip the bellies" (47). His response to characters often differs from that of the narrator. The undead Mathers' story of answering "No" to every question elicits a response from Joe befitting a small-town parish priest. "*This is all extremely interesting and salutary, every syllable a sermon in itself. Very very wholesome*," he responds (30, italics in original). Joe notices the bandage on the neck of Mathers and the wooden leg of the man building the scaffold. This implies that Joe might even have eyes of his own, existing behind or within the eyes of the narrator.[4] This italicised voice that notices things the narrator does not, and applies logic to situations that the narrator does not, attacks the notion of a singular subject. Only Flann O'Brien could create a soul with both Catholic principles and Cartesian skepticism.

O'Brien brings this dualism to the moment of crisis when the narrator imagines Joe as a separate, and perhaps even a frightening, other. Here Descartes' deceiving demon is made literal as the narrator imagines Joe as slimy, or perhaps rough like a cat's tongue, or maybe even scaly: "*That's not very logical—or complimentary either*, [Joe] said suddenly . . . *By God I won't be called scaly*" (117, italics in original). The narrator tries to placate Joe by nonchalantly articulating a mystery of existence that has plagued centuries of philosophers and theologians, "How can I know why I think my thoughts?" but Joe threatens to leave. When the narrator wakes up O'Brien gestures toward another of the great philosophical conundrums: how can we know that we are not dreaming? Unsurprisingly, this question is not answered, but rather met with further theories. Joe replies at first that he will leave the narrator to become part of a system of waiting souls, describing reality like a beam of light travelling on concentric circles. At another point in the novel, Joe thinks he might like to become part of the Lakes of Killarney. O'Brien is not offering answers here, his interest lies instead in conjuring the unanswerable questions. Joe's function as a soul in this novel is not as a channel of communication with God, instead he is just another solipsistic, dislocated line of inquiry no different than de Selby with his theories of waterworks and a sausage-shaped earth.

Hugh Kenner has argued that there are moments in which the narrator gives voice to religious yearnings that O'Brien's orthodox Catholic conscience required him to deny. He offers as an example the narrator's reverie as he stands on the scaffold, awaiting his hanging:

> There are in the great world whirls of fluid and vaporous existences obtaining in their own unpassing time, unwatched and uninterrupted, valid only in their essential un-understandable mystery, justified only in their eyeless and mindless immeasurability, unassailable in their actual abstraction; of the inner quality of such a thing I might well in my own time be the true quintessential pith. I might belong to a lonely shore or be the agony of the sea when it bursts upon it in despair. (O'Brien 159–60)

Kenner argues that these are some of O'Brien's most "deeply felt" passages of writing. "Like much else in the book, they have pagan Irish antecedents" (71). But this reading fails to appreciate the parody at play here and the way the writing mocks exactly this train of thought. The words and images are enchanting and beautiful, but few of the sentences actually mean anything at all. What, for instance, does it mean to obtain in time that does not pass? How can one be the pith of an inner quality? Concepts like these are only possible in the hereafter of the novel: the narrator visits an Eternity filled with useless commodities, obtaining things there in time that does not pass. While there, the policemen tell him of a machine which breaks apart senses to show the bad smells or bad feels within the good ones, as if these qualities can be separated out like so many ingredients. "'We have a machine down there,' the sergeant continued, 'that splits up any smell into its sub- and inter-smells the way you can split up a beam of light with a glass instrument. It is very interesting and edifying, you would not believe the dirty smells that are inside the perfume of a lovely lily-of-the mountain'" (246). But there is no spiritual reality to the narrator's reverie. The evocation of nature—waves bursting on lonely shores—suffuses the passage with a mystical worth, just as the narrator's elevated language suffuses his character with a sentimentality that might lead one to believe that these words are deeply-felt. The sentiment seems to be beautiful and heartfelt in the same way that the narrator's story seems to be progressing forward. Ultimately, however, both the images and the story itself are exercises in futility.

To underscore the worthlessness of the narrator's reverie, it appears in tandem with a story that has its own mysterious spiritual allusions. As Sergeant Pluck prepares to hang the narrator, he tells the story of Quigley from Fermanagh, a man let up in a hot air balloon only to disappear. When the balloon was put back up again, the man returned in it "without a feather out of him if any of my information can be believed at all" (158). Ultimately threatened by the townspeople to tell his story or suffer violent consequences, the man escapes back into the clouds, never to be heard from again. The relationship between Quigley and the narrator seems to be one of opposites—one goes up in a hot air balloon, one goes down in a lift; one remains silent, one struggles to express; one chooses to disappear while the other is damned to unwitting re-experience. By making these connections O'Brien gestures toward the possibility of an experience that is unlike that of the narrator's. There must be a light to his darkness, a peace to his clamour. There must be a place where spirituality is exquisitely ineffable and unyielding to empirical inquiry. There must be experiences that exist despite an analytical understanding of their workings. There is the experience of Quigley from Fermanagh who does not (or cannot) articulate his experience in the sky. In opposition to this, there is the narrator, who tries to write his experience, and even tries to write of his imaginings of the afterlife, yet cannot succeed with either.

Bodily assumption into heaven is one of the Catholic Church's most intriguing mysteries. Catholic dogma teaches that the Virgin Mary "having completed the course of her earthly life, was assumed body and soul into heavenly glory," and the feast day of the Assumption, 15 August, is a holy day of obligation in Catholic Churches. Pope Pius XII proclaimed the dogma of the assumption in his *Munificentissimus Deus* in 1950. He wrote that the bodily assumption is a truth "which surely no faculty of the human mind could know by its own natural powers . . . [and] is a truth that has been revealed by God and consequently something that must be firmly and faithfully believed by all children of the Church" (Pars. 44, 12). In refusing to speak, Quigley seems to offer implicit assent to Pope Pius's estimation of the capabilities of the human mind.

In his creation of the policemen who hound the narrator with their impossible logic and even more impossible inventions, O'Brien provides the funniest and most confounding consideration of "un-understandable mystery." MacCruiskeen's light mangle or infinite boxes within boxes show the narrator shocking realities beyond what he thought possible. And while these impossibilities find their origin in scientific advancements of the twentieth century, the real punishment for the narrator lies in how to understand and express the inconceivable. These are revelations of an unholy sort, and they bring the narrator to prayer too late: "At this point I became afraid. What he was doing was no longer wonderful but terrible. I shut my eyes and prayed that he would stop while still doing things that were at least possible for a man to do" (O'Brien 73). These are fitting revelations for a narrator who has put more work into ensuring the posterity of de Selby's theories than he has into ensuring the safety of his own immortal soul. The human struggle to express revelation, along with the need to reconcile faith with science, was particularly important to Catholic modernists. In his *livre inédit*, Alfred Loisy considered the concept of revelation and dogma in the Catholic Church as attempts to express and understand the ineffable. These explanations rely on symbols and metaphors which are presented to humanity in a way that can be understood through human experience, and Loisy argues that these symbols can be mistakenly interpreted as the revelation itself:

> These symbols and metaphors, in relation to the experiences to which they give utterance, are a creative stimulus, but they are not wholly adequate or final and their utility varies with its dependence on man's intellectual and moral progress. The fault of the traditional teaching was in having so fastened its attention upon the forms of the symbols themselves as almost to have forgotten the reality for which they stand. (Reardon 23)

In *The Third Policeman*, however, there is no reality for which any of these revelations stand. There is no divine truth for which these invisible spear points or infinite boxes are symbols. There is only the fear of the impossible.

At the core of the narrator's punishment is the inconceivable notion of eternity. Joseph Devlin writes of the way in which O'Brien focuses on the impossibility of eternity rather than the torments of hell. "In the retreat sermon in Joyce's *A Portrait of the Artist as a Young Man*, the priest tries to make the eternity of hell comprehensible by using the image of a bird carrying away a mountain, one grain of sand at a time. But for O'Nolan it is the incomprehensibility of eternity that is hellish" (Devlin 327–28). After the endless complexities and convolutions of the Parish, this never-ending sameness torments the narrator because it offers nothing but time. Joe's obstinate refusal to accept that Eternity can be reached by a lift stems from his ability to understand the notion of multiple levels of meaning. Eternity he takes to mean the realm of heaven (or perhaps even hell). But this Eternity is in keeping with the notion of empty spirituality found throughout *The Third Policeman*. This Eternity is located just to the right of Mr. Jarvis's outhouse on the map MacCruiskeen found on his bedroom ceiling (O'Brien 123–4). Earlier in the story, the sky above that spot is described as "serene, impenetrable, ineffable and incomparable, with a fine island of clouds anchored in the calm two yards to the right of Mr. Jarvis's outhouse" (86). Just as with the story of Quigley, this imagery gestures toward another level of divine experience. But it comes as no surprise that the narrator's destiny is to go into the ground under the outhouse, not into the ethereal ether over it.

Spirituality in Eternity becomes as empty and useless as any of the items that can be summoned forth from its hellish oven doors. To remark on the narrator's stockpile of meaningless merchandise, the Sergeant says, "Lord, save us" (137). This echoes Joe's earlier exclamation "Lord, save us!" as the group plummeted in the lift to arrive in Eternity (130). With the Sergeant, though, the saying is only a meaningless oath to express mild astonishment, rather than a prayer for mercy. Overcome with emotion on the way back up in the lift, the narrator sobs as the policemen discuss sweets. Suddenly, the candy becomes metaphorical for an undiscerning, insincere religion. It soothes, stupefies, tempts, and punishes. There is "supernatural pleasure" in the candies. Sobbing and snuffling, the narrator stuffs his mouth with them as the Sergeant proclaims, "Lord, I love sweets." He says that the carnival assorted has a "very spiritual" flavor but resists the temptation of Pluck's offered bag because of the punishment of indigestion he will suffer later (142). Truly, nothing has worth in this hellish Eternity, and for all the religious imagery, the characters' elevation upward is only a farce—and a lift. Rather than inspired or even reborn by the visit to Eternity, the narrator emerges hopeless and desperate to escape back into sleep: "Compared with this sleep, death is a restive thing, peace is a clamour and darkness a burst of light" (143).

John Cardinal Newman, an early rector of O'Brien's alma mater of University College Dublin, compared skepticism to an epidemic that was "wonderfully catching." He argued that the imagination was the cause of the infection in that it provided plausible ways of thinking that could overcome one's mind:

> We begin by asking "How can we be sure that it is not so?" and this thought hides from the mind the real rational grounds on which our

faith is founded. Then our faith goes, and how in the world is it ever to be regained, except by a wonderful grant of God's grace. May God keep us all from this terrible deceit of the latter days. (Newman 32)

In *The Third Policeman*, however, imagination and faith are intertwined in such a way that the two become stronger rather than weaker. O'Brien took as his inspiration the impossibilities inherent to Catholic faith, and while the story is certainly one of "back-chat and funny cracks," there is also an uneasy exploration of the unknown that informs the work. So much of O'Brien's imagined hell is a twisting of the mysteries that define his faith. The soul fractures and doubles the sense of self rather than bringing that self into solidarity with divine being. Prayers and the articulation of spiritual longings are empty and meaningless. Revelations lead to confusion and terror rather than truth and hope. The answers offered by science were frightening, but they were nothing compared to the mysteries demanded by faith. For as much as scientific advancement boggles the mind at what is possible in the now, the mysteries of Catholicism go on into eternity.

NOTES

1 This is not to say that *The Third Policeman* should be considered a Catholic novel. The struggle between good and evil, which is a defining characteristic of these works, plays no part in O'Brien's novel. Because the narrator tells his story from hell, that struggle, if indeed one existed at all, took place in the narrator's experience well before the novel itself begins. Graham Greene was the reader at Longmans who recommended the publication of *At Swim-Two-Birds*. He also wrote a letter congratulating O'Brien on the publication of *The Hard Life* and is the person to whom the book is dedicated.

2 The narrator says that he and the mastermind of the murder, John Divney, were inseparable for three years after Divney hid the black box in a place he kept secret from the narrator (O'Brien 18). Upon seeing the undead Mathers, Joe tells the narrator, "*There is nothing dreamy about your stiff shoulders.* No, I replied, but a nightmare can be as strenuous physically as the real thing" (25–6).

3 Both Joe and the readers have eyes within those of the narrator, much like the horrible image of Mathers with eyes "with a tiny pinhole in the centre of the

'pupil' through which the real eye gazed out secretively and with great coldness," (O'Brien 24).

4 There are also similarities between the story of Quigley and the story of a man "caught up to the third heaven" in 2 Corinthians 12: 2–5. This is a passage that Augustine considers at length in his *Works*.

WORKS CITED

Booker, M. Keith. *Flann O'Brien, Bakhtin, and Menippean Satire*. Syracuse: Syracuse Univ. Press, 1995.

Brooker, Joseph. *Flann O'Brien*. Devon: Northcote House, 2005.

Catholic Encyclopedia. Vol. 9. New York: Universal Knowledge Foundation, 1910.

Clarke, Richard F. *Logic*. London: Longmans, Green & Co., 1889.

Cohen, David. "Arranged by Wise Hands: Flann O'Brien's Metafictions." *Conjuring Complexities: Essays on Flann O'Brien*. Eds Anne Clune and Tess Hurson. Antrim: W. & G. Baird, 1997.

Cronin, Anthony. *No Laughing Matter: The Life and Times of Flann O'Brien*. New York: Fromm International, 1998.

Devlin, Joseph. "Flann O'Brien." *British Writers*. Ed. George Stade, Supplement II. New York: Charles Scribner's Sons, 1992: 327–28.

Kenner, Hugh. "The Fourth Policeman." *Conjuring Complexities*. Eds. Anne Clune and Tess Hurson. Antrim: W. & G. Baird, 1997.

Newman, John Henry. *The Living Thoughts of Cardinal Newman*. Ed. Henry Tristram. New York: David McKay and Co., 1946.

O'Brien, Flann. "A Sheaf of Letters." *A Flann O'Brien—Myles na Gopaleen Number*. Eds. Robert Hogan and Gordon Henderson. Special issue of *The Journal of Irish Literature*. 3.1 (1974): 65–92.

—. *The Third Policeman*. Normal, Illinois: Dalkey Archive Press, 1999.

MACIEJ RUCZAJ

Infernal Poetics/Infernal Ethics: *The Third Policeman* Between Medieval and (Post)Modern Netherworlds

> "an observer placed at the lower end of a cylindrical verti-
> cal shaft 5000 ft deep sunk from the surface towards the
> centre of the earth" (Joyce, *Ulysses*, 1922)

In one of the pioneering analyses of Flann O'Brien's *The Third Policeman*, Hugh Kenner stated: "The book is a black joke, a comic turn; it is not a *Divina Commedia,* and never dreamed of being one" (69). Although the author himself describes the setting as "a sort of hell," which the nameless narrator "earned" for his crime, and intended to entitle the book "Hell Goes Round and Round" thus inscribing it in the generic tradition culminating in Dante's poem, Kenner felt obliged to authoritatively disperse any notion that O'Brien's "back-chat and funny cracks" (O'Brien 200) may have something in common with the canonical Western representation of the netherworld.

Dante and his *opus magnum* is a presence hovering over the poetics of Anglo-American modernism. O'Brien, however, is to a large extent excluded from the companionship of "high modernists" for whom *La Divina Commedia* was—in Joyce's words—the main "spiritual food."[1] Although both attempted a similar venture into the world of the dead, there is a deep incongruity in the "public image" of the two authors. For a long time, O'Brien was a victim of a kind of "biographical criticism," which succumbed to the sense of a consciously staged farce surrounding the writer's career and which rendered any imaginable connection between the sombre, eagle-nosed Dante of Romantic paintings and the clownish figure of Myles na gCopaleen unthinkable (Hopper 18–21).

Subsequently, O'Brien was salvaged from this kind of criticism and *The Third Policeman* was rediscovered as "a novel of ideas" (Booker 48). In this new critical wave, particular attention was paid to the subversive and distorting qualities of the text: it was inscribed either in the tradition of Menippean satire—as an ironic assault on the dogmas of Western Cartesianism (Lanterns, Booker)—or as a paradigmatic proto-postmodernist metafiction deconstructing the monologic concept of authorship (Keith Hopper). Admittedly, critics such as Hopper detect "the Catholic conscience" or "a morality tale," "at the deep core of the novel," yet even in this case any closer affinity seemed improbable due to the disparity between the postmodern open structure of the novel and the closed, monologic universe of Dante (Hopper 192).

What if we reverse this attitude and "take hell for granted," at the same time realizing the major difference in the ontological status of Dante—the pilgrim from the world of the living, and O'Brien's narrator—the inhabitant of the first of the eschatological realms?[2] Without claiming a direct intertextual relation between the *Commedia* and *The Third Policeman*, and without attempting to contradict the "postmodernist" or Menippean interpretations, I would like to propose that a reading of O'Brien's novel centred on the theme of the netherworld and realized by means of an analogy with Dante's *Commedia* makes it possible to resolve the inherent paradox between the heteroglossic poetics of the novel and the dimension of the "morality tale" at "the heart" of the text.

There are several perspectives from which the relation between the two texts can be approached. The least controversial would be to detect in O'Brien's texts a similar tendency to the "poetics of perversion" that Van Hulle describes in relation to Beckett, calling the process "putting Dante on his head" (Anspaugh 31–2; Caselli 2, 21). For instance, the passage about the "trip to Eternity" abounds in ironic play with the motifs both from Dante (*selva selvaggia*) and the Celtic otherworldly literature (especially the lands of plenty and eternal youth). The present paper, however, aims at disclosing a deeper structural affinity between the eschatological realms presented in the two texts, an affinity that transcends the mere level of literary free play. The focus is on two exemplary dimensions connected to the structuring of the "place of damnation." Firstly, the paper examines the theology of crime and punishment as the basic structuring principle of the "place of damnation," before turning to the allegorical tension inherent in the infernal topography and exemplified by the dualism of "right and left."

The Anatomy of Inferno

In Canto XIV of *Inferno,* Virgil explains the origins of the rivers of Hell: he describes the gigantic monument in Crete, a symbol of the corruption of human history, whose tears "force a passage through that cavern / taking their course from rock to rock into this depth" (XIV, 94–120). As Dante, the pilgrim, points out, the hellish rivers "si diriva così dal nostro mondo" (flow from *our* world). The essence of Hell is poignantly expressed by means of the allegorical image: Hell is not a place where anything can be originated or created; the whole essence of Inferno starts and feeds itself "outside," by man's own doings (Durling 84). It can thus be said about the damned of the *Commedia* that "the torments and punishments of Hell are images of what they have elected" (Collins 80).

As David Pike notes, each of the Dantean *figurae* "reveals the truth of his life as a fixed, emblematic moment of sin" (208). The world of the netherworldly "Parish" that the narrator—Noman[3]—enters is said to possess a specific nightmarish atmosphere, which (as Francis Doherty points out) contains nothing other than projections of Noman's mind materialized in the infernal setting: "everything being generated by himself, from dreams, fantasies, fictions" (Doherty 58). In fact, it may be claimed that the world of the Parish is to a large extent reduced to the participants in the story of Noman's crime—the murder of old Mathers. In *The Third Policeman,* Noman's hell is peopled with killers and robbers like himself, and by policemen he invokes implicitly just after the killing when he is overwhelmed by fear of "the gallows." The first person he encounters on "the other side" is his victim, and old Mathers returns to haunt him at the end in the form of Policeman Fox ("The great fat body in the uniform did not remind me of anybody that I knew but the face on the top of it belonged to old Mathers," 183). Concetta Mazullo suggests that even the prominence of bicycles in the Parish can be explained by a reference to the moment of crime: after all, it was on bicycles that Noman and Divney arrived at the scene of the murder, and it was with "a special bicycle-pump" that the first blow was struck (7).

In Canto XIV, the pilgrims encounter the blasphemer Campaneus who claims with hopeless pride: "Qual io fui vivo, tal son morto" (That which I was in life, I am in death) (XIV, 51). As Pike suggests, this statement provides a summary of the infernal condition of the damned: "the reification of the souls into an eternal present that merely reflects the absolute past of their failed lives." Hell "eternally freezes the poses of the damned into the essence of what they were" (103). The motif of "reification" within the "emblematic moment of sin," an entrapment in the deed, is seen in O'Brien's novel in the very first scene after Noman enters old Mathers' house (i.e. after his death). Noman notices the "resurrected" Mathers and feels "a stiffness" spreading "across my own shoulders . . . from my exertions with the spade" (25), which in turn prompts the reader to make the only possible connection—to the scene of the murder and burying of Mathers' corpse, both actions being carried out with a "spade." Only after a while do we realize that the narrative is deliberately discontinuous here, violating the mimetic temporal relations. After all, the murder and Noman's "visit" to Mathers' house are divided by a period of three years in the narrative. Nevertheless, old Mathers still has his "body bandaged," and the shoulders of the narrator are still "stiff." The moral dimension thus seems to invade and overwhelm the mimetic level of the narrative, introducing a meaningful discontinuity instead of a chaotic linearity.

The nature of infernal torments in Dante's poetic vision is organized according to the principle of *contrapasso*, an aesthetic rather than theological concept of the mechanics of Divine Justice. Although Noman's Hell seems to follow Foucault's precept of the shift from corporeal punishment and torture towards "the play of much more subtle sufferings" of the mind, deprived of their medieval "visual grandiosity" as the defining feature of the modern understanding of punitive justice (Foucault 39–63), it nevertheless preserves the Dantean principle. In what seems to be a metafictional allusion from the author himself, O'Brien's Noman states at the beginning: "Perhaps it is important in the story I am going to tell to remember that it was for de Selby that I committed my first serious sin. It was for him that I committed my greatest sin" (9). According to the principle of *contrapasso*, his punishment has a peculiarly "de Selbyian" air, abounding with strange pseudo-scientific theories and the overwhelming atmosphere of "life as hallucination."[4] Some of Dante's damned are burnt to ashes, others torn to pieces by demons; in the case of Noman, it is his perception and his consciousness that come under attack. The core of the subversive strategy reveals itself in the complete violation of the cooperation between the mind and the senses. The "awful alteration of everything" makes the connection and agreement between the two faculties impossible.[5] The mind is suddenly unable to grasp and comprehend the data delivered by the senses, leaving the narrator completely disoriented in the new environs.

Reading *The Third Policeman* as a text displaying the failure of language and human perception/reason found its expression in the current analyses of the novel within the tradition of Menippean satire. Noman is described as a "godless Cartesian" led by a belief in a reality that is ultimately graspable and decipherable by his perception. The world is—as in Maritain's definition of Cartesianism—transparent to his sight, which joins in a single act "seeing and interpreting." The basis of infernal torture is thus provided by the assault on his senses and mind rather than body (the mere instrument of *ratio* in Cartesian philosophy). In the famous scene in the underground "Eternity," Noman is confronted by the phenomena that "lacked an essential property of known objects . . . their appearance, if even that word is not inadmissible, was not understood by the eye and was in any event indescribable" (135). Both the human episteme ("not understood by the eye") and the expressive powers of language ("indescribable") are disclosed as essentially limited and fallible. The futility of the Cartesian epistemological hubris and of the aspirations of the "monologic" author in full control of the discourse are thus displayed, confirming the "Menippean/postmodern" core of O'Brien's text.

Nevertheless, the deficiency of human epistemic and intellectual capacities provides also the basic poetic principle of Dante's *Inferno*. In a striking metaphor that merges the sense of perception, the cognitive powers, and the ethical dimension, Virgil describes the damned as having "squinted minds" during their lifetime, and this sensual/intellectual/moral handicap is reified in Hell (VII, 40). Epistemology is by no means a central issue in Dante's *Commedia*; however, it plays a prominent role in the poetics of its first canticle. *Inferno* is a zone of corporeality and sense perception, which in other eschatological realms are exchanged for the spiritual and super-rational modes of existence and cognition (Miller 93, 127). As Wallace Fowlie notes, "occhio" (eye) is one the most frequently used words in this part of the *Commedia* (38). It is the realm of mirrors reverting and deforming reality, of human perception deposed from its throne of the interpreter of reality. *Inferno*'s corruption reveals itself not only as epistemic deficiency but also spatial disorientation, and—above all—in the textual distortions, malapropisms, and misquotations, i.e. textual features also ascribed to O'Brien's novel. According to Teodolinda Barolini: "the mimesis of the first canticle is dedicated to reproducing the instances of textual distortion. Textually, the governing principle of *Inferno* is misuse . . ." (4).

In his study of Beckett, Kenner juxtaposes the allegedly "Irish" tradition of "epistemological comedy" (Swift, Sterne, and Beckett) that exposes the limited nature of perception and language with the "ethical" one (seemingly an allusion to Dante), which inevitably operates within the stable axiological frame (37). Dante's *Inferno*, however, proves that the two do not necessarily form an antithetical pair. Poetics and ethics of Dantean vision are inherently related and indivisible and as such may provide an alternative instrument for the analysis of the chaosmos of Noman's "Parish."[6]

The Unbearable Leftness of Being

Allegory is a governing trope of Dante's poem, uniting each detail into the overarching meaningful structure of the God-centered universe. In the *Commedia,* the medieval belief in the allegorical coincidence of the physical and the spiritual is conveyed, inter alia, by the references to "leftward and rightwards" movement. Whereas in *Inferno* the pilgrims are descending "toward the bottom on the left" (Canto XIV), purgatorial ascent is repeatedly described as rightwards movement. This emphasis is particularly disturbing when we realize that they travel down the circles of Hell and up the slopes of Mount Purgatory—thus in a circular trajectory—rendering the terms "right" and "left" quite meaningless. Dante of course refers to the "absolute right and left," i.e. invested with an allegorical significance, the point of reference being the theological topography of the Last Judgment scene with the damned on the left and the saved on the right of the divine throne.

The disconcerting dialectics of right and left also suffuses the text of *The Third Policeman*, especially the discourse of the policemen, to find its climax in Sergeant Pluck's "rules of wisdom" of which the fourth is: "take left turns as much as possible." When describing the madness of Policeman Fox, Pluck points to his belief in the existence of "the right turn of the road" and of "getting all the leftness from his blood"; the reader is manipulated into a feeling of uneasiness concerning the mimetic level of the text and seduced to "take every detail as significant" (Clifford 84), i.e. to ascribe to it allegorical meaning. Hopper has convincingly proved how O'Brien's narrative constantly produces such "surpluses of meaning," only to laugh at the reader's expense (204–5). The discussion of Policeman Fox's attitude to "rightness and leftness" is just another example of such an authorial seduction: intimations of some—moral?—dimension of the duality are immediately destroyed by Pluck's confirmation of the superiority of left over right by means of a rhetorical question: "Did you ever in your life . . . mount the bicycle from the right" (153)?

The obsession with left and right may thus be taken as nothing more than playing with the absurd, similar to the obsession with odd and even numbers in *At Swim-Two-Birds*. Just as in Brian McHale's comment on Kafka, the text creates "constant promises of allegorical meaning, everything can be allegory but nothing actually is . . ." (141). Nevertheless, if we examine the dialectics of right and left in the text as a whole, we may see a peculiar consistency in the use of this motif. Firstly, the theme is developed by means of a crucial anatomical detail: Noman's wooden leg is the left one. Booker makes a striking comparison regarding this: whereas the wooden limb is a feature that connects Noman with several characters of Beckett's fiction and drama, there is a considerable difference as far as the function of this motif is concerned. Beckett's heroes are presented as really physically handicapped, their bodies are in a state of constant decomposition, which serves as a crucial defining element of their status. On the other hand, on the mimetic level, Noman's wooden leg seems "to offer little hindrance to [his] physical capabilities" (Booker specifically mentions the scene of Mather's murder, where Noman is able to transport and bury the corpse almost by himself [24]). The explanation may be quite straightforward: the wooden leg should not be read as a unit on the literal level, but rather one invested with allegorical significance. Interestingly, the description of how Noman broke his leg and finally acquired a wooden one follows almost immediately after the word "sin" occurs for the first and only time in the text. Moreover, it may be added that in the first canto of the *Inferno,* Dante is in fact depicted as limping on his "pie fermo" (firm foot), which in medieval anatomy is synonymous with the left one, and this motif is part of a series of allegorical images referring to his sinfulness such as "dark wood" or "lost path" (Freccero 34–8).

This last analogy is of course rather O'Brienesque in itself. Nevertheless, the theme of the left leg surfaces several times with possible ethical undertones, most prominently when Noman meets "the killer and the robber" Martin Finnucane, a character that fills him with fear and disgust but in reality is simply a mirror of his own self. This coequality is signalled in the text by the ultimate revelation that the robber also has a left leg made of wood. "Funny coincidence," Noman thinks, but it is not.

Secondly, the dualism of right and left embraces the whole topography of the netherworldly surroundings: the police barracks Noman comes across after entering the unknown land are located on the left side of the road, and moreover at the place where the path "gently bends" to the left. The underground Eternity that the narrator is taken to shortly afterwards is also repeatedly described as being situated at "the left turn" of the road.

At the end, the narrator seems to finally realize the hidden meaning of the right-left dialectics. Escaping from the gallows and deciding to leave the Parish, he makes a real theological argument:

> It was on the *left* the Sergeant had gone with MacCruiskeen, [to that quarter the next world lay] and it was *leftwards* that all my troubles were. I led the bicycle to the middle of the road, turned her wheel resolutely to the *right* and swung myself into the centre of her saddle.
>
> (173, emphasis mine)

When read allegorically, this fragment conveys the possibility of the narrator's salvation. And, in fact, the atmosphere of this fragment heavily recalls the imagery of Dante's passage through the boundary between Hell and Purgatory.

Dante leaves Hell through the dark passage along the "blind stream" and at the end he is confronted with the starlit sky. In a similar manner, Noman follows "water by the roadside, always over-shouted in the roistering day," but now performing "audibly in its hidings" (173). Above, he "could see the dim tracery of the stars struggling out here and there between the clouds" (173). The whole journey is in almost complete darkness, just like the passage of the poets to the foot of Mount Purgatory. Dante's "cieco flume" is described by D. Pike as "a truly liminal region," connecting the deepest circle of Hell with Purgatory, though not belonging to either of them (132). Noman's journey through the dark landscape, discernible by sound and touch rather than sight, leads finally to another "liminal zone"—the dwelling of Policeman Fox, situated "inside the walls" of old Mathers' house.

Significantly, the omnipresent "leftness" is exchanged in these closing passages for the "right": old Mathers' dwelling is located on the "right-hand" side, similarly to other reassuringly familiar places (e.g. "Courahan's house," 194). In fact, leaving Policeman Fox, Noman moves on in the mode that resembles not only the closing lines of the *Inferno*, but also the opening of the *Purgatorio*:

> We made our way across the lonely plain,
>
> like one returning to a lost pathway,
>
> who, till he finds it, seems to move in vain. (I, 118–120)

Noman follows a well-known, rediscovered path, indulges in imagining his "old friend Divney" and finally sees his own house "exactly in the point I knew it stood."

He is overwhelmed by the sense of happiness, which, as in the case of Dante, turns the experience of Hell into nothing more than a distant memory (194).

At this point, however, Noman is confronted with the fact of his death and his damnation. The parallel with Dante's passage through the frontier between the two kingdoms turns into a bitter travesty. Crucially, the duality of right and left is rendered obsolete in the light of this new revelation. At the beginning of the novel, Noman's walk towards the police barracks led him through the bleak brown bogland *on the left* and "greener country" *on the right*. The landscape through which he now staggers is, on the one hand, the same region he walked through at the beginning of the narrative. This time, however, the spatial dualism seems superseded by the all-embracing "leftness": "Waterlogged bog and healthless marsh *stretched endlessly to left and right*" (197, emphasis mine).

Thus, O'Brien's novel presents itself as an allegory decapitated, lacking the necessary component of upward progression. Both protagonists seem to follow a similar trajectory through the dialectics of right and left; the difference emerges on the margins of both texts. The breathtaking daybreak of the opening canto of *Purgatorio* is matched by the image of the dawn, which "had come with a bitter searing wind," bringing "black angry clouds" rather than light. The *Inferno*—as Ezra Pound suggests—must be read only as a prelude to the *Purgatorio* and the *Paradiso*. The dawn is also concomitant with the cleansing of the pilgrim's vision and gradual re-establishment of proper relations between words and things. *The Third Policeman* leaves no space for such an upward continuation; the narrator is not a pilgrim but an inhabitant of the realm, and thus the dawn signals only the deathly *repetition* of the infernal punishment. Therefore, the text of the novel cannot provide a complete all-explaining system of the kind the *Commedia* as a whole presents. At the end of Dante's pilgrimage, the final union of "being" and "knowing" is achieved. Conversely, Noman's revelation consists in "non-being" and "ignorance." It stays within the infernal zone of fragmentation, "angry incomprehension" and distortion. It remains horizontal rather than vertical, it moves in circles, rather than—as the pilgrim-poets do—in the gyre.

Inferno *sub specie tempora modernitatis*?

The Third Policeman, as I have attempted to prove, follows a similar path to the *Inferno*, playing on the one hand with the poetics of distortion, ironic inversion and instability of meaning, and on the other—trying to anchor this instability to the moral reality of the fallen human reason and perception. It represents the mode of epistemological comedy, yet is inextricably linked with the ethical one. O'Brien's poetics of "the relative world" that rejects any definiteness is not so far removed from Dante's text as it may first appear to the reader. The sense of alienation between the texts probably emanates from different sources, however.

Whereas in Dante, the endless repetition of torment is necessarily connected to the consciousness of its finality and the acknowledgment of Divine Justice that moulds even Hell into the manifestation of God's universal plan, O'Brien's inferno offers no such reassuring knowledge. The difference is realized by means of the motif of the erasure of the narrator's memory. Noman shares the reality of "changeless there-being" of the damned but not their consciousness. While the infernal existence of each soul starts with confession and its installment in the topography of Hell (Canto V), Noman's netherworld is characterized by a sense of anxiety and incertitude. He belongs to this "new breed" who, to invoke Beckett's early poem:

> . . . shall not scour in swift joy
> the bright hill's girdle
> nor tremble with the dark pride of torture
> and the bitter dignity of an ingenious damnation. (Beckett, "Texts")

The narrator of Beckett's *Texts for Nothing* sums up this hiatus between the medieval and modern "infernal experience":

> I was, I was, they say in Purgatory, in Hell too, admirable singulars, admirable assurance. Plunged in ice up to the nostrils, the eyelids caked with frozen tears, to fight all your battles o'er again, what tranquillity, and know there are no more emotions in store, no, I can't have heard aright. (Beckett 124–5)

John Freccero—dealing with the fundamental generic characteristic of the *Commedia*—speaks of the form of "Christian allegory," which "is identical with the phenomenology of confession, for both involve a comprehension of the self in history within a retrospective literary structure" (Freccero 120). *The Third Policeman* pretends to follow the model with its confessional opening: "Not everybody knows how I killed . . ." yet the rest of the narrative presents us with a *concerto* of "evasions and subterfuge" (to use St. Augustine's description of the story of original sin) on the side of Noman who seems to lack any sense of guilt and sinfulness. The rejection of the generic fundament of the *Commedia* is paralleled by the evasion of its central ethical premise: the existence of the individual "who through the exercise of his freedom of choice is subjected to the rewarding or punishing justice" (Dante, "Epistle to Can Grande").

The rejection of responsibility for one's own guilt and thus one's own subjectivity may evoke Beckett's *Not I*, with one crucial difference, however: the Mouth (just as other protagonists of Beckett's "purgatorial" texts) suffers in some indefinable space "between two lit refugees" of Hell and Heaven for some indefinite transgression (for being born), whereas Noman's sin remains—on the contrary—very "traditional." Although he shares the namelessness and status of "astonishing parade of nullity" of Beckett's characters, Noman still seems to be the subject of the same individualized punishing justice as the damned of Dante's epic poem.[7]

The question of whether this final conclusion should be read as O'Brien's statement on the *conditio humana* of modernity,[8] thus making *The Third Policeman* a specific *Inferno sub specie tempora modernitatis*, remains open and could be the subject of another study.

NOTES

1   Admittedly, passing allusions to the similarities between the *Commedia* and O'Brien's novel can be found in, for example, Morse and M.K. Booker.

2   A solution actually proposed by Booker, though only in a footnote (Booker 60).

3   In using the coinages "The Parish" and "Noman," I follow Keith Hopper's monograph on O'Brien.

4   See, for example, Ondřej Pilný (44), Anne Clissmann (156).

5   See, for example, Pilný 47.

6   See also Booker 60.

7   If we were to look for the closest Dantean model for O'Brien's Hell, it would probably be the infernal vestibule of Canto IV with its state of confusion, namelessness, and liminality.

8   There are several quotes that provide striking parallels to O'Brien's vision in this respect: Walter Benjamin defines modernity as—inter alia—"the endless repetition of the same thing disguised by the illusion of its novelty," literally an "infernal repetition." This last notion bears a crucial significance for the overall interpretation of the novel: it sums up a paradoxical connection between the motifs of infinity (mediated by means of science) and imprisonment that recur in my argument. The world of the Parish seems, in fact, to parallel almost exactly Chesterton's critique of the scientific materialism: "The size of this scientific universe gave one no novelty, no relief . . . The grandeur of infinity added nothing to it. It was like telling a prisoner in Reading gaol that he would be glad to hear that the gaol now covered half the country. The warder would have nothing to show the man except more and more long corridors of stone lit by ghastly lights and empty of all that is human" (cf. the underground "Eternity" of Sergeant Pluck).

WORKS CITED

Anspaugh, Kelly. "Faith, Hope, and—What Was It?: Beckett Reading Joyce Reading Dante." *Journal of Beckett Studies* 5.182 (1996).

Barolini, Teodolinda. *Dante's Poets: Textuality and Truth in the Comedy*. Princeton: Princeton Univ. Press, 1984.

Beckett, Samuel. "Texts for Nothing." *The Complete Short Prose, 1929–1989*. Ed. S. Gontarski. New York: Grove Press, 1995.

Booker, M.K. *Flann O'Brien, Bakhtin, and Menippean Satire*. Syracuse: Syracuse Univ. Press, 1995.

Caselli, Daniela. *Beckett's Dantes. Intertextuality in Fiction and Criticism*. Manchester: Manchester Univ. Press, 2005.

Clifford, Gay. *The Transformations of Allegory*. London: Routledge & Kegan, 1974.

Clissmann, Anne. *Flann O'Brien. A Critical Introduction to His Writings*. Dublin: Gill and Macmillan, 1975.

Collins, James. *Pilgrim in Love. An Introduction to Dante and His Spirituality*. Chicago: Loyola Univ. Press, 1984.

Dante. *La Divina Commedia*. DanteOnline. Accessed 3 March 2011.

—. *Comedy*. Trans. Robert Hollander. DanteOnline. Accessed 4 March 2011.

—. *Epistle to Can Grande*, trans. James Merchand. Accessed 10 March 2011.

Doherty, Francis. "Flann O'Brien's Existentialist Hell." *The Canadian Journal of Irish Studies* XV.2 (1989).

Durling, Robert M. "Deceit and Digestion in the Belly of Hell." *Allegory and Representation. Selected Papers from the English Institute 1979–1980*. Ed. S. J. Greenblatt. Baltimore: The John Hopkins Univ. Press, 1981.

Foucault, Michel. *Dohlížet a trestat*. Trans. Č. Pelikán. Praha: Dauphin, 2000.

Fowlie, Wallace. *A Reading of Dante's Inferno*. Chicago: Univ. of Chicago Press, 1981.

Freccero, John. *Dante: The Poetics of Conversion*. Cambridge: Harvard Univ. Press, 1998.

Hopper, Keith. *Flann O'Brien: A Portrait of the Artist as a Young Post-modernist*. Cork: Cork Univ. Press, 1995.

Kenner, Hugh. "The Fourth Policeman." *Conjuring Complexities. Essays on Flann O'Brien*. Eds. Anne Clune and T. Hurson. Belfast: Queen's Univ. Belfast Press, 1997.

—. *Samuel Beckett: A Critical Study*. New York: Grove Press, 1961.

McHale, Brian. *Postmodernist Fictions*. New York: Routledge, 1987.

Mazullo, Concetta. "Flann O'Brien's Hellish Otherworld: From *Buile Suibhne* to *The Third Policeman*." *Irish University Review* 25.2 (Autumn/Winter 1995).

Miller, Edward G. *Sense perception in Dante's Commedia. Studies in Medieval Literature*, vol. 15. Lampter, Dyfed: The Edwin Mellen Press, 1996.

Morse, Daniel. "Making the Familiar Unfamiliar: The Fantastic in Four Twentieth-Century Irish Novelists." *That Other World. The Supernatural and the Fantastic in Irish Literature and its Contexts*, vol. two. Ed. Bruce Stewart. Gerrards Cross: Colin Smythe, 1998.

O'Brien, Flann. *The Third Policeman*. London: Flamingo, 1993; Normal, Illinois: Dalkey Archive Press, 1999.

Pike, David L. *Passage Through Hell: Modernist Descents, Medieval Underworlds.* Ithaca: Cornell Univ. Press, 1997.

Pilný, Ondřej. "Cycling Round the Bend." *Literaria Pragensia* 13.7 (1997).

ANTHONY ADAMS

Butter-Spades, Footnotes, and Omnium: *The Third Policeman* as 'Pataphysical Fiction

> From a chance and momentary perusal of the Policeman's notebook it is possible for me to give here the relative figures for a week's readings. For obvious reasons the figures themselves are fictitious. (*The Third Policeman* 103 n. 7)

> An anthology devoted to small boxes, such as chests and caskets, would constitute an important chapter in psychology. These complex pieces that a craftsman creates are very evident witnesses of the *need for secrecy*, of an intuitive sense of hiding places. (Bachelard, *Poetics of Space* 81)

A third of the way through Flann O'Brien's *The Third Policeman*, a reader might be encouraged to attempt the anthology Bachelard envisions; by its close, if not before, the same reader will be considerably dissuaded. Discouragement comes with the knowledge that such little boxes, which represent a psychological rather than a physical threshold, serve both to intrigue and mislead; *The Third Policeman* contains such elaborate boxes of misdirection that one might despair of ever finding the keys again. The novel tantalizes with its evocation of a brilliantly self-referential world filled with a most crazed sanity, and written in a relentlessly reflexive language. This style has encouraged readers to declare the novel an early exposition of the postmodern awareness that reality is not given, but written.[1] Especially unnerving is a manifest distrust toward any language that threatens to describe reality, combined with a thrill in the madcap constructs of those who make the effort to do so. If the bulk of the action takes place in a hellish afterlife, or at least an intellectual purgatory, then *The Third Policeman* presents a curiously confusing hell in which inventiveness and verbosity pose greater dangers than any corporal punishment. The novel's humor disquiets readers with a landscape of gendered bicycles, querulous policemen, and lugubrious footnotes. We perceive, alongside a potential fictive world, a potential physics and metaphysics that play with knowledge and limits, an original blend of the antiquarian and the scientific avant-garde, and one that shares elements with the contemporary genre of steampunk, but which surpasses this genre in the inventiveness of its enigmas as well as in its pessimism about mechanical progress. *The Third Policeman* celebrates, albeit skeptically, a metafictional poetics that was also embraced by pataphysics, a concept introduced by Alfred Jarry and embraced by the Oulipo, and which has echoes in writers such as Joyce and Cortázar. The novel makes elaborate display both of the difficulty confronted by seekers of linguistic truth, and of the mechanical lunacy of the modern world, and the hope for physical truth it seems to offer. These comprise, on the one hand, "language objects" (the intellectual trumpery of the policemen, de Selby's tomes, scholarly folderol) and, on the other, "objects to language," the panoply of intricate inventions or gizmos that play such an important role in the police barracks (microscopic chests, water-boxes, mangles). For the former, language serves the typical metafictional function of making the reader aware that it is writing, not reality, one reads; instead of being allowed to proceed in the belief that they are viewing through a transparent glass the functions of the real world, such fiction continually calls attention to itself in the act of being read. For the latter, descriptions of these inventions serve to confuse the reader, and to complicate any image of mechanical reality. They become less like useful objects, less "tool-like," and more like vague and elaborate *things*, amorphic yet powerful in the inscrutability of their construction or purpose. The joint effect of these aspects of O'Brien's writing creates a world whose most uncanny quality is also a diversion: the key that would unlock this set of boxes is itself another box.

Language objects
Although often considered with Joyce and Beckett in the tradition of literary Irish comic writing, O'Brien himself would have been skeptical regarding

his membership in such a club. His admiration for Joyce's artistic genius was coupled with ambivalence regarding his stance toward literary achievement and what O'Brien detected as a particularly Modernist (and perhaps elitist) interest in the all-inclusive work of art. His attitude toward Beckett was more welcoming, and it is to novels such as *Murphy* or *Watt* that *The Third Policeman* seems to compare best.[2] Keith Hopper has noted the attraction both authors felt toward the anti-Cartesianism found in the work of early parodists such as Swift and Sterne (Hopper 226–8). Yet there is another strain of metafictional writing that has not drawn much attention from O'Brien's readers, and it is this concept of pataphysics to which I turn. 'Pataphysics was the name given by the French writer Alfred Jarry to a playful stance and attitude toward scientific inquiry and its notions of exactitude that he pursued throughout his works.[3] It is perhaps best understood as a series of artistic and intellectual gestures, which starts early on in his *Ubu*-writings, and reaches its most explicit form in *Exploits and Opinions of Doctor Faustroll Pataphysician* (1911), and *Siloquies, Superloquies, Soliloquies and Interloquies in Pataphysics* (1906).[4] Jarry offers an extended definition of his imagined "new science" only once, in chapter seven of *Doctor Faustroll*:

> Pataphysics is the science of imaginary solutions, which symbolically attributes the properties of objects, described by their virtuality, to their lineaments. (Jarry, *Selected Works* 193)

Jarry's use of the word "lineaments" here is telling, as he intentionally favors the contours of an entity, which he claims reveal its deepest properties, the way that surface terrain reveals subterranean rifts. What is valuable in geology is patently foolish in other fields, but Jarry's real emphasis is on "solutions imaginaires." His physics pursues only "the laws governing exceptions, and will explain the universe supplementary to this one" (Jarry, *Selected Works* 192). For Jarry, glorifying the exceptions rather than the norms was the pataphysician's desideratum, for he remains aware that "reality is never *as it is* but always *as if it is*" (Bök 8). Pataphysics is not a pseudo-science, because it does not pretend to explain matters in this universe; rather, it imagines, and constructs via language, a supplementary universe whose contours are amusingly similar to our own. To participate in this new science, one proposes the absurd, and then rigorously extrapolates from that point. Among his admirers were the practitioners of potential writing known as the Ouvroir de Littérature Potentielle, or Oulipo. Jarry's pataphysics, along with his notion of the *clinamen*, declares him an early participant in Oulipian techniques *avant la lettre*: "anticipatory plagiarists," Oulipo prefers to call them (Mathews and Brotchie 211).

There are numerous points allowing comparison between Jarry and O'Brien: the elaborate games played regarding books; the playful use of language to provoke unexpected contradictions; the ludicrous description of Faustroll himself; the loss of language of the "dogfaced baboon" Bosse-de-Nage, whose only utterance is "Ha ha"; even a shared interest in bicycles.[5] But two examples must suffice. As he embarks on a voyage, Faustroll explains to his companion that what appears to be a "polished copper bed" is both a fantastic sieve and their boat, and explains the specific scientific and technological principles at work:

> It is probable that you have no conception, Panmuphle, writ-carrying bailiff, of capillarity, of surface tension, nor of weight-less membranes, equilateral hyperbolae, surfaces without curvature, nor, more generally, of the elastic skin which is water's epidermis . . . But this bed, twelve meters long, is not a bed but a boat, shaped like an elongated sieve. The meshes are wide enough to allow the passage of a large pin; and the whole sieve has been dipped in melted paraffin, then shaken so that this substance (which is never really *touched* by water), while covering the web, leaves the holes empty—the number of which amounts to about fifteen million four hundred thousand. (Jarry, *Selected Works* 188)

In this "perpetually dry boat" the trio conduct themselves on a voyage worthy of Saint Brendan. Faustroll also informs Panmuphle that he has an improved vessel, fortified with the deposition of 250,000 drops of castor oil, which vibrate under a certain proportion in conformity with principles of elasticity (a favorite word of Jarry's). Faustroll's boat, like O'Brien's bicycles, are described and operate according to the strictest suggestions of pataphysics.

The second example is the clinamen, Jarry's rediscovery that endeared him most perhaps to the Oulipo (Mathews and Brotchie 126–7). The term has its origins in the atomic theories of the Roman Epicurean philosopher and poet Lucretius, where it represents the "swerve" of particles that is expressly creative in force. Lucretius considered the clinamen the basis for free will in living creatures. For the practitioners of potential literature, it becomes the term for when a writer chooses to voluntarily abandon one of his or her chosen "constraints," so as to avoid mere artifice in the search for art.[6] Jarry makes such exceptions a cornerstone of his pataphysical art. In *Faustroll* he declares the clinamen an "unforeseen beast," which functions "to maintain a sufficient level of chaos in the universe" (Motte 266).

The Third Policeman revels in these very pataphysical exceptions, in which the opaque language of this world acts as a barrier to understanding, seeming to multiply and condense, or stand aloof and suggest cryptically, all while proceeding within the most seemingly straightforward dialogues. We see it first in the delightfully difficult way that the narrator must go about gaining information in this world. His conversation with the supposedly-murdered Mathers is exemplary. The shocking presence of the dead man in his kitchen begins a verbal exchange of nullity for curiosity. In contrast to the narrator's "meaningless" superfluity of words as plentiful as if "produced by machinery," Mathers offers a sequence of head-shakes and negations. "He negatived my inquiry about his health, refused to say where the black box had gone and even denied that it was a dark morning. His voice had a peculiar jarring weight like the hoarse toll of an ancient rusty bell in an ivy-smothered tower. He had said nothing beyond the one word No" (O'Brien 26). With the assistance of his newfound soul Joe, the narrator eventually learns the method to Mathers's obstinacy, and learns some facts, although not precisely those that he originally sought. To make one's way in this world is a crooked proposition. His first impressions and subsequent interview with Martin Finnucane go along much the same lines: "He was tricky and smoked a tricky pipe and his hand was quavery. His eyes were tricky also, probably from watching policemen" (O'Brien 43). At Joe's insistence that he seek the man's occupation, our narrator suggests a series of eccentric choices: is he perhaps a bird-catcher, a tinker, a man on a journey, a fiddler, a man out after rabbits, a water-works inspector?[7] His eventual arrival at the police barracks brings more circumlocution. "What would you say a bulbul is?" asks MacCruiskeen. We learn that a bulbul is not "one of those ladies who take money," nor "the brass knobs on a German steam organ," has nothing to do "with the independence of America or such-like," is not a "mechanical engine for winding clocks," or a "tumour, or the lather in a cow's mouth, or those elastic articles that ladies wear" (O'Brien 65–6). "MacCruiskeen was giving you his talk," says Sergeant Pluck to the narrator; but the universe here is nothing *but* talk, nothing but the (often perverse) thrill in language itself. One might imagine these rather one-sided dialogues as being a comic gloss on the world, as clever observers seek to mold it, and police it, for their pleasure.

Such a pataphysical delight in language finds even stronger energy in the elaborately sophomoric learning of the sage de Selby, for the sake of whose commentaries, it might be remembered, the narrator put himself in peril in the first place. The narrator's obsession with the bizarre philosopher offers a perverse rationale for much that happens. He first discovers de Selby after having "just earned the privilege of lying late" (O'Brien 9). He goes on to steal the book from school, committing his "first serious sin." He is meditating on the cost of de Selby's books when he has the accident that takes his leg. And it is for the purpose of publishing his "De Selby Index" that he consents to murder. The enigmatic figure of de Selby emerges in the narrator's musings and in the twenty-seven footnotes that populate the pages of *The Third Policeman*, which consider his inept theories on houses, names, night, mirrors, sleep, percussion, film, and women and men. As the novel comes near its close, these notes become gradually, though not predictably, longer, yet offer more information on the scholarly quarrels and melodramas that congeal around his work than on the work itself.

Footnotes have often been a target for those wishing to lampoon the excesses and neuroses of academia (Hauptman 112–15). Often seen as a cornerstone of pedantic indulgence, or as the spoor of insecure scholarship, interest in the mock footnote is another metafictional delight.[8] The footnotes in *The Third Policeman* would seem at first to provide a welcome oasis from the hurly-burly chaos of the main narrative; instead, they cycle us back again to the humorous yet uncanny lack of insight that can be sustained by any of the linguaphones in the novel. "De Selby has some interesting things to say on the subject of houses" (O'Brien 21), we learn at the beginning of chapter two, and immediately our eyes drop to the bottom of the page, to scan our first footnote. The immediate effect is reassuring, for this note offers conventional information about where we might find more about what de Selby has to say. We are quickly disabused of this false security. The sage attributes a number of great evils to dwelling in houses, rather than outdoors. Houses are "coffins" and "warrens," encouraging ignoble activities such as "reading, chess-playing, drinking, marriage and the like," and de Selby suggests replacing four walls and a roof with his radical redesign: roofless structures with tarpaulins for walls, the whole surrounded by a latrine-like moat, an experiment in human improvement that led to "more than one sick person [losing] his life in an ill-advised quest for health in these fantastic dwellings" (O'Brien 21). The third footnote is lengthy, but tells how the commentator Le Fournier attributes de Selby's bizarre ideas about houses to misinterpretations of his own absent-minded doodles: "The next time he took it up he was confronted with a mass of diagrams and drawings which he took to be the plans of a type of dwelling he always had in mind and immediately wrote many pages explaining the sketches" (O'Brien 21–2 n. 3). In a nutshell, we have the uncanny humor shared by *The Third Policeman* and Jarry's pataphysics: imagine the absurd, even the impossible, and justify it with language.

Much later, as we listen to the hammering of a gallows being constructed, the narrator muses upon de Selby's "water-box," "probably the most delicate and fragile instrument ever made by human hands" (O'Brien 144 n. 1). De Selby imagines heaven to be closely associated with water, a substance the philosopher praises for its "circumambiency, equiponderance and equitableness" (O'Brien 146). As de Selby drenches passers-by with hoses, nearly drowns in his bath, and is harried by the police for water-hoarding, the narrator notes that the primary result of these misadventures in scientific method was a miserable spate of "persecutions and legal pin-prickings unparalleled since the days of Galileo" (O'Brien 148). Turning to the thick cluster of notes featured on these pages (one extends over an entire page), a reader learns that while de Selby's "water-boxes" might well have led to a "esoteric water science" that would have banished "much of our worldly pain and unhappiness," none of the authorities on the man can give an account of what they did, or how they were constructed. We learn in a footnote that one scholar thinks they were used to "dilute" water, although this "speculation must not be allowed the undue weight which his authoritative standing would tend to lend it" (O'Brien 147 n. 4). Amidst such meandering observances is a lengthy footnote that introduces the reader to the de Selby "Codex," a "collection of some two thousand sheets of foolscap closely hand-written on both sides. The signal distinction of the manuscript is that not one word of the writing is legible" (O'Brien 145 n. 2). Attempts at comprehension have resulted in widely divergent conclusions: one passage is declared a "penetrating treatise on old age" by one scholar, "a not unbeautiful description of lambing operations on an unspecified farm" by another. Amidst these unavoidable squabbles, and amidst claims of forgery and obscenity, the novel unfolds a tale not of de Selby himself or his work, but of the vanities and ephemeral indulgences of scholarship, of clever readers' claims to comprehend.

Objects to language

The enigmatic water-box is only one of the objects of wonder encountered in the novel. *The Third Policeman* features a world of intricate and indescribable handicrafts, and their "thick description" (to steal a term from anthropology) is similar to the crooked linguistic efforts people must make to gather information in this universe. The effect is to render these "machines" less like objects, and more like *things*, a much trickier state of being. Things are not objects—not fixed in place, not docile for the purposes of study—the thing is the object in chaotic blur, or in pieces, with a certain agency of its own that encourages creativity. Can this scrap be salvaged? Can this thing be re-stored, re-used, renewed? We cannot study things directly, we can only catch glimpses; they remain partial, oblique, peripheral. Once we look at things, we render them objects. We can look through a window, and watch the city street, or at it, and see the smudged glass, but the window as a thing remains aloof.[9] The handicrafts of *The Third Policeman* are definitely things, and, like Faustroll's sieve-boat, perversely evade language and easy description. They supplement the written universe with their own inscrutable construction, and impenetrable purpose, which tends to "mangle" the light of understanding, producing only "ragged shout[s]" (O'Brien 108).

One contemporary movement that attempts to restore some of the thing-ness to the objects of the mechanized world is the loose amalgamation of artists, tinkerers, and clothiers who associate themselves with steampunk.[10] Steampunk (or clockpunk) is at its heart a means of renewing the connec-tion of contemporary technology with the technology and engines of the past. It remains basically optimistic in its approval of the notion of progress and technological advancement. Where it departs from mere technophilia is in its interest in maintaining a visible human connection with the technology itself. One could say that steampunk is opposed to the aesthetic smoothness and near-invisibility of contemporary technologies, favoring a return to a clunky and hands-on gadgetry. The steampunk aesthetic of brass knobs, gears, and goggles stresses the desire of its adherents to tinker with the very stuff and en-gines of early industrial modernity, do-it-yourselfers engaged with Victorian-era science and its accompanying urban squeal, seeking a "perverse and play-ful trawl through the dusty corners and back alleys of the nineteenth century in order to generate alternative pasts and encase cutting-edge gadgets in the patina of outdated technology" (Pike 872).

Yet the steampunk attitude toward machinery remains an optimistic one at heart, to which the dark artifacts of *The Third Policeman* stand in uncanny contrast. The admiration elicited by MacCruiskeen's sequence of miniature chests-within-chests comes from their eerie beauty:

> Never in my life did I inspect anything more ornamental and well-made. It was a brown chest like those owned by seafaring men or

lascars from Singapore, but it was diminutive in a very perfect way
as if you were looking at a full-size one through the wrong end of a
spy-glass . . . "It is unmentionable," I said. (O'Brien 70)

He removes another perfect chest from within it, a feat that makes our narrator "half afraid to think" what this second chest might contain. At this point, MacCruiskeen gets

two thin butter-spades from the shelf and put them down into the
little chest and pulled out something that seemed to me remarkably
like another chest . . . [He] got two straight-handled teaspoons and
put the handles into his last chest. What came out may well be
guessed at. He opened this one and took another out with the assistance of two knives. He worked knives, small knives and smaller
knives, till he had twelve little chests on the table, the last of them an
article half the size of a matchbox. (O'Brien 72)

When there are twenty-nine such objects on the table, and the policeman
begins working at the last indescribable chest with another invisible pin, this
display of craftsmanship becomes "no longer wonderful but terrible" (O'Brien
73). The illusion of wonder and value in this progressively infinitesimal sequence of perfect chests is exploded, with a classic move of Flannian absurdity, in the comic scene where the tiniest (and microscopic) chest is knocked
to the floor: "*This is amusing*," Joe says, "*You are going to be hung for murdering
a man you did not murder and now you will be shot for not finding a tiny thing
that probably does not exist*" (O'Brien 113). More eerie, but also emblematic of
the emptiness of seeking value in such things, is the musical instrument the
policeman plays, a "little black article like a leprechaun's piano with diminutive keys of white and black and brass pipes and circular revolving cogs like
parts of a steam engine or the business end of a thrashing-mill" (O'Brien 69).
His hands move over this device as if he were playing an instrument and his
face appears to be perceiving some lovely tune, but the narrator hears only
a "tremendous overpowering silence." MacCruiskeen later tells him that the
notes he plays "are so high in their fine frequencies that they cannot be appre-
ciated by the human earcup. Only myself has the secret of the thing and the
intimate way of it, the confidential knack of circumventing it" (O'Brien 75).

MacCruiskeen's "great rusty mangle" is, like all of his mechanisms, not as it first seems; its complexity and apparent delicacy is undermined by its rusty and plain appearance, for the narrator thinks that the policeman "was making preparations for mangling his washing and his Sunday shirts." After "screwing down the pressure-spring and spinning the hand wheel and furbishing the machine with expert hands," he begins to assemble his machine for "stretching the light":

> He went over then to the dresser and took small articles like dry batteries out of a drawer and also an instrument like a prongs and glass barrels with wires inside them and other cruder articles resembling the hurricane lamps utilized by the County Council. He put these things into different parts of the mangle and when he had them all satisfactorily adjusted, the mangle looked more like a rough scientific instrument than a machine for wringing out a day's washing . . . MacCruiskeen kept on adding small well-made articles to his mangle and mounting indescribably delicate glass instruments about the metal legs and on the super-structure . . . All in all it was the most complicated mangle I ever saw and to the inside of a steam thrashing-mill it was not inferior in complexity. (O'Brien 106)

This passage builds its effect slowly. Unlike a steampunk gadget, this contraption resists admiration. The juxtaposition crucial to O'Brien's sense of the absurd is that of the sublime and the profane. This combination is referenced often in *The Third Policeman*, creating a humorous aloofness from science that is shared with Jarry's pataphysics. But O'Brien goes further than Jarry in his relentless consideration of the ordinary danger inherent in the phenomenally complex, although all this danger is undercut by laughter. The policeman is about to "mangle" the substance he introduces to the narrator as omnium, and a most powerful substance it would seem to be. It is like and unlike light and matter and everything:

> "You are omnium and I am omnium and so is the mangle and my boots here and so is the wind in the chimney."
>
> "That is enlightening," I said.

"It comes in waves," he explained . . .

"Some people," he said, "call it energy but the right name is omnium because there is far more than energy in the inside of it, whatever it is. Omnium is the essential inherent interior essence which
is hidden inside the root of the kernel of everything and it is always
the same . . .

Some people call it God." (O'Brien 109–11)

The purpose of the improved mangle is to "stretch the light," to attempt to
get to the secret message at the core of this universal kernel. By means of his
machinery, MacCruiskeen can "stretch a ray out until it becomes sound," and
he enlists the narrator's help to hear the sound of God:

The unearthly voice had roared out something very quickly with
three or four words compressed into one ragged shout. I could not
be sure what it was but several phrases sprang into my head together
and each of them could have been the contents of the shout. They
bore an eerie resemblance to commonplace shouts I had often heard
such as *Change for Tinahely and Shillelagh! Two to one the field! Mind
the step! Finish him off!* I knew, however, that the shout could not be
so foolish and trivial because it disturbed me in a way that could only
be done by something momentous and diabolical . . . "I could not
make it out," I said, vaguely and feebly, "but I think it was railway-
station talk." (O'Brien 108)

Such claptrap is the unlocked mystery of mysteries, the "supreme pancake." This
horrible secret is used with shock and humor at the end of the novel, when we
at last encounter the third policeman, Policeman Fox. When the narrator asks
after his long-sought cashbox, this unsettling figure asks lightly, his eyes bright
as the sun: "Do you like strawberry jam?" (O'Brien 186). The cashbox contains
four ounces of omnium; with omnium one could do anything, Fox says, such
as have a house full of jam, easily remove muck from leggings, produce perfect
hard-boiled eggs. This omnipotent substance, for which the narrator devises
uses both grandiose and grim (O'Brien 188–9), Policeman Fox proposes using
in the home to keep things "spick and span" (O'Brien 183). O'Brien's pataphys-

ics, his imaginary solutions, combine the humdrum and sublime. We laugh along with him at the awful contiguity of sense and nonsense, at the constructions that defy or tease our understanding while alluding to potential meaning in themselves and in the strange boxes within which we find and lose ourselves repeatedly, but delightedly, with great wit and greater wonder.

NOTES

1   The most valuable discussion of O'Brien in this tradition is Hopper; see also Booker.

2   See treatments by Hopper, Kennedy, and McHale.

3   Jarry explains that he added the apostrophe only to indicate the Greek origin of the term, avoiding a cheap pun in French, in which tongue his neologism could sound like *pattes à physique*.

4   *Siloquies* was compiled by Jarry in 1906, but published only in 1992. Translated in *Adventures in 'Pataphysics*, ed. Brotchie and Edwards.

5   See Jarry's "The Passion Considered as an Uphill Bicycle Race" (1894), "How to Construct a Time Machine" (1899), and the significant portion of *The Supermale* (1902) that describes a race between a locomotive and a five-man bicycle.

6   The term has been used most frequently in a critical context by Harold Bloom. On the sense of the term in Lucretius and its reanimation among contemporary writers, see Motte.

7   Such locutions of O'Brien's bear similarity to the celebrated "taxonomies" of Borges, and should be given greater critical consideration.

8   Worth mentioning in the context is perhaps the surreal emblem of the footnote offered by Jeremy Hilary Boob PhD, the "nowhere man" whom the Beatles meet in *Yellow Submarine* (1968).

9   Essential criticism for "thing theory" remains *The Social Life of Things* (ed. Arjun Appadurai, Cambridge: Cambridge Univ. Press, 1988) and numerous essays by Bill Brown.

10   See Onion for a contemporary overview of the genre. Although best-known for its developments in fashion, design, and music, the roots of steampunk remain literary: see William Gibson and Bruce Sterling, *The Difference Engine* (New York: Bantam

Spectra, 1991), and Paul Di Filippo, *The Steampunk Trilogy* (New York: Four Walls Eight Windows, 1995), for two dissimilar visions. China Miéville's *Perdido Street Station* (London: Macmillan, 2000) also contains elements of this aesthetic.

WORKS CITED

Bök, Christian. *Pataphysics: The Poetics of an Imaginary Science*. Chicago: Northwestern Univ. Press, 2002.

Booker, M. Keith. *Flann O'Brien, Bakhtin, and Menippean Satire*. Syracuse: Syracuse Univ. Press, 1995.

Hauptman, Robert. *Documentation: A History and Critique of Attribution, Commentary, Glosses, Marginalia, Notes, Bibliographies, Works-Cited Lists, and Citation Indexing and Analysis*. Jefferson, NC: McFarland, 2008.

Hopper, Keith. *Flann O'Brien: A Portrait of the Artist as a Young Post-modernist*. 2nd ed. Cork: Cork Univ. Press, 2009.

Jarry, Alfred. *Selected Works of Alfred Jarry*. Ed. Roger Shattuck and Simon Watson Taylor. London: Eyre Methuen, 1965.

—. *Adventures in 'Pataphysics. Collected Works of Alfred Jarry*, vol. 1. Trans. Paul Edwards and Antony Melville. Ed. Alastair Brotchie and Paul Edwards. London: Atlas Press, 2001.

Kennedy, Sighle. "The Devil and Holy Water: Samuel Beckett's *Murphy* and Flann O'Brien's *At Swim-Two-Birds*." *Modern Irish Literature*. Ed. Raymond A. Porter and James D. Brophy. New York: Iona College Press, 1972. 251–60.

Mathews, Harry and Alastair Brotchie. *Oulipo Compendium*. Atlas Press: London, 1998.

McHale, Brian. *Postmodernist Fiction*. New York: Routledge, 1991.

Motte, Warren F., Jr. "Clinamen Redux." *Comparative Literary Studies* 23.4 (Winter 1986): 263–81.

O'Brien, Flann. *The Third Policeman*. Normal, IL: Dalkey Archive Press, 1999.

Onion, Rebecca. "Reclaiming the Machine: An Introductory Look at Steampunk in Everyday Practice." *Neo-Victorian Studies* 1.1 (Autumn 2008): 138–63.

Pike, David L. "Buried Pleasure: Doctor Dolittle, Walter Benjamin, and the Nineteenth-Century Child." *Modernism/modernity* 17.4 (November 2010): 857–75.

JOSEPH BROOKER

"That Carrousel Inside and Outside My Head": Flann O'Brien and *Pale Fire*

"You can always count on a murderer for a fancy prose style" (9): Humbert Humbert's sidelong reflection as *Lolita* starts is among Vladimir Nabokov's prime bids for any dictionary of quotations. The formulation seems crazily unreliable, yet it is oddly transferrable to Flann O'Brien's *The Third Policeman*: a novel likewise narrated in fabulously eccentric style by a largely unrepentant criminal who tells us of his travels across country and brushes with the law, and finally faces a belated kind of doom for his actions.

The parallel is teasing, but would be a slim basis for any sustained comparison of the two authors. Dissimilarities readily present themselves, and might as well be listed now. One was Russian, one Irish; one travelled the globe, the other stayed at home. One was long uxorious, the other married late; one's writing became a byword for scandalous concupiscence, the other's is reticent about desire, let alone romance. One published a shelf's worth of novels, as well as performing academic and editorial duties; the other expended most of his creative energy in the *Irish Times*. Neither writer seems to have read the other; Nabokov's correspondence and voluminous biography offer no sudden cameo for the Brother.

This article suggests, though, that the juxtaposition is worthwhile. I will consider especially Nabokov's *Pale Fire* (1962) in a Mylesian light, considering how far it shows resemblances to O'Brien's work and in what ways they more pointedly differ. But I start from the assumption that O'Brien and Nabokov lived, part of the time, on the same literary continent. Where was it?

Both Vladimir Nabokov (b. 1899) and Flann O'Brien (b. 1911) were flamboyant, experimental contributors to mid-twentieth century writing. O'Brien's best work dates from the late 1930s and early 1940s, but his novel-writing career ultimately extended to the mid-1960s. Nabokov's career, like his life, was longer and, in the writing of novels, far more prolific. But in reaching from the 1920s to the 1970s, and scaling a peak in the 1950s and early 1960s, he can also be reckoned to have centred on the century's middle decades. In literary-historical terms, this places them in the wake of the high modernists born a decade or two before Nabokov. Along with other ludic penmen like Borges (b. 1899) and Beckett (b. 1906), they worked a passage from the time of *transition* to the heyday of *Playboy*.

As accounts of literary postmodernism were formulated through the 1970s and 1980s, O'Brien and Nabokov were both drawn in on its tractor beam. In work like Brian McHale's influential *Postmodernist Fiction* (1987) they appear as luminal, pioneering figures. Both, more specifically, were also post-Joycean writers. Brian O'Nolan's unlikely claim that he had "met [Joyce] in Paris several times" (Cronin 247) is trumped by Nabokov's more reliably documented acquaintance with him in the same city (Ellmann 616). If Joyce gave a line of praise to *At Swim-Two-Birds* that has stayed on the book's jacket for decades, he also agreed to attend a lecture by Nabokov "to save his young friend from [the] undue embarrassment" of addressing an empty hall (Ellmann 699). Nabokov's most acclaimed mature novels, *Lolita* and *Pale Fire*, carry a stylistic verve that comes closer than most to Joyce's prose. Among the most explicit homages in the fiction itself is Humbert Humbert's sudden aside that *"J'ai toujours admiré l'oeuvre ormonde du sublime Dublinois"* (207). The reference to the Ormond Bar of "Sirens" also punningly creates a new adjective suggesting both "golden world" (*monde d'or*) and, in Nabokov's own later gloss, "out of this world" (*hors du monde*) (*Selected Letters* 410); it thus offers a Wakean pirouette while admiring *Ulysses*. The closest equivalent in Flann O'Brien's fiction may be Mick Shaughnessy's tribute to Joyce in *The Dalkey Archive*, "for his dexterity and resource in handling language, for his precision, for his subtlety in conveying the image of Dublin and her people, for his accuracy in setting speech down authentically, and for his enormous humour" (96). Late Flann O'Brien here makes a pedestrian contrast to peak Nabokov.

In fact both writers offered a mixed response to Joyce. O'Brien's alter ego Myles na gCopaleen, as David Powell has shown, had as much abuse as praise for Joyce, mention of whose name he said could make him "froth at the gob" (Cronin 216). Nabokov considered *Ulysses* central to twentieth-century writing but drew the line at *Finnegans Wake* and was unimpressed by the *Portrait*. The anxiety of influence was far stronger in the case of O'Brien who, as Anthony Cronin has proposed (ix), inherited Joyce's cultural legacy as a Dublin Catholic and was frequently accused of replaying the maestro's record. Nabokov, travelling from St Petersburg to Ithaca and Montreux via Berlin and Paris, faced no such local difficulties. His readiness to lecture students at length on the virtues of *Ulysses* shows a correspondingly more detached relation to Joyce than O'Brien's. His criticisms of Joyce bespeak the haughtiness of the citizen of the world, rather than the *ressentiment* of a corner of the Palace Bar.

In Cedarn, Utana in 1959, with Brian O'Nolan pondering the reiusse of *At Swim-Two-Birds* across the Atlantic, Nabokov's Charles Kinbote declares that he needed a disguise to work at a Zemblan university and "present to rosy youths *Finnigan's Wake* as a monstrous extension of Angus McDiarmid's 'incoherent transactions' and of Southey's Lingo-Grande" (59). Kinbote's spelling would have been marked down heavily by Myles na gCopaleen, who repeatedly complained about Irish scribes' insertion of an apostrophe into Joyce's last title. But it is to Kinbote's book that I wish to turn as a means to compare Nabokov and O'Brien. Other novels would offer their own points of comparison. *The Real Life of Sebastian Knight* (1941), for instance, is narrated by a figure whose determined anonymity oddly parallels the protagonist of *The Third Policeman*, written at almost the same time. But *Pale Fire* displays an attitude to fiction that arguably chimes most loudly with O'Brien's: the novel as high-wire act, the entire text a brilliant parody of another genre of writing. Flann O'Brien's novelistic career began with a book within a book: it tells of the characters of Dermot Trellis, who is being written by the UCD student, who himself appears on the pages of a novel attributed to Flann O'Brien. "*Pale Fire*, a poem in heroic couplets" (9), is also a book within another book. We could even identify three *Pale Fires*: John Shade's poem; Charles Kinbote's scholarly edition of it, a larger book containing the first; and Nabokov's novel, effectively identical to the second *Pale Fire* but signed with another name, and hence framing Kinbote's labours in their own ironized arena.

Nabokov's layering is not so flagrantly metafictional as O'Brien's. He is not concerned here to show characters rebelling against their authors, or a fiction's distinct ontological levels colliding—though he is tempted into teases that confound clear distinctions, like Kinbote's late speculation that he might "turn up yet, on another campus, as an old, happy, healthy, heterosexual Russian, a writer in exile" (229). Shade's reference to "Hurricane Lolita" in 1958 (185–6) is another dance on the edge of involution. Nabokov gave that title to a notebook as his novel's effects swirled that year (Boyd 361). He can veer close to one of O'Nolan's great motifs, the play with authorial identity. *Lolita* itself offers a "Vivian Darkbloom" (31), an anagram of Nabokov's name; in a letter he later explained that it had been "planted at a time (1954) when I toyed with the idea of publishing *Lolita* anonymously but wished to affirm my authorship in code." The letter was signed "Vladimir Nabokov (Vivian Bloodmark)" (*Selected Letters* 391). *Lolita*, like *Pale Fire* (and like *The Poor Mouth*), has a foreword by a fictional character, and Nabokov sees that his "impersonation of suave John Ray" makes his own discourse seem like "an impersonation of Vladimir Nabokov talking about his own book" (*Lolita* 311). A scholar in *The Third Policeman* likewise accuses another of having spent his entire career posing as himself (176). But the difference between O'Brien and Nabokov remains, along with the resemblance. *At Swim-Two-Birds* and *Cruiskeen Lawn* are happy to scramble worlds. The gap between levels of reality turns out to be as fragile as the sheet of paper on which a character is written, or the space between two columns in the *Irish Times*. The world of *Lolita*, though, is apparently different from that of *Pale Fire*: in the latter, as in our world, Lolita is not the real Dolores Haze but a scandalous book. Nabokov opens subterranean spirals between books, discreet and delicate enough for a fast reader to miss. But he remains more intuitively faithful to the idea of the novel and the temporary integrity of its world than Brian O'Nolan, who commenced novel-writing with an anti-novel and ended it with symptomatically botched attempts at more straightforward stories (Taaffe 196–7).

Yet the tricky structure of *Pale Fire* does represent one of the closest convergences between the two writers. The novel poses as a scholarly edition of a poem, complete with Foreword, Commentary, and Index. Kinbote's surrounding material is over six times the length of the poem. It commences in soberly factual mode: the Foreword's opening paragraphs inform us of the lengths of Shade's Cantos, the type of index cards that he wrote on, and his working methods. Within the first three paragraphs, though, the sobriety quickly blurs. The Cantos are referred to with curious familiarity as though they are texts we already know: "Canto One, with all those amusing birds and parhelia," and "Canto Two, your favourite." Kinbote is allowing his role as editor— of a poem that no one else has yet seen—to be invaded by his own intense responses to the text. Then in the third paragraph comes Kinbote's attempt to clarify his own statement about Shade's corrections, followed by the sudden, blunt declaration: "There is a very loud amusement park right in front of my present lodgings" (9). In a sense much of the book is adumbrated here. It is crucial to the book's effect that it maintains to the end the presumption or pretence of being a contribution to scholarship—making it a considerable rarity, a novel with a functioning index. But this aim, as a reader of Kinbote's notes quickly enough sees, cannot be fulfilled. The book is a wild swerve away from its ostensible subject: it gives Shade's delicate poem space to speak for itself, but then accelerates across a wide plain of comical misconstrual and feverish digression. In Kinbote's preposterously myopic declaration that "I have no desire to twist and batter an unambiguous *apparatus criticus* into the monstrous semblance of a novel" (67), Nabokov lets the book summarize itself.

Kinbote's notes, almost despite themselves, do give us much information about John Shade's life and work. But they do so in the service of the editor's larger conviction that Shade's meditation on life and death was really intended to be a commentary on Kinbote's own secret history as the exiled king of Zembla. Kinbote ultimately admits that the poem has not fulfilled these hopes (226), but this has not stopped him from filling the greater part of the book with his own extravagant story. As his foreword closes he refers again to "that carrousel inside and outside my head" (21). He means that the amusement park is distracting him; also probably that its distraction is the greater for having penetrated him, for having become mirrored in his mind. We may think that Kinbote's head contains a "carrousel" anyway, a whirl of fantasy; and in that sense the ride is an image for the crazy energy of the book. "Hell Goes Round and Round" was among Flann O'Brien's proposed titles for *The Third Policeman* (Cronin 101). Kinbote at this moment might agree, even if he later revises the distraction down to mere "camping tourists" (180): the carrousel was only ever inside his head.

"The modern novel should be largely a work of reference," declares the student narrating *At Swim-Two-Birds* (25). *Pale Fire* could be considered one of fiction's fullest responses to that injunction. It does not do what the student really has in mind—"reference" for him means rehashing characters who already exist—but it manages to be a novel while also being from end to end a work of textual commentary and exegesis, however unhinged. Something about this mode was very congenial to O'Brien. Within *At Swim* itself we can think of the italicized headings that pedantically puncture the text with information:

> I derived considerable pleasure from the casual quality of his sugges-
> tion and observed that it would probably do us no harm, thus ex-
> pressing my whole-hearted concurrence by a figure of speech.
> *Name of figure of speech:* Litotes (or Meiosis). (20)

In the many moments like this, even *At Swim*'s primary narrative becomes a text of two levels: a first-person discourse that also has recourse to a secondary level of reference and clarification, as though a dictionary has been opened or, in an image from our own century, a hyperlink clicked on. The novel is not so much a work of reference as a work containing its own commentary. In this sense it shares a mischievous impulse with *Pale Fire*, though the novel it produces has a very different shape. The impulse to commentate and amend is basic to *Cruiskeen Lawn*, too: many of Myles na gCopaleen's energies derive from the desire to correct or explicate a pre-existing text. Even the title of *The*

Dalkey Archive (which accords with the sense that the novel has in part been pulled together from O'Brien's files of existing material) hints at this sense of literature as scholarship.

In one sense the closest thing to *Pale Fire* in O'Brien's oeuvre is *The Poor Mouth*, which is presented as a text that has been received and edited by Myles na gCopaleen. By 1973 it had two Prefaces and a Foreword (in the last of which the Gaels, heading the other way from Kinbote, are "setting their faces toward Siberia in the hope of better weather" [9]), and a brief set of Notes from the allegedly real Patrick C. Power. Yet O'Brien's major engagement with scholarly paratext is *The Third Policeman*. The novel's entire plot is initially driven by the narrator's desire to fund his research into de Selby's philosophy. Anon (to call him that) believes that "if my name was to be remembered, it would be remembered with de Selby's" (10). Chapters of the novel are thus apt to begin with a reflection on de Selby that prompts the text to digress into footnotes. Some notes are simply pseudo-scholarly citations: "*Golden Hours*, vi.156" (37). Others extend into elaborate accounts of fictional scholarship and debate. We learn of "Le Fournier, the reliable French commentator" and author of *De Selby—L'Enigme de l'Occident* and *Homme ou Dieu* (21, 32); of the English scholars Hatchjaw and Bassett; of the alternately "credulous" and "shadowy" German Kraus (116, 119). The fiction of a scholarly industry is elaborate enough, and comedy runs from the inaptly pastoral names of de Selby's works themselves (*Golden Hours, Country Album*) to the brisk tone in which some research is dismissed: Hatchjaw "has many ingenious if not quite convincing arguments . . . The theory is, however, not one which will commend itself to the serious student" (93). It enters another plane in the book's second half: for three pages in Chapter Eight a footnote scales half the height of the page, and the final note in Chapter Eleven stretches over seven pages (166–72). A text ostensibly meant for secondary clarification has effectively displaced the primary narrative. In this last note, furthermore, a record of scholarship has pullulated into an adventure story, in which Hatchjaw sets off armed to the teeth on a vain quest to annihilate Kraus in Hamburg.

An immediate analogy suggests itself: Anon is to de Selby as Kinbote is to Shade, the "beloved old conjurer" (21) whose last work he obsessively annotates. The vertiginous expansion of Anon's footnotes is akin to Kinbote's shifts between serviceably succinct notes on John Shade and wildly digressive accounts of his own escape from Zembla, which are apt to run on for several pages at a time. In both cases the jest thrives on the text's vestigial maintenance of the pretence of scholarly seriousness. Neither narrator acknowledges that a note has become disproportionate, though Kinbote solemnly urges us to cut up the book to make it easier to move between poem and notes (21). Anon's tales of the skirmishes of Hatchjaw and company are echoed by Kinbote's bitter rebukes to the critics—"Professor Hurley and his clique" (10), pointedly banned from his Index (234–5)—seeking to wrest editorial control from him. The polemics between de Selby's commentators are tonally very close to Kinbote's complaint, at once fiddly and furious, that

> the imputations made (on July 24, 1959) in a newspaper interview with one of our professed Shadeans—who affirmed *without having seen the manuscript of the poem* that it "consists of disjointed drafts none of which yields a definite text"—is a malicious invention on the part of those who would wish not so much to deplore the state in which a great poet's work was interrupted by death as to asperse the competence, and perhaps honesty, of its present editor and commentator. (10)

The comedy of metalanguage ballooning to outperform its ostensible subject is perhaps the most distinctive connection between O'Brien and Nabokov. The analogy is imperfect, certainly. Anon's notes, however lengthy, are only a fraction of his book, whereas Kinbote's amount to a pointed satire on the scholarly edition whose literary original is dwarfed by its apparatus. (This may be satire, but Nabokov did not disdain such labour: he produced lengthy paratexts for his edition of Pushkin's *Eugene Onegin*, and stated that forging Kinbote had involved "retwisting my own experience" as an editor [*Strong Opinions* 77].) The main text of *The Third Policeman* itself is not de Selby's: the notes pull us away from Anon's story toward de Selby's, while Kinbote's tend to pull us away from Shade's. Whereas Nabokov dazzlingly gives us Shade's entire poem, de Selby's work is only spotted in brief extracts; part of O'Brien's joke is the sense of energy and intellect being devoted to a body of writing that doesn't actually exist. Finally, de Selby is utterly unlike Shade. The eccentric and hapless "savant" resembles not so much the gruff and worldly Appalachian poet as his commentator Kinbote.

I have suggested elsewhere ("Myles' Tones" 27–31) that O'Brien's novels tend to centre around figures less sharp-witted than himself: writerly omnipotence is saved for the commanding alter ego of Myles. The most extreme instance would be *The Poor Mouth*'s simple-hearted peasant Bonaparte. Kinbote partially echoes this strategy. He has Nabokov's supreme eloquence, but not his nous; he makes Humbert Humbert look a master of cunning. Some of *Pale Fire*'s broadest humour involves Kinbote's persistent misconstruals. The moment when he discovers a cryptic note accusing him of halitosis but assumes that the relevant word is "hallucinations" (76) is so broad as almost to belong to another writer. His impercipience also includes the running joke of his failure to understand the poem's title (11, 62, 63), and more damagingly his egotistical inability to see the importance and pathos of Hazel Shade, whose "dull" story has ousted "rarer and richer matters" from the poem (127–8). In a sense he has proved a systematically inept reader of the poem he cherishes, and the passionate ineptitude is more like de Selby's than any other of O'Brien's figures. It is not just that de Selby's ideas are absurd, but that he cuts a constantly preposterous figure: trying to travel by locking himself in a room (51), being fined by the local authority for hoarding water (147). His theory that night is made of "black air" is excused by the fact that he was "*hors de combat* from his long-standing gall-bladder disorders" at the time (116).

A strong strain of tomfoolery in *Pale Fire* recalls these solemn accounts of misadventure. Kinbote's aviator father would regularly crash-land in "some remote valley" where he would be forced to "make a speech to his subjects," "a group of gaping Zemblan yokels." Kinbote himself recalls arriving in America by parachute, "a matter of mere sentimental tradition rather than a useful manner of transportation" (188–9). He intended to stay at the same mountain resort as the Shades and to surprise them with a "sudden emergence in Tirolese garb from behind a boulder" (141). A Zemblan revolutionary, in a truly de Selbian scene, "had lost a leg in trying to make anti-matter" (117). Kinbote recalls lecturing students "in a heavy make-up, with wig and false whiskers" (59). It is all less Stephen Dedalus, more Inspector Clouseau. What this most resembles, even more than de Selby's hapless travails, is a note struck in Brian O'Nolan's early writing. His first alter ego Brother Barnabas, in the student magazine *Comhthrom Féinne*, travels through Germany, encounters the writer Politicus while "walking down the corridor of an express-train in search of a bottle of lemonade," and fights him in Baden-Baden: Barnabas wearing "College colours" and Politicus "clad becomingly in a singlet of Abbey Street puce" (*Myles before Myles* 63–4). In an uncanny foreshadowing of Kinbote's career, the protean Barnabas elsewhere recounts his daring escape from Russia, where he "in the palmy days before the revolution was responsible for a tiny but gilded principality in the wilds of the Siberian steppes" (73). Seeing that "terrible flight" is "the only alternative to my imminent dissolution," Barnabas "quitted my peoples," taking on international aliases and settling in Dublin with relief at the "almost entire absence of communism in the city" (73–4). The stentorian tone and dashing cosmopolitan matter recur, to an extent, in the spoof letters that O'Nolan and friends sent to the *Irish Times* in 1940: so "Josephine" Conrad acquires "proficiency in the argot of the sea" and, passing as a man, runs away to sea as "a humble heaver aboard a coal boat bound for distant Wigan," ultimately to become "an object of respect in every gin-palace from Bermuda to the Barbary coast" (193). In these writings O'Nolan achieves not just an elaborate, deadpan eloquence but, quite unusually for him, an exotic flash of international colour. The high-spirited irony verges on high camp—which is noteworthy, as camp is not usually the word for O'Nolan's humour, but is irresistibly a word for *Pale Fire*, whose narrator hankers after every passing delivery boy and recalls attending a ball with "two guardsmen disguised as flowergirls" (134).

It is in the matter of literary style that Nabokov and O'Brien finally converge and diverge. Another significant parallel merits notice here. Both were writers whom history had strung across languages, and hence made the more watchful of them. Nabokov fled revolutionary violence to Europe, where he wrote ten novels in Russian. In 1940 he left Nazi-occupied France for the United

States, and subsequently all his fiction was written in English. In an interview he declared that the "complete switch from Russian prose to English prose was exceedingly painful—like learning anew to handle things after losing seven or eight fingers in an explosion" (*Strong Opinions* 50). He elsewhere announced that his "private tragedy" was "that I had to abandon my natural idiom, my untrammelled, rich, and infinitely docile Russian tongue for a second-rate brand of English, devoid of any of those apparatuses—the baffling mirror, the black velvet backdrop, the implied associations and traditions—which the native illusionist, frac-tails flying, can magically use to transcend the heritage in his own way" (*Lolita* 316–7).

There is a kind of comedy in Nabokov's avowals of linguistic loss, for their sheer eloquence makes them cases of performative contradiction. Surely, no one who could write this way could really think their English second-rate. In any case, as Michael Wood observes, while Nabokov's exile was enforced, he did not need to exile himself so brutally from Russian prose. The second exile, Wood proposes, is a performance in homage to the first: the abandonment of Russian is a "voluntary miming" of the loss of Russia (4). Nabokov's fictional treatment of the matter can rarely be rawer than Kinbote's gloss on Shade's phrase "two tongues": it simply lists a slew of East European languages in apposition to English, with "English and Russian" unique among them in appearing four times, before the differently angled pair "American and European" closes the note (180). The meaning may be that Kinbote is really Russian, not Zemblan; but one might also infer a nod to the author's self-proclaimed situation.

Brian O'Nolan was raised in a house in which, as Cronin says, "no English at all was spoken" (9). Language was a politically sensitive subject in Ireland, after the British authorities' attempt to crush and diminish the Irish language in the previous two centuries. This is replayed in *The Poor Mouth*, where the young Bonaparate O'Coonassa is beaten by his schoolmaster for not realizing that his name, like every other boy, is now "Jams O'Donnell" (30–1). Subsequently, at the other extreme, a collector of folklore arrives to record the Gaelic grunting of the household pig for posterity (45). O'Nolan would retain a double attitude to Irish. He praised the suppleness of his first tongue, in which much of *Cruiskeen Lawn* initially appeared; but he decried those who were making careers of reviving it in the independent state.

These two tales of linguistic transition are only loosely alike. Only one involves peril and transcontinental exile. O'Nolan did shift *Cruiskeen Lawn* from Irish to English, but he bore no nostalgia for a Gaelic idyll. Yet we can observe a likeness in the two writers' attitudes to the English language. Both are at once peculiarly at home in it, and peculiarly detached from it. They are masters of a tongue that was not their first, and the mastery involves the quizzical eye of the outsider—or, less dramatically, of the multilingual reader for whom a given sentiment could always be translated back and forth across several languages. (O'Nolan might have made his own list: "English and Irish, English and German, English and Latin, English and Irish . . .") Both were fastidious around English: O'Nolan most obviously in the Catechism of Cliché and those many moments when Myles lengthily lambasts a solecism. There is a strong streak of rationalism in O'Nolan, a preference for the measurable and correctable over the emotional and ineffable, which finds an echo in Nabokov's public pronouncements—notably his always brisk dismissals of Freud. Yet Nabokov's style conjoins exactitude with something less native to Myles.

Nabokov's mature fiction renders objects, people and actions through an almost matchlessly vivid idiom of assonance, alliteration, economy, and surprise. Admittedly, in delegating narration to Humbert and Kinbote, he blurs the matter of his own mastery, at once lending them his gifts and leaving a diegetic margin of excuse for stylistic excess. When Kinbote, carrying Shade's poem, feels that "fireflies were making decodable signals on behalf of stranded spirits" or "a bat was writing a legible tale of torture in the bruised and branded sky" (221), do we admire Nabokov's dexterity or stand warily back from Kinbote's emotive exaggeration—or both? But over the course of the novel we cannot doubt its stylistic felicity, from the most functional phrase—"Sybil whom a shrub had screened from my falcon eye" (67), "an ovation of crickets" (189), Manhattan's "smoke-blue morning" (209)—to the lyric bursts above, or the long swoop over Wordsmith's campus to land on a boy flying a model aeroplane under "pale plumes of cirrus" (72).

Myles ought to have approved. Yet to talk of lyric also indicates the last contrast, which replays his divergence from Joyce. O'Nolan was a writer of supreme competence, but distrustful of art. I have noted elsewhere his tendency to promote writing as a job of work (Brooker, *Flann O'Brien* 103–5). It is of a piece with his contempt for "corduroys": Dublin bohemians and aesthetes. O'Nolan could write crisply, polemically, or hilariously, but he rarely sought to write beautifully. The very idea is incongruous. Nabokov postulated "aesthetic bliss" (*Lolita* 314) as literature's primary value, proclaimed that a major writer was predominantly an "enchanter" (*Lectures on Literature* 5), and insisted that a work would endure for "its art, only its art" (*Strong Opinions* 33). Such talk might have made Myles shuffle and mutter. He too was a kind of conjuror of style, but he had no wish to let spells linger. The heights of bliss are foreign to O'Nolan's writing—which is partly just to say that he was a more thoroughly, exclusively comic writer than Nabokov. Michael Wood justly writes of the "fabulous, freaky, singing, acrobatic, unheard-of English" (5) that Nabokov found in exile. The closest that Brian O'Nolan came to such an English was in the strange idiom that appeared from nowhere to fuel *The Third Policeman*. It was a fancy prose style he never repeated.

WORKS CITED

Boyd, Brian. *Vladimir Nabokov: The American Years*. Princeton: Princeton Univ. Press, 1993.

Brooker, Joseph. *Flann O'Brien*. Tavistock: Northcote House, 2005.

—. "Myles' Tones." In *"Is It About a Bicycle?": Flann O'Brien in the Twenty-First Century*. Ed. Jennika Baines. Dublin: Four Courts, 2011. 17–31.

Cronin, Anthony. *No Laughing Matter: The Life and Times of Flann O'Brien*. London: Grafton, 1989.

Ellmann, Richard. *James Joyce*, 2nd ed. Oxford: Oxford Univ. Press, 1982.

McHale, Brian. *Postmodernist Fiction*. London: Routledge, 1987.

Nabokov, Vladimir. *Lectures on Literature*. Ed. Fredson Bowers. New York: Harcourt Brace Jovanovich, 1980.

—. *Selected Letters 1940–1977*. Ed. Dmitri Nabokov and Matthew J. Bruccoli. London: Weidenfeld and Nicolson, 1990.

—. *Strong Opinions*. New York: Vintage International, 1990.

—. *Pale Fire*. London: Everyman, 1992.

—. *Lolita*. London: Penguin, 2000.

O'Brien, Flann. *At Swim-Two-Birds*. Harmondsworth: Penguin, 1967; Normal, IL: Dalkey Archive Press, 1993.

—. *The Best of Myles*. London: Picador, 1977; Normal, IL: Dalkey Archive Press, 1999.

—. *The Third Policeman*. London: Grafton, 1988; Normal, IL: Dalkey Archive Press, 1999.

—. *Myles Before Myles*. Ed. John Wyse Jackson. London: Paladin, 1989.

—. *The Poor Mouth*. London: Flamingo, 1993; Normal, IL: Dalkey Archive Press, 1996.

—. *The Dalkey Archive*. London: Flamingo, 1993; Normal, IL: Dalkey Archive Press, 1993.

Powell, David. "An Annotated Bibliography of Myles na gCopaleen's 'Cruiskeen Lawn' Commentaries on James Joyce." *James Joyce Quarterly* 9:1 (Fall 1971): 50–62.

Taaffe, Carol. *Ireland through the Looking-Glass: Flann O'Brien, Myles na gCopaleen and Irish Cultural Debate*. Cork: Cork Univ. Press, 2008.

Wood, Michael. *The Magician's Doubts: Nabokov and the Risks of Fiction*. London: Chatto & Windus, 1994.

W. MICHELLE WANG

Lightness of Touch: Subtracting Weight from the Narrative Structure of *At Swim-Two-Birds*

Writing of his own fiction, Italo Calvino explains how "my working method has more often than not involved the subtraction of weight. I have tried to re-move weight, sometimes from people, sometimes from heavenly bodies, some-times from cities; above all I have tried to remove weight from the structure of stories and from language" (3). Calvino's concepts of lightness and weight offer a useful critical apparatus with which to approach Flann O'Brien's first novel, *At Swim-Two-Birds*. The use of lightness as a critical lens to examine O'Brien's novel is particularly compelling precisely because its lightness is not immediately apparent. While the novel may initially appear convoluted and dense—embodiments of weightiness—in the unlikely, discordant medley of Western cowboys and Irish mythological giants, a closer examination reveals a finely-spun texture that pervades the storyworld, imbuing it with the touch of lightness that Calvino views to be central to imaginative fiction.

This essay examines how structural lightness is created in *At Swim-Two-Birds* through the subtraction of weight from its characters and narrative structure. The novel is deftly suspended by the insubstantiality of the char-acters and by the flattening of its narrative layers, which are unremittingly transgressed by this riotous troop of borrowed and invented personalities who refuse to respect the ontological boundaries of the worlds they inhabit. *At Swim-Two-Birds* demands that we forsake all reliance on secure ontological boundaries and precisely delineated narrative levels—gritty fiction-reading conventions that add to the weightiness of a novel—to flit in, out, and be-tween narrative levels as we experience reading the novel. Both conventions of fiction and of reading fiction are hurled into the fire as readily as Teresa tosses parts of Trellis's manuscript into the blaze at the end of *At Swim-Two-Birds*, where the novel finally tends toward unmeaning.

The use of Calvino's writing as a lens to read O'Brien's novels is an interesting one, especially since several critics have remarked on the literary connections between the two novelists. In a 1970 issue of *Modern Languages*, one reviewer suggests that "Italo Calvino is in many respects an Italian Flann O'Brien"—for like the Irish writer, he was, at that time, "by no means as well known as he should [have been]" (136). Russell Davies's 1981 review of *If on a winter's night a traveler* establishes Calvino's familiarity with the works of the Irish novelist. Calvino, Davies writes, "has conceded to enquirers that the works of Flann O'Brien, [amongst others], come closest to the spirit of invention generated by this book" (774). Robert Looby makes a similar observation about Calvino's novel when he remarks that it "ow[es] much to Flann O'Brien's spirited complexities" (n. p.). Concetta Mazzullo, in fact, goes as far as to suggest that "Flann O'Brien was metamorphosed into [the character] Silas Flannery" in *If on a winter's night a traveler* (185).

What's significant about Mazzullo's remarks for my argument is her observation that both Calvino's and O'Brien's "characters are marked by *lightness*[:] Calvino's *The Baron in the Trees* strangely recalls Sweeny flying and jumping from tree to tree in the deserted lands of Erin . . . O'Brien's characters who try to free themselves from the heaviness of the world end up in tragic falls" (203).[1] In his entry on Flann O'Brien in *The Modern Word*, Looby also uses "lightness" at one point to characterize O'Brien's style of writing, though he does not explicate what he means by the term. That O'Brien's characters are marked by lightness, as Mazzullo suggests, is certainly part of the way I make the term concrete in my essay. However, my use of lightness as a critical framework functions in a more extensive manner. I propose that it is not merely the visual lightness evoked in Sweeny's leap from tree to tree that is at stake here; rather, it is the formal workings of lightness, particularly at the levels of narrative structure and character construction, that gives *At Swim-Two-Birds* its dynamic inventiveness.

Infused with dimensions of insubstantiality, O'Brien's characters are frequently shifting vestiges, which lend a peculiar lightness to their existences: Finn Mac Cool, "a hero of old Ireland," for instance, "came out before me *from his shadow*," while the Good Fairy is altogether invisible (O'Brien 6; emphasis added). Finn, whose "superb physique and development" would seem to convey the very stalwart weightiness of his existence, is rendered evanescent when the extradiegetic event of the student-narrator's toothache rudely intrudes upon his existence without warning, thus dispelling the solidity of his being.

> *The third opening*: Finn Mac Cool was a legendary hero of old Ireland . . . Each of his thighs was as thick as a horse's belly, narrowing to a calf as thick as the belly of a foal. Three fifties of fosterlings could engage with handball against the wideness of his backside, which was large enough to halt the march of men through a mountain-pass.
>
> I hurt a tooth in the corner of my jaw with a lump of the crust I was eating. (2)

John Furriskey, meanwhile, is "born at the age of twenty-five and entered the world with a memory but without a personal experience to account for it" (1). Born thus with the stirring vestiges of a past consciousness, Furriskey is endowed with the lightness of *thoughts* of things past, yet without the encompassing historical baggage of the actual experience of it. In this way, O'Brien's characters take on a "rarefied consistency" (Calvino 16), where their existences are lightened to such a degree that they seem less dense than the usual array of literary characters readers are accustomed to. This semi-porosity gives them the license to drift between narrative levels in flagrant transgressions of the ontological worlds they are supposed to inhabit.

Characters are also afflicted with profoundly absurd or bizarre qualities that lighten the density of their existences. For instance:

> Dermot Trellis practised [a] curious habit in relation to his reading. All colours except green he regarded as symbols of evil and he confined his reading to books attired in green covers. Although a man of wide learning and culture, this arbitrary rule caused serious chasms in his erudition . . . For many years he experienced a difficulty in obtaining a sufficiency of books to satisfy his active and inquiring mind, for the green colour was not favoured by the publishers of London. (O'Brien 104)

Following closely on the heels of this flagrantly absurd qualifier of Trellis's apparent erudition—of reading only books with green covers—is the humorous remonstrance against the unsympathetic London publishers' failure to favor the color. Their lack of appreciation for green covers, the student-narrator informs us, comes at the tragic expense of the impoverishment in learning in one of the great minds of the time. The juxtaposition of such absurdity in this earnest, contrived manner subverts the rounded "wholesomeness" readers have come to expect of conventional literary characters, bestowing them with lightened consistencies that allow O'Brien's characters to hover just above the text, dissolving the solidity of the storyworld.

The novel's final paragraph, in particular, celebrates these ethereal brush-strokes through mentions of Sweeny, the moon, and the eventual erasure it tends toward, as "Sweeny in the trees hears the sad baying as he sits listening on the branch" (237). Sweeny or Suibhne, the legendary mad Irish king who leaps like a bird from tree to tree, is the very epitome of lightness. The image of the old king who refuses to stay grounded and sits up in a tree, and the as-sonance of "Sweeny in the trees" lends the moment a touch of lightness that is almost like a nursery rhyme. J. C. C. Mays, Stephen Knight and especially Anne Clissmann have pointed to the suggestive significance of the Sweeny plot in *At Swim-Two-Birds*. Clissmann's remarks on "the central importance of Sweeny in the structure and vision of *At Swim*" suggest that the embedded tale of the frenzied Irish king is pivotal to the narrative structure of O'Brien's novel (*Alive-Alive O'* 120). Leaping lightly from tree to tree in his madness, Sweeny is a fitting metaphor for the narrative leaps between the constantly-violated ontological layers of *At Swim-Two-Birds*.

Calvino also accords particular privilege to imagery of the moon (which brings with it a sensation of "suspension, a silent calm enchantment" [24]) in his discussion of lightness, which complements the way O'Brien uses it in the conclusion to his novel: "Soon the moon comes forth from behind her cur-tains riding full tilt across the sky, lightsome and unperturbed in her imme-morial calm. The eyes of the mad king upon the branch are upturned, whiter eyeballs in a white face, upturned in fear and supplication. His mind is but a shell" (O'Brien 238). Ancient beyond both memory and record, the moon sails lightsome and tranquil across the night sky as Sweeny stares into it with mad eyes upturned. Both pitiful and fearful, the image of Sweeny is of one who has been literally hollowed-out and lightened or emptied, as his mind remains but a shell. At every turn in O'Brien's writing, we find that "quick, light touch" Calvino valued in his own writing that attests to the lightness of *At Swim-Two-Birds*.

The author's artful assimilation of Finn and Sweeny—in their dislodgment from Irish mythology and subsequent transfiguration in O'Brien's narrative— keep the atmosphere of the novel from sinking under "a vise of stone" (Calvino 4) in the plethora of stories they invoke. Dynamic versions of the myth handed down through the generations (in the plurality of ways stories about Finn end, for instance), introduce a rich intertextuality to O'Brien's writing. A "palimp- sestic" effect is achieved in the partial erasure of the multitude of stories these Irish mythological figures bring with them as they are transfigured (Shea 275; Herman 139). This erasure and re-writing, in fact, happens quite literally in *At Swim-Two-Birds* when the lore of Sweeny, as faithfully retold by Finn earlier in the novel (O'Brien 63–95), is moved from that initial hypo-hypodiegetic to a hypodiegetic level of the narration (that is, one level up) when Jem Casey and Sweeny himself literally fall into the thick of things from the top of their re- spective trees (O'Brien 126–135). The result of such rewritings is a Sweeny and a Finn Mac Cool of considerably lightened densities in the palimpsest of sto- ries told about them. The use of mythological images in this way thus prevents the petrification of fiction, which Calvino warns against, in O'Brien's novels.

There is no sense of weighty agglutination despite the amalgamation of texts and characters assembled in *At Swim-Two-Birds*. These are drawn from sources as diverse as the fictional forty-volume *Conspectus of the Arts and Natural Sciences* to recitations of Sweeny's lays across the novel. Anne Cliss- mann notes that "by the time the book ends[,] it has presented some thirty-six different styles and forty-two extracts" (*Flann O'Brien* 86), yet these symbioses never weigh the novel down because they constitute mere shadows of char- acters rather than characters themselves. For instance, Rüdiger Imhof points to the moment when a group of Red Indians are momentarily called upon to help Shanahan and company fight off their opponents (said Red Indians never re-visit the novel again, although, in an O'Brien universe, there is every chance that they might): "Sensing that they would be defeated by their opponent Red Kiersay unless someone came to their rescue, they called in 'a crowd of Red Indians' Tracy was writing about at that time in another book" (Imhof 166; O'Brien 79). William Tracy, "author of Western romances"—another invented O'Brien personality—was writing these Red Indians into existence at the very moment the characters in Trellis's novel (Shanahan and friends) assimilated them into their battle. Such porosity allows characters to shuttle between texts, set lightly adrift in the sprawling network of literary landscapes; all (story)worlds are their literal oyster.

Structural lightness is also achieved in *At Swim-Two-Birds*, despite the complexity of its narrative organization, through the flattening of its multiple levels of diegesis. Such treatment of the narrative structure works in two ways. First, it deautomatizes readers' perceptions of fiction, as the Russian Formalists have it, such that we "come to grips with the [story]world in a more strenuous and thus, more rewarding fashion" (Erlich 178). Foregrounding the frequent metalepses in *At Swim-Two-Birds* thus facilitates this process of deautomatization. Second, by unraveling the ponderous traditions of reading inherited from realism and the weighty and serious allusiveness of modernism, O'Brien generates a structural lightness that abandons the onerous baggage of conventional (automatized) ways of reading fiction that weigh both the text and the reader down.

At least two dimensions of the narrative structure in *At Swim-Two-Birds* contribute to the complexity of the novel: the "flat" rather than hierarchical presentation of narrative levels and overt, frequent transgressions of said narrative levels. Where multiple narrative levels are invoked in a novel, they are conventionally "nested" (to use Brian McHale's term) within hierarchically arranged frames, in which the outermost frame or primary narrative level tends to be privileged since it technically enables the existence of all other narrative levels (McHale 113). In *At Swim-Two-Birds*, however, O'Brien flattens all notion of hierarchy by resolutely refusing to privilege the primary narrative level occupied by the student-narrator, or any other narrative layer for that matter. He achieves this in several ways. For one, M. Keith Booker points out that "there are many segments of the text that are clearly subsections within larger sections, but the subheadings of these subsections are given in the same [italicized] style as the headings of the sections themselves" (33). The effect of this is that the texts appear, at least stylistically, to be presented on the same level. Furthermore, no one character (and by extension, the narrative levels which they inhabit) is given central significance over any of the others, which heightens the sense of parity between narrative levels. The effect of using the device of *mise-en-abyme* in this curious fashion thus "rob[s] events of their solidity" (McHale 125), suspending the novel in a delightful lightness. The ending of *At Swim-Two-Birds* demonstrates O'Brien's flagrant disregard of conventional privileging of primary narrative levels, for the homodiegetic (first-person) frame narration has all but disappeared by the final "Conclusion of the book, ultimate" (O'Brien 237). In this way, a flat rather than hierarchical presentation of narrative levels is upheld.

O'Brien also subverts our dependence on traditional delineations of narrative levels in order to make sense of his novel. This is evident in the metaleptic transgressions that occur throughout the novel, where characters from a hypo-hypodiegetic level of the narrative leap one up into the hypodiegetic level to drug their creator (Trellis) in order to lead lives that they prefer (O'Brien 162). As Thomas Shea puts it, "O'Brien deliberately befuddles the reader and frustrates the mind which wants to sort and organize. Any attempt to accommodate the novel to a systematic structure falls short because the text deliberately resists procedural patterns grounded in traditional rules of coherency" (59). An appreciation of its varying levels of diegesis is imperative to the reader's sense of logical flow in the narrative, but even that finally collapses in *At Swim-Two-Birds*. In the "Conclusion of the book, ultimate," while the final narrative level presented should ostensibly be the student-narrator's end to his novel, there are no identifying tags to attribute this narration to him. In fact, the first-person narrative voice is replaced by a third-person narration, which undermines readers' expectations and dependence on narrative frames/levels to make sense of the novel. In this case, the "I," which O'Brien has used to condition his readers to recognize the presence of his student-narrator thus far, is pulled from beneath our feet with this unanticipated leap—another reminder of its lightness—from first- to third-person narration. The unnamed student-narrator is thus effectively effaced by the end of *At Swim-Two-Birds*, as the diegetic level of narration that attests to his existence (which in turn gives existence to all other narrative levels) is erased.

The structural lightness achieved in the compression of diegetic levels in this manner has the effect of unraveling traditions of fiction-reading and -writing, serving to deautomatize conventional reading practices. Readers, for instance, would be hard-pressed to refer even to the student-narrator, whose narration ostensibly frames the stories within his story, as the "protagonist" of *At Swim-Two-Birds*—the word "protagonist" defined as "[t]he chief character in a plot, on whom our interest centers" (Abrams and Harpham 265)—because our interest in him remains relatively peripheral throughout the novel and even this tangential interest is undermined by his disappearance at the close of the novel. The absence of a protagonist-figure creates a "weightless gravity" (Calvino 19) whereby the reader need not be anchored, weighed down or committed to the story of any one character or narrative thread— which, anyhow, all tend toward eventual erasure. Conventions of fiction, such as the concept of a protagonist or of precisely delineated narrative levels, are utterly subverted as the reader no longer has to follow, identify with, or empathize with any one central character, or commit themselves to any particular narrative layer as espousing a "truthful" reality; the reader is free to revel in the lightness that O'Brien's writing testifies to.

Erasure of the characters' existences occurs at multiple levels in *At Swim-Two-Birds*: first in the penultimate conclusion, where "the pages which made and sustained the existence of Furriskey and his true friends" are burnt by Teresa, the maid at the Red Swan Hotel, and then in the ultimate conclusion, where the reader registers the notable absence of the student-narrator and encounters, more dramatically, the exit of "the poor German" who commits suicide in the very last line of the novel (O'Brien 239). O'Brien thus erases the significance, or at least the tendency to meaning, of everything that has come to pass, pushing his use of metafictive devices, as Neil Murphy writes, "to hitherto unseen limits, to the point of the extinction of the narrator, and perhaps even the text itself" (Murphy 10). The implications of this are twofold. First, as Anthony Burgess, Ninian Mellamphy, Sue Asbee, and David Herman amongst others, observe, no particular narrative layer is privileged over another, for each narrative level is "openly reveal[ed]" to have "no more legitimacy than any other" (Murphy 38); they are all equally meaningful or tend equally toward unmeaning, depending on your perspective. Second, such erasure lends an eventual lightness to the text, despite its initial, apparent convoluted weightiness. O'Brien, above all, removes the weight of any single authoritative author (as manifested by the multiplicity of writerly figures in *At Swim-Two-Birds*: the student-narrator, Dermot Trellis, Orlick Trellis, William Tracy) and even of his own authorial powers. When his friend Niall Sheridan remarked that the initial manuscript of *At Swim-Two-Birds* was far too long, O'Brien authorized him to pare it down, which Sheridan did by eliminating a third of the original before turning it over to the publishing offices (Gass xii). By stripping *At Swim-Two-Birds* of a single author's control, O'Brien effectively removes weight from the storyworld until what is left is only an image of an image, the very lightest of things, which is almost erased by the end of the novel as well.

Subverting fiction's traditional function of holding "a mirror up to society," *At Swim-Two-Birds* instead "holds up a mirror to the mirror" (Hopper 6) as O'Brien uses parody and satire to laughingly expose fiction-reading conventions that readers and critics have come to depend upon. Asbee, for instance, explains that modernist writing had cultivated the convention of having readers "do a great deal of work before they can catch every nuance intended by the writer, and can admire what may subsequently emerge as aesthetic coherence and organization of the work. It is this new expectation that readers will expend inordinate amounts of time and effort on understanding such a work of fiction that O'Brien mocks in *At Swim*" (21). By tracing the digressive and "purely gratuitous" allusions O'Brien makes in his novel (which could be "intended" or "entirely fortuitous"), Asbee shows how the novelist's fiction-making techniques undermine such reading practices (21–22). These satirical tendencies arguably generate lightness in the structure of *At Swim-Two-Birds* by subtracting the weighty traditions of reading we inherited from realism in the nineteenth century and the allusory impulses of the early twentieth, to demand that we learn to read fictions like O'Brien's in new ways. The image in the mirror to the mirror that O'Brien holds up is one that demands we toss out such ponderous conventions that weigh our experience of fiction-reading down.

The complex narrative structure of *At Swim-Two-Birds* also works against what Victor Shklovsky calls the "process of automatization," which "eats away" at our ability to see things, inducing readers to pass cursorily over the surface of objects in an "abstractive" manner that cues a "generalizing perception" (5). Such practices of seeing, which lead only to a "recognition" rather than a "vision" of things, are antithetical to the artistic impulse, which works to "intensify the impressions of the senses" (3). The "hallmark" of artistry, Shklovsky argues, is to remove the literary work from the domain of automatized perception, allowing the reader to pause in his/her reading and "dwell" on the text—for "[t]his is when the literary work attains its greatest and most long-lasting impact" (12). It is in this way that art becomes the means by which readers can "experience the process of creativity" (6). The task of the novelist is thus to forestall such "generalizing perception" that causes the literary work to gradually "fade away" and lose its significance (5). O'Brien's foregrounding of the frequent metalepses in *At Swim-Two-Birds* therefore serves to facilitate this process of deautomatization.

As William Gass observes, "[a]lthough *At Swim-Two-Birds* has the form of a classic frame tale, the four books [(B1:O'Brien's), (B2:N's), (B3:Trellis's), (B4:the son's)] are not hermetically sealed from one another as these parentheses seem to indicate. Like salvage from the sea, flotsam from this or that wrecked narrative washes up on foreign shores" when these frames eventually collapse into each other (ix). Metalepsis, as Herman explains, can be formally defined as "one or more illicit movements up or down the hierarchy of diegetic levels structuring narrative discourse" (133). For instance, the narration in B4 takes flight and ascends to an indeterminate position between B2 and B3 when "Orlick Trellis metaleptically migrates to a frame positioned somewhere between O'Brien's narrator and Dermot Trellis" (Herman 137). Herman observes that it is "Orlick's diegetically unstable status that allows him to exact revenge on Dermot Trellis by narrating a story (236 ff.) that details torments as cruel as any Sweeny ever experienced" (138). To elucidate, as if the fact that Orlick was begotten as a result of Dermot's assault of his own fictional creation, Sheila Lamont, was not bizarre enough, *At Swim-Two-Birds* takes an even stranger turn when Orlick's narration in B4 metaleptically transgresses the hypo-hypodiegetic level of the narration to effect changes on events occurring in B2. At the level of Orlick's narration, which should ostensibly take place in B4, Trellis is thrown out of bed by the Pooka—both of whom are characters from B2 who have never been allowed to meet, since they belong to two of three different stories that the student-narrator is telling (O'Brien 188). In this surreal mad circus, Trellis is first physically tortured and then severely taken to trial by his own fictional creations (191ff).

The Russian Formalists contend that the use of such devices to "enstrange" (*priëm ostranenija*), or to deautomatize our perceptions of the novel, is "an omnipresent principle of imaginative literature" (Shklovsky 6; Erlich 177). The enstrangement perpetuated through these metaleptic devices counteract the "inexorable pull of routine" reading practices, in order to defeat "stock responses attendant upon" the text (Erlich 177). Such impulses against automatization likewise characterize Calvino's partiality toward the quality of lightness in fiction-writing.

> Whenever humanity seems condemned to heaviness, I think I should fly like Perseus into a different space. I don't mean escaping into dreams or into the irrational. I mean that I have to change my approach, *look* at the world from a different perspective, with a different logic and with fresh methods of *cognition* . . . In the boundless universe of literature there are always new avenues to be explored, both very recent and very ancient, styles and forms that can change our image of the world. (Calvino 7, emphasis added)

Lightness, Calvino suggests, lends a different lens with which we can look at the world, to properly see it "from a different perspective, with a different logic and with fresh methods of cognition," which is exactly the effect of O'Brien's structural lightness on the reader's image of the fictional world we encounter in *At Swim-Two-Birds*. Accustomed ways of reading fiction—a perceptual "recognition" rather than "vision" of things—become deautomatized by the radical subversions of conventional reading practices through O'Brien's subtraction of weight from his characters and from the narrative structure of his novel (Shklovsky 3, 10). O'Brien "lays bare the device[s]" of his art through his use of such techniques, decisively pulling the rug out from under our feet, and marches readers down new roads for experiencing fiction (Shklovsky 149). The quality of lightness is thus intimately related to the new ways of fiction-making and fiction-reading that *At Swim-Two-Birds* attests to.

As Booker observes, "[b]ecause of the inherent ambiguity of the text, *At Swim* offers itself to a wide variety of interpretations, depending on the perspective and strategy that the reader brings to the text" (42). In a novel that celebrates so much ambiguity, any critical reading that aspires toward solving its central "mystery," or claims to provide an authoritative "key" to interpretation, necessarily falls into the novelist's sly trap of mocking any and all futile attempts to impute authoritative meaning on a text that tends so much toward erasure and unmeaning by the end. That lightness of touch that characterizes the satirical nature of O'Brien's work ultimately eludes all attempts to circumscribe his writing within fixed critical or interpretive frameworks.

NOTE

1   Though Mazzullo's essay is entitled "O'Brien and Calvino: Between 'Lightness' and 'Heaviness,'" her emphasis lies in making connections between characters from both authors' novels and is not, as its title somewhat misleadingly suggests, focused specifically on issues of lightness and heaviness. The single reference she makes in her entire essay to the subject of lightness is quoted in my essay.

WORKS CITED

Abrams, M. H. and Geoffrey Harpham. *A Glossary of Literary Terms*. 9th ed. Boston: Wadsworth Cengage Learning, 2009.

Asbee, Sue. *Flann O'Brien*. Boston: Twayne Publishers, 1991.

Booker, M. Keith. *Flann O'Brien, Bakhtin and Menippean Satire*. Syracuse, NY: Syracuse Univ. Press, 1995.

Burgess, Anthony. "Probably a Masterpiece" in *Alive-Alive O': Flann O'Brien's At Swim-Two-Birds*. Ed. Rüdiger Imhof. Dublin: Wolfhound Press, 1985. 70–72.

Calvino, Italo. *Six Memos for the Next Millennium*. New York, NY: Vintage, 1988.

Clissmann, Anne. *Flann O'Brien: A Critical Introduction to his Writings (The Story-Teller's Book-Web)*. Dublin: Gill and Macmillan, 1975.

—. "The Story-Teller's Book-Web" in *Alive-Alive O': Flann O'Brien's At Swim-Two-Birds*. Ed. Rüdiger Imhof. Dublin: Wolfhound Press, 1985. 118–140.

Davies, Russell. "The Writer Versus the Reader." *Times Literary Supplement* (10 July 1981): 773–774.

Erlich, Victor. *Russian Formalism: History – Doctrine*. 3rd ed. New Haven and London: Yale Univ. Press, 1981.

Gass, William. Introduction. *At Swim-Two-Birds*. By Flann O'Brien. 1951. Normal, IL: Dalkey Archive Press, 1998. v–xviii.

Herman, David. "Toward a Formal Description of Narrative Metalepsis." *Journal of Literary Semantics* 26.2 (1997): 132–152.

Hopper, Keith. *Flann O'Brien: A Portrait of the Artist as a Young Post-modernist*. Cork: Cork Univ. Press, 1995.

Imhof, Rüdiger. "Two Meta-Novelists: Sternesque Elements in Novels by Flann O'Brien" in *Alive-Alive O': Flann O'Brien's At Swim-Two-Birds*. Ed. Rüdiger Imhof. Dublin: Wolfhound Press, 1985. 160–190.

Knight, Stephen. "Forms of Gloom" in *Alive-Alive O': Flann O'Brien's At Swim-Two-Birds*. Ed. Rüdiger Imhof. Dublin: Wolfhound Press, 1985. 86–101.

Looby, Robert. "Flann O'Brien: A postmodernist when it was neither profitable nor popular." *The Modern Word: The Scriptorium*. The Modern Word, 28 Jul. 2004. Web. 18 Apr. 2011. <http://www.themodernword.com/scriptorium/obrien.html>

Mays, J. C. C. "Literalist of the Imagination" in *Alive-Alive O': Flann O'Brien's At Swim-Two-Birds*. Ed. Rüdiger Imhof. Dublin: Wolfhound Press, 1985. 81–86.

Mazzullo, Concetta. "O'Brien and Calvino: Between 'Lightness' and 'Heaviness'" in *The Cracked Lookingglass: Contributions to the Study of Irish Literature*. Ed. Carla de Petris, Jean Ellis D'Alessandro and Fiorenzo Fantaccini. Roma: Bulzoni, 1999. Print. 185–204.

McHale, Brian. "Chinese-Box Worlds." *Postmodernist Fiction*. London: Routledge, 1987. 112–130.

Mellamphy, Ninian. "Aestho-Autogamy and the Anarchy of Imagination: Flann O'Brien's Theory of Fiction in *At Swim-Two-Birds*" in *Alive-Alive O': Flann O'Brien's At Swim-Two-Birds*. Ed. Rüdiger Imhof. Dublin: Wolfhound Press, 1985. 140–160.

Murphy, Neil. "Flann O'Brien." *Review of Contemporary Fiction* 25.3 (2005): 7–41.

O'Brien, Flann. *At Swim-Two-Birds*. 1951. Normal, IL: Dalkey Archive Press, 1998.

Shea, Thomas. *Flann O'Brien's Exorbitant Novels*. Cranbury, NJ: Associated University Presses, 1992.

Shklovsky, Viktor. *Theory of Prose*. Trans. Benjamin Sher. Normal, IL: Dalkey Archive Press, 1991.

Unsigned. Rev. of *Barone Rampante*, by Italo Calvino. *Modern Languages: Journal of the Modern Language Association* Sept. 1970: 136.

NEIL MURPHY

Flann O'Brien's *The Hard Life* & the Gaze of the Medusa

> "Average reality begins to rot and stink as soon as the act of individual creation ceases to animate a subjectively perceived texture."
> Vladimir Nabokov (*Strong Opinions*)

The range of critical views that Flann O'Brien's *The Hard Life* has attracted since its modestly successful public reception in 1961 is more diverse and frequently contradictory than that received by any of his other novels. Many critics have observed, for example, that the conversations between Collopy and Father Fahrt are empty rhetorical games, a view supported by the decidedly inexpressive narrator, Finbarr's, observation that "[a]s usual, the subject under discussion was never named" (30). Anthony Cronin suggests that these conversations represent the central achievement of the novel, claiming that they are "classics of pointless dialectic" (215), a point echoed by M. Keith Booker, but extended to suggest that almost "all of the language in *The Hard Life* is . . . without the backing of any firm conviction" (93). Similarly, Thomas Shea contends that the novel becomes an exploration of how "discourses collapse, sounding only a desperately squalid void" (142), and Keith Donohue argues that throughout the novel, "[w]ords, things, and events are treated as epistemological uncertainties" (185).

Despite the frequency of such poststructuralist-inclined perspectives, Anne Clissman describes the novel as "O'Brien's most normal picture of reality" (272), while Jonathan Bolton considers *The Hard Life* to be a "comic bildungsroman: a peculiar hybrid formulation that mimics the expectations of self-cultivation, but then subverts its own narrative trajectory" (18) and he also argues that the novel is a "cynical representation of a culture and way of life that is beyond reform or hope or change" (121). Bolton's view of the novel as cultural critique is clear and in particular he points to the novel's representation of a culture of "neglect, alcohol dependency, and an absurdly unstable surrogate family environment" (121), concluding that the "narrator's symbolic splurge at the end of the novel confirms O'Brien's cynical attitude towards reform in Ireland" (128). However tenuous this final assertion might be, Bolton's essay is indicative of a general movement, in critical terms, away from a consideration of the novel as a postmodern or poststructuralist text, or as self-referential epistemological satire, towards an emphasis on the socio-political implications of a novel that, in O'Brien's catalogue, offers a relatively direct realist focus. For example, Joseph Brooker rightly points out that *The Hard Life* significantly develops the O'Brien canon in its representation of "two subjects largely absent from the early fiction: women and the church" (76), and Keith Hopper argues that the novel is a "post-colonial satire of de Valera's Ireland (with its anti-pluralist constitution which privileged the role of the Catholic Church)" (54). He also suggests the need for, and offers, a feminist reading of *The Hard Life*. These observations are rooted in what Hopper terms a "surface commitment by O'Brien as a cultural observer to show the structures and ideologies which underlie his society" (55). While Hopper is cautious enough to acknowledge the "surface" nature of this commitment, it is clear that O'Brien's level of engagement with social reality is more direct than in his previous novels. Despite this, Hopper points to O'Brien's misogynistic tendencies, to which the novelist himself appears blind. There is ample textual evidence in *The Hard Life*, and elsewhere, to support Bolton's, Brooker's and Hopper's readings and what their respective arguments register is that this novel offers a site for discussion of ideological readings that *At Swim-Two-Birds* and *The Third Policeman* do not. Female characters have greater presence, if not necessarily active importance, in *The Hard Life* than in any of the other novels and the biting satire of Dublin life, the Catholic Church, and Irish political structures, are all evident. Also obvious, parodic or otherwise, is that it was the first time that O'Brien situated his satirical mode in such a literal, socially charged context. This essay, however, contends that the satire is poorly executed for several reasons, although this is not the primary reason for its failure as a major work in O'Brien's canon. Instead, I will illustrate that *The Hard Life* fails, not only because it is "structurally flawed and thematically erratic" (Hopper 52), which is most certainly is, but because for the first time O'Brien constructed a fictional world that is radically different to the worlds that bear the mark of his genius, the world of sublime invention and daring imaginative risks that we find in the first three novels.

There appears to have been some desire, on O'Brien's part, to attract notoriety with *The Hard Life*, particularly via the school-boy puns and vulgar humour directed towards Father Fahrt, and Carol Taaffe has convincingly suggested that financial motivation and other contextual reasons may have been significant factors in the author's switch to a more realist focus (182–193). In any event, the end-result is a fiction that permits social reality a far greater presence than in any of the previous fictional work. Unfortunately, in his efforts to make more of a direct impact, there is a sense, as Taaffe argues, that the "conventional linear narrative" that he offers is restrained to the point of "dullness" (183). For the first time, O'Brien abandons the radically inventive surfaces that had always characterised his work, and that had placed him in a literary tradition defined by authors like Sterne, Cervantes, Calvino, Nabokov, Kundera, and Borges. While *The Hard Life* is far from being a conventional realist novel, it nevertheless abandons the sophisticated self-conscious humour and narrative inventiveness of the earlier work and instead offers a grim self-deflation and largely linear skeletal plotlines. More serious, ultimately, is that unlike its predecessors it simply doesn't offer the self-containment, the inner cohesion that the most successful storyworlds offer. The novelistic balance that Brian McHale speaks of as "the special logical status of the fictional text, its condition of being in-between, amphibious—neither true nor false, suspended between belief and disbelief" (33) is not convincingly achieved in *The Hard Life* because the grim ordinariness of things, the flat humour, the excessive reliance on bland conversation, all deaden the special "amphibious" power that fiction at its best usually has—the "reality" overburdens the fiction.

The Hard Life initially mimics the generic form of the nineteenth century realist novel, featuring deceased parents, orphans, urban squalor, an element of social commentary, and clearly discernible historical and geographical frames in late nineteenth-, early twentieth-century Dublin. However, this 'Oirish' variation of English realist fiction also echoes Joyce's *Dubliners, A Portrait of the Artist as a Young Man*, and *Ulysses*, unlikely source texts for a realist novel, although O'Brien clearly parodies or negates the Joycean model in several ways, most notably in that Dublin is sketched with almost no precise detail, no inner reflection, and none of Joyce's linguistic inventiveness. For example, Booker points out that the recurring ellipses, or gaps in communication that one encounters so frequently in *Dubliners*, serve similar textual functions in *The Hard Life*, most obviously in "the consistent refusal to name Collopy's project, a refusal that keeps the nature of this project not only from the reader but also from Finbarr and Manus, who frequently witness the conversations of Collopy and Fahrt on this topic" (89). Finbarr, of course, is neither sure of what he is saying much of the time nor particularly concerned about his lack of clarity. He concedes, for instance, at an early stage that "[t]hat's merely my recollection of the silly sort of conversation we had. Probably it is all wrong" (5). He proceeds to acknowledge his vague apprehension of events when, after describing Mr. Collopy, he swiftly withdraws the validity of the description: "There is something misleading but not dishonest in this portrait of Mr. Collopy. It cannot be truly my impression of him when I first saw him but rather a synthesis of all the thoughts and experiences I had of him over the years, a long look backwards" (9). This essentially subversive self-reflexive commentary conditions much of his recounting of events and his awareness of the requirements of his narratorial role is frequently coupled with an open admission of failure: "It is seemly, as I have said, to give that explanation but I cannot pretend to have illuminated the situation or made it more reasonable" (14). The key implication is that he will fulfill his obligations as narrator of an ostensibly real set of events but he is unable to admit to their absolute veracity. Furthermore, his glib lack of overall coherence is often very lightly passed over, like at the beginning of chapter four when one discovers that six years have been skipped, causing a lack of continuity in terms of temporal development: "And still the years kept rolling on, and uneventfully enough, thank God" (22).

Despite the use of familiar metafictional tropes like the subversion of linguistic validity, the self-reflexive deflations, and the parodic treatment of temporal clarity and sequence, the use of the linear realist novel structure is maintained throughout, including elements of the epistolary novel for much of the final third, essentially a series of aimless and increasingly fantastic letters from his brother Manus. Even within the epistolary frame, there is an endless procession of trivia, far-flung fantasy, and verbiage, a point recognised by the narrator: "Well that was a long and rather turgid letter but I found myself in agreement with the last paragraph [take no action for the present]. In fact I put the whole subject out of my head ..." (129). Finbarr's response points to a pattern of general disdain of the merits of language in the text as a whole, as does Manus's catalogue of bogus books of questionable expertise acts—constant reminders of the dubious nature of the written word and the perils of high-flown rhetoric. For example, his first book on tight-rope walking whose title pages reads "THE HIGH WIRE—Nature Held at Bay—Spine-chilling Spectacle Splenetizes Sporting Spectators—By Professor H. Q. Latimer Dodds" (47), is composed in jargonized prose whose only function is to generate the illusion of authority. The sense that textual items like books and letters are essentially hollow forms of discourse is extended to include many other linguistic formations in the novel, and the prognosis is that language, at least in social modes of discourse, is ultimately empty. *The Hard Life* may actually be the most radically dismissive of all of O'Brien's works in that it allows language to have no significant purpose and words achieve very little in this nauseating world of recycled conversations and, as Booker observes in the case of Manus, a "commodification of language," whose sale-value is its only significance (94).

Therefore, the novel that initially loosely resembles a Dickensian social commentary ends up acting as an unsettling and intensely negative text, simultaneously expressing the author's revulsion at a Dublin provincial mind and a deep lack of faith in language systems. Of course, critics like Bolton, Baines,

Brooker, Hopper, Taaffe, *et al* have pointed to the social implications of the novel, and the mirror held up to the world in *The Hard Life* is far less obtuse than in *At Swim-Two-Birds* and *The Third Policeman*, neither of which make any meaningful attempt to offer clear representations of social reality although, of course, one could argue that both novels are deeply connected to human concerns by virtue of the philosophical implications of their imaginary frames. While *The Hard Life* gives us a singular fictional frame with often vague, but uncomplicated, characters, the two earliest novels offer instead multiple fictive frames and characters who represent varying levels of ontological complication, from death to mere invention. *The Hard Life* is far more grounded in what might be described as the "real" but it is also very clearly more complex than that. There is also a peculiar sense of not being able to get to grips with anything in particular, something that is suggested by Manus's adjustment of Keats's epitaph ("Here lies one whose name is writ on water") to read "Here lies one whose name is writ in water," that is, invisible (172). He takes an already precarious scripted image and makes it vanish completely, and the world of the novel becomes less and less tangible, a quality that also extends to the narrator himself. Finbarr, as a character, is incapable of any meaningful intervention in the life of the text, and this accounts for the sense that the novel doesn't have a centre, a point made by Tess Hurson (120). It seems that what Hurson notices is a hollow centre of significance, of absent meaning, because the reportage-style of the narrator offers little by way of ambition, intent, or focus. In fact, many critics have variously adjudged *The Hard Life* to be an incomplete novel, a structurally flawed, muddled social commentary, an "insecure, imperfect novel" (Baines 143), which "lacks coherence" (Clissman 290), and is neither "plausible nor metafictional" (Brooker 76). It is difficult to argue with all of these demonstrably accurate observations but it is also clear that many of them are rooted in a sense of implicit disappointment that the novel's ostensibly realist frame is so insecure or, alternatively, that the novel's merit lies in its social engagement. As Bolton suggests, "the social and cultural representation of endemic problems of growing up Irish" are important but have been "neglected by critics focused on poststructuralist issues" (121). The reason that both views can be validated rests on the novel's equivocal status as social docu-ment. Yes, there is more social engagement here than elsewhere in O'Brien, but that engagement is compromised by the relentless parodic treatment of these elements to the extent that it is difficult to ascertain a coherent social point. The equivocal nature of the novel is also ultimately a symptom of the main under-lying technical problem: the social elements compromise the fictional achieve-ment and it is thus the contention of this essay that it is precisely because of the attempt to reflect a social reality at all that the novel fails.

In all three previous O'Brien novels, the structure of the fictional ontol-ogy is derived from what Denis Donoghue refers to as "the wrenching of lan-guage from the propriety of its normal reference," or catachresis (135), and argues that "there are entire works which are catachreses in principle, such as *Finnegans Wake* and the Alice books" (137). *At Swim-Two-Birds*, *The Poor Mouth*, and *The Third Policeman* perpetually subvert any possible anchoring to social reality by radically destabilising temporal, spatial, and rational norms; their primary characters are more fundamentally at odds with what we might consider encyclopaedic reality than those in *The Hard Life*, and there are no serious substantive rhetorical attempts to register direct observations about society. Flann O'Brien's great power as an artist lay precisely in the fact that he constructed such powerful catachretic fictional worlds, and when in *The Hard Life* there was an attempt to moderate this approach, to allow more direct social engagement into its fictional frame, the potency of his illusory story-world is greatly diminished. The kind of Art that O'Brien had previously cre-ated always retained a distance from the more rationalised, linear energies of the social world, and the ceding of this distance appears to have allowed a dull predictability into *The Hard Life* or, as Yeats argues, "all imaginative art remains at a distance and this distance, once chosen, must be firmly held against a pushing world" (224). While, of course, there is nothing implicitly wrong with direct social engagement in fiction, one can argue that the pecu-liar strengths of O'Brien's imaginative process were previously more closely linked with a tradition in European (and world) fiction that privileges dis-tance, obtuse focus, and highly stylised fictional ontologies. It is no accident that Borges was an admirer of O'Brien and that Calvino very likely based his Silas Flannery, from *If on a winter's night a traveller*, on the student-narrator of *At Swim-Two-Birds*.[1] What these authors, among others like Nabokov, Kundera, and Beckett, share is akin to the quality that Susanne Langer ascribes to every "work of art": the "tendency to appear . . . dissociated from its mundane environment," or the sense of "otherness from reality—the impression of an illusion enfolding the thing, action, statement, or flow of sound that constitutes the work" (45). Similar to Donoghue's catachretic quality, Langer argues that every work of art ultimately "detaches itself from its actual setting and acquires a different context" (47).

O'Brien's early fictional landscapes clearly resonate with the self containment of Langer's "otherness." For example, in his early review of *At Swim-Two-Birds*, Borges cites Schopenhauer's view that dreaming and wakefulness are the pages of a single book, which we read in order to live, and suggested that books that branch into other books, like O'Brien's first novel, "help us sense this oneness" between the dreaming and wakefulness (162). Langer's identification of dissociation as a primary quality of art occupies similar ground in that while the remnants of the real are everywhere in the novels, it is the multi-dimensional layering of the fictional experience that speaks of the quality of dreaming, the quality of imaginative otherness that ensures that the fictions achieve the crucial quality of illusion.

The Third Policeman does not extend the Chinese box fictive space of *At Swim-Two-Birds*, but the imaginative range of its hellish, carnivalesque world ensures that the novel retains the central anti-realist focus of the first novel. The primary frame narrative of *The Third Policeman* is a heterocosmic space that exists in opposition to the "real" world, although it certainly has a relationship with that world. In addition, within the primary frame there are several spatial and temporal levels, including a series of in-between spaces, or zones, like the "Eternity" to which the narrator journeys with Sergeant Pluck, and Policeman Fox's tiny police station in the walls of Mathers's house. The construction of several such spatial zones echoes the effect of *At Swim-Two-Birds'* Chinese box narrative in that the multiple, competing levels of reality occupy the central ontological frame of the novel, and ultimately contribute to a deep sense of illusion, or otherness, and also resonates with Borges' sense of the co-presence of waking and dreaming in a way that is perhaps even more unnerving than *At Swim-Two-Birds*, because life and death coexist—a dark parallel to waking and dreaming.

Similarly, in *The Poor Mouth*, the presence of multiple ontological levels proves to be deeply unsettling to a linear, one-dimensional, notion of reality. Sitric O'Sanassa, for example, grows so despondent with his misery-laden impoverished life that he takes up residence in a large spacious room embedded in rock beneath the sea, an underground cave where he can have both company and nutrition: "Where he was, he had freedom from the inclement weather, the famine and the abuse of the world. Seals would constitute his company as well as his food" (98). Living in the textual space that is O'Brien's invented version of inclement Ireland, O'Sanassa chooses to live among the creatures of the sea rather than to live among the half-living on shore, which spurs stories among Bonaparte's neighbours that O'Sanassa has turned into a fish. Similarly, Bonaparte locates the mythical Maeldoon O'Poenassa, plundered from the ancient Gaelic story from the eighth or ninth century, *Immram Curaig Máele Dúin*, in a magic cave where whiskey both fuels a fire and provides sustenance via a spring in the earth. Furthermore, the entire novel is spatially compromised by virtue of Bonaparte being able to see the length of the entire country from his window. That such strategies often represent parodic intent is clear but in addition, as with the earlier novels, the originality of the multi-layered, fictional zones produces an invented reality that allows the reader to explore a variety of perspectives.

This is the source of the artistic problem at the heart of *The Hard Life*. In some respects the novel is a predictable extension of the savage parodic and subversive spirit that dictates almost everything in his work. Whether the parody is of fictional forms (*At Swim-Two-Birds*), rationalism (*The Third Policeman*), or Irish nationalism and Gaelic literature (*The Poor Mouth*), the spirit of comic dissent has always been the commanding intellectual directive, and in *The Hard Life* this spirit finds expression in its overt dismissal of language systems. Whatever else *The Hard Life* is, it is clear that there is a deep parody of the pretensions of language and communicative systems and, stripped of the imaginative elaborations that one finds in the earlier novels, it may well be O'Brien's most nihilistic novel. Finbarr displays none of the humour, or occasional humanity that we encounter in his fictional predecessors and his sense of emotional and intellectual disengagement is deeply unsettling while, finally, the surge of vomit that he expels at the close of the novels generates a quality of bleakness that O'Brien hadn't previously achieved.[2]

So while the parodic intent is perhaps more bleak than in the earlier novels it remains typically O'Brien-esque in its satirical spirit. The primary difference is that *The Hard Life* never achieves that sense of haunting otherness that marks the early novels, that sense of operating solely within their own fictional regulatory systems. In attempting to effect an essentially realist frame, albeit parodically, O'Brien compromises what Langer calls the "air of illusion, of being a sheer image" that he had been so extraordinarily good at (46). Quite simply, there is too much reality in the novel. So while many O'Brien scholars are accurate in itemising the socially-relevant elements, the gender question, Catholicism, dreary provincial Dublin life, I would argue that it is precisely because of the excess of such elements that the artistic core of the novel is undermined. As Langer argues, with respect to art objects, buildings and vases, the aura of illusion is crucial to the self-contained quality that complete fictional forms require (Langer 46). All of O'Brien's previous novels have this quality, they have a sense of belonging to themselves only, or being entirely self-reliant, while *The Hard Life*, despite its parodic intent, never manages to erect a fictional ontology that speaks of the complex levels of unique experience.

In effect, despite its clear satirical intent, *The Hard Life* is the first O'Brien novel that doesn't obviously belong to the same novelistic tradition as Sterne, Diderot, de Assis, Nabokov, Calvino, and Kundera. The early O'Brien novels always had the quality of "lightness" that Milan Kundera associates with Sterne's *Tristram Shandy* and Diderot's *Jacques le Fataliste*, two eighteenth century novels that "reached heights of playfulness, or lightness, never scaled before or since." After those early masterpieces, Kundera argues that "the novel got itself tied to the imperative of verisimilitude, to realistic settings, to chronological order" (15). Similarly Calvino writes of the "adventurous, picaresque inner rhythm" or the "quick light touch" that he aspired to in his own work, as an antidote to the "weight, the inertia, the opacity of the world—qualities that stick to writing from the start, unless one finds some way of evading them" (4). Appropriately availing of the Greek mythic frame of Perseus and Medusa, he argues that the only way to avoid the "slow petrification" of the world "turning into stone," to escape "the inexorable stare of the Medusa," is to do as Perseus did, to fly with winged heels and to gaze at the Gorgon only via the reflection in his bronze shield. Perseus manages to defeat the death-gaze of the Medusa, emblem of all heaviness, by supporting himself "on the very lightest of things, the winds and the clouds, and fixes his gaze upon what can be revealed only by indirect vision, and image caught in a mirror" (4). Calvino allegorises the myth to mean that the poet can only avoid the weight of the real by "indirect vision," by constructing glittering images derived from, but not of the world (4). The heaviness of life is too much to bear for his kind of fiction except by containing its image in poetic image. Of course, this doesn't inevitably mean a retreat from the real because Perseus does gaze at the Medusa but on his terms, through the reflected image, and he thereafter keeps the severed head concealed in a bag to be used as a weapon when necessary, or as Calvino puts it, "he carries the reality with him and accepts it as his particular burden" (5). Thus, this is not a negation of reality but a reconstitution of reality in the forms of art. For Calvino, it represents an alternative method to approach human experience; it was a matter of looking at "the world from a different perspective, with a different logic and fresh methods of cognition and verification. The images of lightness that I seek should not fade away like dreams dissolved by the realities of present and future . . ." (7). The formal reconstruction of reality thus offers the opportunity to re-conceive of reality and allows one to re-envision the constituent parts of the reflected reality. So, while *The Third Policeman* contains a world that is so radically destabilised that it bears little direct resemblance to reality, the fundamental epistemological systems of humanity are subjected to profound reconstruction and, ultimately, dismissal. This corresponds to what Nabokov terms "true reality," which is reflected in fiction only by the construction of "real, authentic worlds," or those that seem "unusual" (118). *The Hard Life*, on the other hand, by virtue of its author's clear desire to render the novel more socially recognisable, relinquishes the lightness of touch and gazes directly at the Medusa's face. This results only in the reflection of what Nabokov terms "average reality," the reality of "general ideas, conventional forms of humdrummery, current editorials" (118). The ultimate satirical point of the novel isn't fundamentally different to that of its predecessors but by training its lens on more direct social material, O'Brien allows the Gorgon's head out of the bag with the result that the imaginative intensity and unpredictable humour is lost.

O'Brien's particular imaginative prowess depended on him averting his gaze from the social. The social critique that is present in *The Poor Mouth* is potent as a fictional presence precisely because it isn't too literal, too direct. When that same impulse finds expression in *The Hard Life* it has the quality of complaint rather than successful satire, weighed down as it is with the concrete issues of Catholicism, and parochial, drab, Dublin life. It relinquishes what O'Brien's work always had, the self-sufficient quality of art or, in Langer's terms, "the impression of an illusion enfolding the thing, action, statement, or flow of sound that constitutes the work" (45–6). What this means, for Langer, is that the work "detaches itself from its actual settings and acquires a different context" (47) and in the process liberates perception "from all practical purposes" (49). With *The Hard Life*, such a process doesn't happen because the work is too firmly anchored to the human reality from which the fiction emerges, and it never attains the sense of unique self-sufficiency that is so apparent in *At Swim-Two-Birds*, *The Third Policeman*, and *The Poor Mouth*.

NOTES

1   Borges was one of the first major favourable reviewers of *At Swim-Two-Birds*, and Concetta Mazzullo has argued that Calvino's Silas Flannery is based on Flann O'Brien,

although it would be more accurate to point to a close family resemblance between Silas Flannery and O'Brien's student-narrator. Mazzullo convincingly argues that Calvino must have read O'Brien, and also draws parallels between the self-reflexive games played out by both Silas and the student of *At Swim-Two-Birds*. It is fitting, of course, that a copy of a Flann O'Brien character ultimately makes an appearance in a work by one of his closest fictional European counterparts.

2   Jennika Baines offers a very useful summary of the various interpretations of the closing 'vomit scene' by a variety of critics, and she also adds her own view that it represents Finbarr's final loss of control faced with having to deal with that trap of his own life (155–6). My own view is that it represents a final self-reflexive gesture, one of many in the novel, a kind of revulsion at itself-as-text.

WORKS CITED

Baines, Jennika. Ed. *"Is It About a Bicycle?": Flann O'Brien in the Twenty-First Century*. Dublin: Four Courts Press, 2011.

Booker, M. Keith. *Flann O'Brien, Bakhtin, and Menippean Satire*. Syracuse: Syracuse Univ. Press, 1995.

Borges, Jorge Luis. *Selected Non-Fictions*. Ed. Eliot Weinberger. New York: Penguin, 1999.

Brooker, Joseph. *Flann O'Brien*. Tavistock: Northcote House, 2005.

Calvino, Italo. *Six Memos for the New Millennium*. New York: Vintage, 1993.

Clissmann, Anne. *Flann O'Brien: A Critical Introduction to his Writings*. Dublin: Gill & Macmillan, 1975.

Cronin, Anthony, *No Laughing Matter: The Life and Times of Flann O'Brien*. New York: Fromm International, 1998.

Donoghue, Denis. *Speaking of Beauty*. New Haven: Yale Univ. Press, 2003.

Donohue, Keith. *The Irish Anatomist: A Study of Flann O'Brien*. Bethesda, MD: Academica Press, 2002.

Hopper, Keith. *Flann O'Brien: A Portrait of the Artist as a Young Post-modernist*. 2nd Ed. Cork: Cork Univ. Press, 2009.

Kundera, Milan. *The Art of the Novel*. Trans Linda Asher. New York: Perennial Classics, 2003.

Langer, Susanne Katherina Knauth. *Feeling and Form: a theory of art.* New York: Scribner, 1953.

Mazzullo, Concetta. "O'Brien and Calvino: Between 'Lightness' and 'Heaviness'" in *The Cracked Lookingglass: Contributions to the Study of Irish Literature.* Ed. Carla de Petris, Jean Ellis D'Alessandro and Fiorenzo Fantaccini. Roma: Bulzoni, 1999. 185–204.

McHale, Brian. *Postmodernist Fiction.* London: Routledge, 1996.

Hurson, Tess. "Conspicuous Absences: *The Hard Life*" in *Conjuring Complexities: Essays on Flann O'Brien.* Eds. Anne Clune and Tess Hurson. Belfast: Queen's University of Belfast, 1997. 119–131.

Nabokov, Vladimir. *Strong Opinions.* New York: Vintage, 1990.

O'Brien, Flann. *At Swim-Two-Birds.* New York: Penguin, 1976; Normal, IL: Dalkey Archive Press, 1993.

—. *The Hard Life.* Normal, IL: Dalkey Archive Press, 1989.

—. *The Poor Mouth.* Trans. Patrick C. Power. Normal, IL: Dalkey Archive Press, 1998.

—. *The Third Policeman.* London: Flamingo, 1988; Normal, IL: Dalkey Archive Press, 1999.

Shea, Thomas F. *Flann O'Brien's Exorbitant Novels.* Lewisburg, PA: Bucknell Univ. Press, 1992.

Taaffe, Carol. *Ireland Through the Looking Glass: Flann O'Brien, Myles na gCopaleen and Irish Cultural Debate.* Cork: Cork Univ. Press, 2008.

Yeats, W. B. *Essays and Introductions.* New York: Macmillan, 1961.

FLORE COULOUMA

Tall Tales and Short Stories: *Cruiskeen Lawn* and the Dialogic Imagination

1. Introduction: a reply to *Cruiskeen Lawn*'s detractors

Although Myles na gCopaleen's chronicles have acquired a cult status in Ireland, *Cruiskeen Lawn* has never been a favorite of literary critics, who generally favour O'Brien's most famous novels, *At Swim-Two-Birds* and *The Third Policeman*. Not only are the chronicles rarely studied, they are also regularly credited with O'Brien's "failure" to become a literary master like his predecessor, Joyce, and his contemporary, Beckett. For most critics, O'Brien's flaw as a writer is to have squandered most of his energy on twenty-six years' worth of *Cruiskeen Lawn* columns. The chronicle ran several times weekly from 1940 until his death in 1966, with decreasing frequency towards the end of his life. Ironically, the chronicle is regularly mentioned along with Flann O'Brien's notorious and devastating alcoholism as the other nail in his creative coffin: "Was it the drink was his ruin, or was it the column?" (Kenner 255). Following Anthony Cronin, O'Brien's ambiguously sympathetic biographer, Kenner brutally states that when O'Nolan started the column as Myles na gCopaleen, "a great future lay behind him" (257). For Cronin, "the Great Myles" could never free himself from the provincialism of Dublin life (*Dead as Doornails* 112). More recently, Declan Kiberd accused the Stage-Irishman side of Myles na Gopaleen (with the later spelling used by O'Brien, after Boucicault) of entrapping Flann O'Brien in the limitations of the colonial subject towards his metropolitan center: when Myles "succumbed to the temptation to placate his newspaper audience," Flann O'Brien took on the role of licensed jester, which led him to "exploit, rather than express, his material" (512), in the hope of reaching London audiences. The unavoidable subservience of the authorized funnyman thus wasted O'Brien's potential as a truly subversive writer. Joseph

Brooker sums it up bluntly: "Flann O'Brien was a failure, and Myles na Gopaleen was to blame" (87). However, Brooker himself notes a changing attitude in the latest critics towards the chronicles, acknowledging them as an innovative piece of writing (88).

The aim of this article is to show that far from being detrimental to his writing, the chronicles are part and parcel of Flann O'Brien's literary imagination and cannot be separated from his so-called major work. My contention is that to criticize the chronicles as provincial and lacking in literary ambition is to fall into the same essentialist trap as the one denounced in the first place by post-colonial critics. Indeed, the colonial opposition between centre and periphery is at stake here; *Cruiskeen Lawn* does not conform to the traditional format of great works of literature, meaning, implicitly, the voluminous novels of the English canon, including, ambiguously enough, Joyce's. Four decades down the line, the very structure and themes of *Cruiskeen Lawn* cannot be ignored as they are integral to Flann O'Brien's satirical genius. My hypothesis is that they are also essential to understanding O'Brien's writing as a whole.

At Swim-Two-Birds and *The Third Policeman* are masterpieces of fragmented narratives. They have been commended as early post-modern works, and they share with *Cruiskeen Lawn* some defining features of post-modern writing: irony and a closeness to Menippean satire; the use of nonsense and self-referential language games; a critical stance on discourses of authority— be they scientific, academic or political; the fascination for relativity theories; and, finally, an ambiguous relation to both the Irish literary tradition and the English(-speaking) canon (Hopper; Booker). In *At Swim*, the first-person narrator's famous "theory of the novel" is comically echoed by Lamont's ferocious rant about how a story should be told: "whether a yarn is tall or small I like to hear it well told . . . I like to meet a man that can take in hand to tell a story and not make a balls of it while he's at it" (63). This no-nonsense Dublin character is clearly an early instance of the *Plain People of Ireland*. He highlights O'Brien's satire of "common sense," which is also a crucial theme in the chronicles. But Lamont's tirade also suggests that *writing* is really *tell-*

ing a story. This complex relation between orality and literacy finds a perfect setting in the chronicles, a hybrid genre between journalism and literature, reality and fiction.

I will examine how Lamont's theory of storytelling applies to *Cruiskeen Lawn*, using a pragmatics approach based on the so-called theories of ordinary language. Starting with Austin's Speech Acts theory, pragmatic analysis focuses on implicit meaning, illocutionary effects, relevance, and cooperative communication, taking into account the context of utterance and the inter-subjective relation between speakers (Searle; Grice; Sperber & Wilson). Such an approach is equally relevant to textual analysis, and I will consider the chronicles as one long on-going conversation between Myles and his readers. Flann O'Brien largely devoted his writing to the representation of language through his depiction of the ordinary, native-speakers of Irish, English, and "Dublinese." In *Cruiskeen Lawn*, Myles, The Brother's brother, Keats and Chapman and The Plain People of Ireland all tell us stories directly and perform a representation of storytelling. This raises a number of questions concerning the narrative structure of *Cruiskeen Lawn*: its linguistic status of ironical stance, its ambiguous relation between orality and the written word, and the importance of dialogic and polyphonic discourse. Two structural themes will help us address these questions: the anecdote and the digression, which are woven together in the meandering narratives of Flann O'Brien's writing.

2.   The ultimate dialogic genre

The pragmatic context of a newspaper chronicle points to its hybrid nature, between a direct address to a real audience, and a written text physically remote from its readers. As in oral interaction, newspapers adapt their content to daily events and the constantly evolving news. They offer a narrative whose very existence is based on temporality, and is therefore at odds with the traditional opposition between oral and written discourse: oral speech unfolds in time while written discourse spreads on the space of the printed page.

Thus the constantly renewed *Cruiskeen Lawn* column made the presence of Myles na gCopaleen felt in many households on a near-daily basis, for over two decades. Despite the unavoidable hiatus between emission and reception that we find in the written word, a daily newspaper partially breaches such a discrepancy by printing reactions from its enthused or disgruntled readers. Brian O'Nolan, for one, knew it and used it to his advantage when he sent a string of controversial letters to the *Irish Times*, as a student; the hoax was exposed but it earned him his job (*No Laughing Matter* 110). The complex nature of the chronicle, pertaining to both oral and written genres, can thus be related to a form of epistolary interaction. From sending letters to responding to them in his column, Myles deftly manoeuvres the dialogic dimension of epistolary exchange, based on spontaneity (however fake, in his case) and reciprocity.

Let us turn to a concrete example, from *The Best of Myles*:

A few weeks ago I was interrupted when about to give the public my long-awaited description of my own face. Several anxious readers have written in asking when they might expect it. My answer is that they might expect it to-day. Let us take the features one by one and then stand back, as one stands back from a majestic Titian or Van Gogh, and view the whole magnificent—

The Plain People of Ireland: Is this going to be long?

Myself: Not very.

The Plain People of Ireland: How long roughly?

Myself: Well, say ten lines for the vast Homeric brow, the kingly brow that is yet human wise and mild. Then the eyes, peerless wine-green opal of rare hue, brittle and ebullient against the whiteness of Himalayan snow—

The Plain People of Ireland: Another ten lines?

Myself: Say seven each. That's fourteen altogether.

. . .

The Plain People of Ireland: And how about the gob and the snot?

Myself: If you mean the finely-moulded masterful—

The Plain People of Ireland: Did you ever hear this one: As a beauty I am not a star. There are others more handsome by far—

Myself: I did, I did. Stop!

The Plain People of Ireland: But my face I don't mind it, For I am behind it, It's the people in front get the jar!

Myself: Lord save us!

The Plain People of Ireland: Could we not leave the whole thing over to another time?

Myself: Very well. But heaven knows whom we are disappointing in this matter. (81–82)

In this episode, Myles explicitly acknowledges the existence of his audience from the beginning ("the public," "several anxious readers"). Although it refers to the readers in the third person, the column posits itself as a reply in a previously started conversation ("my answer is . . ."). Myles then addresses us directly with the imperative "Let us take," and switches to a conversation in the direct style between himself and his *Plain People* audience. The column first reminds us of the physical distance between columnist and reader, and of the temporal hiatus in the exchange. Then, Myles stages the conversation itself, offering us a literal representation of oral interaction. The final words give a sense of interrupted conversation, thus creating expectation: we are waiting for a sequel.

Here, Myles displays his agonistic representation of conversation: each speaking turn is a struggle, with both parties intent on telling their jokes and anecdotes. In an agonistic dialogue, the aim is to silence one's opponent, which is partially the case here (Myles gives up). The irony pervading the scene also reminds us of its many narrative levels (as the column's audience, we are also the *Plain People*), as well as its meta-narrative dimension: Myles offers us a reflection on the column's pragmatic status as a conversation. The dialogic theme finally contributes to the very structure of the *Cruiskeen Lawn* narrative, since most chronicles feature a dialogue in the direct style—between Myles and The Brother or The Plain People of Ireland, or between Keats and Chapman—or directly address readers in the second person.

For all his insistence on the oral dimension of linguistic exchange, Myles's working material is the written word: thriving on the hybrid status of his newspaper chronicle, he plays up the complex relation between orality and literacy at work in his stories, for his readers' viewing (or is it listening?) pleasure. Representing orality can be deemed a thankless task since the written word is only a poor substitute for the voices and accents of native Dubliners, but Myles steps up precisely where the written word falls short. His task is not about *transcribing* the sounds of oral speech so much as showing how entangled they are with written discourse, in a fictional context and in ordinary language. The example quoted above playfully highlights our common assumption that written and oral discourses correspond to language registers: pompous Myles describes his own face in a very formal, convoluted—understand "written"—style, while the *Plain People*'s speech is, of course, *plain,* and fraught with slang ("how about the gob and the snot?"). The written word adds up on the page, allowing a syntactic complexity that is harder to follow when spoken. In speech, words chronologically replace each other, which makes it crucial, in O'Brien's agonistic conversations, to have the last word; what remains of the spoken word is the punch line. Here, the conversation is about Myles's face, which is strikingly relevant: *saving face* is at stake in the dialogue, hence the Plain People's insistence against Myles's refusal ("Stop!— But my face I don't mind it, For I am behind it . . .").

Much like the typographical digressions in *At Swim* and the footnotes in *The Third Policeman, Cruiskeen Lawn* exploits the visual dimension of the printed text. Its many pictures and punctuation marks ironically point to their own artificiality as substitutes for oral speech and its context of utterance. Even the Plain People are not immune to such ambiguity; the limerick they recite here has the fixed quality of a written poem, as attested by the ironic use of capital letters after commas: "But my face I don't mind it, For I am behind it, It's the people in front get the jar!" They too have fallen victim to the artifices of the written word, and they love it.

3. Anecdotes and the master storyteller

In light of Myles's games with orality and literacy, let us turn to the etymological sense of "anecdote" provided by the Oxford English Dictionary (a Flann O'Brien favourite):

> From Greek, *things unpublished.*
>
> 1. *pl.* Secret, private, or hitherto unpublished narratives or details of history.
>
> 2. The narrative of a detached incident, or of a single event, told as being in itself interesting or striking. (At first, an item of gossip.)

The first meaning is that of an unpublished (i.e. not public) story, which brings us back to the written story versus the story told. The potentially infinite reproduction of the printing press makes stories public with no limit in time and place, or as to audience. On the other hand, a private story told orally is necessarily limited to its unique speaker and context of utterance: however gifted of gab Myles and his fictional co-speakers are, each version of the same story changes with its context and narrator and becomes a single, distinctive story in its own right.

As always, Myles na gCopaleen thrives in the *in-between*. As a satirical chronicle, *Cruiskeen Lawn* publicly comments on the "great story" of Irish politics and public events. As Myles's inimitable collection of stories, it recounts the trivial (fictional) anecdotes of the Dublin common man. In both cases, its readership can be considered large—twenty-six years' worth of *Irish Times* readership—or relatively private—the column was only intended for its contemporary *Irish Times* readership, not for the international audience it gained after *Cruiskeen Lawn* was re-published in book form. Myles also blurs the distinction between history—the story worth publishing—and its "details," targeting the authority traditionally imparted to the written word. Myles's self-conscious anecdotes from the colonial periphery seem all the more irreverently relevant since they are defined as marginal by the OED, a linguistic symbol of the colonial centre.

What makes anecdotes worth writing? Let us examine another example:

> I'll tell you a good wan.
>
> *Indeed?*

I'll give you a laugh.

How very welcome.

The brother's studyin' the French. The brother has the whole digs in a right state and the nerves of half of the crowd up there is broke down.

How truly characteristic of your relative.

The brother comes down to breakfast there about a fortnight back, ten minutes late. And I'll tell you a good wan. What be all the powers had the brother up here at the neck.

I do not know.

A bow tie begob.

I see . . . (Best of Myles 68)

Here, the main story (The Brother learning French) is embedded in the framing scene, where the storyteller inflicts his insignificant anecdote on the listener (Myles/reader). Narrator Myles then depicts the scene as an anecdotic, marginal event of everyday life: meeting a loquacious acquaintance at the bus stop. What makes these stories interesting is their ironic *mise-en-abyme*: Myles's ironical stance disconnects them from their original context of utterance, the better to show their comic absurdity. We laugh at the storyteller's self-importance and at his irrepressible love for talk. The storyteller's fatuous pronouncements also mirror Myles's pedantic attitudes: he too loves the sound of his own voice. The multiple narrative frames makes telling the anecdote an event in its own right, no less worthy of telling, and so on and so forth.

Framing the anecdote into another narrative enables us to examine its nature, function, and effects. Myles's ironic distance thus fulfills his comic goal and offers us a reflection on anecdotes as speech acts. At a literal level, the information provided by the anecdote is neither complete nor relevant to the listener, whose calculated reserve facetiously highlights the speaker's incontinent verbosity. From a Gricean point of view, then, the speaker does not follow the rules of cooperative conversation, which are to provide clear, true, complete, and relevant information to one's co-speaker (41–58). He fulfills the pragmatic condition of sincerity, however, despite Myles's disingenuous account of the whole scene. The encounter is much more important than Myles's mocking irony would falsely suggest: as a speech act, it performs what Jakobson call the *phatic function* of language; it establishes and maintains linguistic communication by drawing and keeping the co-speaker's attention (217). (In our example, almost a third of the entire column is taken up by phatic expressions such as "I'll tell you a good wan" and the co-speaker's ironic replies "How very welcome," "I see"). Myles's obsession with such expressions is in keeping with his depiction of ordinary language and his interest for the pleasure of utterance as distinct from meaningful content.

Anecdotes provide a broad range of stories, from utter fiction and nonsensical jokes to straightforward comments on the political Irish news. With Myles na gCopaleen, everything becomes anecdote material: limericks, overheard conversations, but also the great political story of the nation. This has a double consequence: on the one hand, insignificant, irrelevant stories acquire an essential pragmatic and social importance which is only enhanced by their comic effect. Making fun of anecdotes and their tellers (the Brother's brother, The Plain People of Ireland) also results in a celebration of the footnotes of Dublin life. On the other hand, since the constant use of anecdotes presents the column itself as harmless banter, it brings down the serious, political news to the level of anecdotic (and often comically absurd) fun. Myles debunks the solemnity—and indeed, the very notion—of a national linear story represented by its great characters, such as in the following example:

> Certainly Costello was not lacking in courage when, the other day, he introduced in Parliament his Arts Bill: this I take to be a thinly veiled plan to give Paddy Kavanagh a pension for life. I object, of course. Taking the papal Bull by the horns, I assert it is contrary to Catholic teaching. Number two, I was not consulted. (*Further Cuttings* 130)

Fragmenting the "great" story brings it down to the level of the anecdote, and makes it material for linguistic fun. Myles subverts the authority of political discourse in the same way as Flann O'Brien does in the novels, blurring the boundaries and hierarchy between narratives as a satirical device against linguistic and literary oppression.

Last but not least, anecdotes respond to a pleasure principle and illustrate the erotic dimension of language: Myles, the Plain People of Ireland and the talkative characters of the novels all share an insatiable love for proffering utterances sententious or poetical, simply to bask in the music of the human voice: "there's a lilt in that," says Lamont about the "Pint of Plain" poem, in *At Swim* (77). With the added ambivalence of Myles's ironical point of view, both melodious voice and printed text point to the physicality and opacity of language, and to its inaccessible, nonsensical dimension. In this respect, the "Keats and Chapman" stories perfectly illustrate the purely reflexive function of puns (e.g. "He's reading between the lions" in *The Various Lives*, 58).

In all of Flann O'Brien's writing, and particularly in *Cruiskeen Lawn*, anecdotes embody the fragmented narratives of everyday life, as much as they contribute to questioning the notion of monologic discourse. Myles's stories always involve a number of dissenting voices, both explicitly depicted in conversation scenes, or implicitly present through his many levels of narrative irony. This dialogic and polyphonic dimension is also expressed by the digressive nature of the anecdotes themselves. We now need to examine digression more closely, in relation with the notions of non-cooperative conversation and diglossia.

4.   Digression and subversion

At Swim and *The Third Policeman* are famous for their highly digressive narrative structures, and the theme of digression itself is essential to their stories. The novels present digression as a discursive phenomenon but also in its moral and spatial senses: characters and narrators go astray, literally on their wandering bicycles, and morally, leaving the straight and narrow to take paths that go round and round and make them "lose the plot." Digression also plays an essential part in the chronicles, and, again, needs to be acknowledged within Flann O'Brien's representation of language as a whole.

Narrative digression partially defines a newspaper chronicle, since the columnist follows the accidents of daily life and news, and, in the case of Myles na gCopaleen, his unpredictable and facetious imagination. When the chronicles were collected for their publication as books, they were arranged under the titled sections we know them by: "The District Court," the "Catechism of Cliché," "Bores," and so on. However, there were no such titles in the original layout, as Kevin O'Nolan notes in his preface to *Further Cuttings From Cruiskeen Lawn*: "Through half its history the column appeared under the name 'Cruiskeen Lawn' . . . without further clue as to what readers were actually having on any particular day" (11). Thus the column consists of the many digressions from—and cyclical returns to—its narrative threads:

> This is part II of my series, the Roasting of Architects. In part I we saw that most cities have become dangerous and uninhabitable, and that architects wish to be permitted to remedy these conditions, which have been created by architects . . . (*Further Cuttings* 109)

The constant back and forth movement between different storylines removes all sense of a single, linear thread throughout the entire column, which echoes the subversion of narrative conventions in *At Swim*. On the other hand, punchlines make each episode a self-contained unit. Myles's multi-faceted persona and his use of characters as narrators of their own stories increase the number of digressions in the column. This leads to a highly polyphonic, often chaotic and nonsensical effect on the delighted reader.

Let us now examine how digression is used within narratives:

> In the Dublin Court yesterday, an elderly man who gave his name as Myles na gCopaleen was charged with begging, disorderly conduct, using bad language and with being in illegal possession of an armchair . . .
>
> Defendant: *Quid immerentes hospites vexas canis ignavus adversum lupos?*[1]
>
> Detective Sergeant: This man had no difficulty in speaking English when he was lying on the street. This sort of thing makes a farce of the language movement . . .

Justice: Are you married?

Defendant: Are you?

Justice: Impertinence won't help you.

Defendant: It won't help anybody. The question you put is apparently equally offensive to both of us. I am a victim of circumstances. *Maioribus praesidiis et copiis oppugnatur res publica quam defenditur propterea quod audaces homines et perditi nutu impelluntur et ipsi etiam sponte sua contra rem publicam incitantur.*[2]

Detective Sergeant: This is a very hardened character, Your Honour. He was convicted for loitering at Swansea in 1933.

Justice: I must convict. There is far too much of this sort of thing in Dublin and I am determined to put it down.

Defendant: What sort of thing?

Justice: The larceny of armchairs.

Defendant: It wasn't an armchair. There were no arms on it . . .

(*Best of Myles* 148–9)

The trial scene—a recurring feature in O'Brien's writing—hails the traditions of Menippean satire and Victorian Nonsense, and abounds in pointless questions and irrelevant answers. This questioning session represents an extreme version of the agonistic dialogue. For the defendant, flouting the rules of cooperation is key; Old Myles uses irrelevant digressions as strategic devices in this aggressive language-game. The judge attempts to bring him back to the main point of order ("behave yourself"), but Myles turns the discourse of authority against him. Fittingly enough, the master-digresser is also a "loiterer" whose wandering activities must be "put down."

The Latin quotes add to the comic effect, being both seemingly incongruous and perfectly relevant to mock the rigid, monologic discourse of oppressive law. The first quote directly insults the police officer; the second quote is a thinly veiled attack against the "enemies of the Republic," with the Irish subtext lending Myles's tirades more piquancy. Myles's hilarious defence is also a case for free-flowing digression and fragmented, polyphonic narratives. It puts down linear, unambiguous, monologic discourse as oppressive and unnatural. Finally, the Latin quotes remind us that Flann O'Brien's digressions are also about subverting not simply discourse, but language itself. Foreign words hinder the flow of English speech and contradict its given authority over the absent native tongue. Here, Latin outshines English as a symbol of academic, social, and religious authority, while Myles's conviction for "bad language" comically hints at the status of Irish under English rule.

Digressions now take on a political dimension. More than being merely post-modern devices for disrupting linear narratives and canonical stories, anecdotes and digressions naturally follow from O'Brien's diglossic view on language and his satiric charge against linguistic oppression. The term *diglossia* refers to the complementary use of two languages or dialects within one speech community, based on the opposition between official and vernacular languages (Ferguson 214–34). Diglossia is not bilingualism: not all speakers can use both languages at will. This leads to complex attitudes of social evaluation and linguistic self-consciousness. O'Brien's novels and chronicles illustrate the full panel of speakers' attitudes to their own language: some speak a Dublin, working-class variety of Irish-English (*Cruiskeen Lawn, At Swim*); some only speak Irish (*An Béal Bocht*); some, such as Myles na gCopaleen, master all languages and registers. O'Brien/Myles constantly denounced the linguistic hypocrisy of his time and the difficulty of the man in the street to position himself as a native speaker in a newly independent Ireland. Writing *Cruiskeen Lawn* mostly in English was not a decision by his inner stage-Irishman, nor was he shirking his duties as an Irish-speaking author. My contention is that the chronicles truly represent the linguistic complexity of O'Brien's Ireland, with all its contradictions and ambiguities.

Ireland's primary diglossic opposition is of course English versus Irish, the colonial language versus the native tongue, as depicted in *An Béal Bocht*. Yet Myles's Dubliners are in fact native English speakers. They have lost their original linguistic identity, and their dialect of English is still dominated by the "standard," dictionary variety regularly caricatured in the chronicles. On the other hand, they must face a paradoxical situation where Irish has become the new official language, and English the everyday life vernacular. Myles, who was truly bilingual, was keenly aware of the damages caused both by linguistic colonialism and by compulsory linguistic revival. True to his satirist's nature, he always denounced hypocrisy but never took a stance one way or the other. His regular use of languages other than English and Irish makes a point: in the example above, Old Myles's mischievous use of Latin shows how absurd, fickle, and ultimately damaging the notion of superiority of a language can be.

In *Cruiskeen Lawn*, the "language question" indifferently refers to English or Irish, ironically highlighting the disingenuous interest of politicians for the native tongue:

> The language problem again—I *am* sorry but we must, you know. First, pronunciation; this is very important. Carelessness in the formation of vowels and consonants, when it is accompanied by im-proper breathing, bad phrasing and the forcing of the voice, leads inevitably to slovenly speech . . . You cannot give too much attention to this matter—with it is bound up the whole question of national prestige . . . If the language is permitted to die the consequences will be terrible. (*Further Cuttings* 95)

Here, Myles refers to English, not Irish. He goes on: "one thinks immedi-ately of the words: 'Cow,' 'Man' . . . You know how they come out: 'Kehaouw,' 'Mhaaanh' . . ." His conclusion turns the table on the "language movement": "any given nation should have . . . *some* language. If we fail to make the most of what little English as we now remember it may bode ill for us" (96).

Myles indiscriminately attacks snobs, whatever their allegiance. His linguis-tic satire translates into his storytelling, a free-flowing form concerned with representing the digressive and fragmented nature of language itself, its dif-ficulties and its epiphanies. Just as there is no such thing as a superior form of language, Myles refuses allegiance to canonical and conventional forms of writing. Thus, subverting monologic discourse enables him to show how contradictions and conflicts are the very substance of language and stories: anecdotes and the "great" narrative of history, digressions and storyline, co-operative and agonistic dialogue.

We can now answer Myles na gCopaleen's accusation of provincialism. The chronicles, as a constantly changing, always subversive collection of stories, find their inspiration in the absurdity of daily life and in Flann O'Brien's tireless exploration of the recesses of ordinary language. That he always kept Dublin as his main material, and the chronicles as his primary form of storytelling attests not to his provincialism but to the relevance of his representation of language. *Cruiskeen Lawn* is not an insignificant part of O'Brien's work but its defining core: a true *genre mineur* for a *littérature mineure*.

NOTES

1   This is a quote from Horace, *Epode* VI: "Why pester harmless passers-by, you cringing cur? Are you afraid of wolves?" (trans. D. West 10).

2   Quoted from Cicero, *Pro Sestio*, 47: "The Republic is attacked with more force and means than it is defended, because there only needs one sign to raise perverts and impudents; They even do not need to be prompted, they raise themselves against the Republic" (my translation).

WORKS CITED

Austin, John L. *How to Do Things with Words*. Oxford: Oxford Univ. Press, 1962.

Booker, M. Keith. *Flann O'Brien, Bakhtin, and Menippean Satire*. Syracuse: Syracuse Univ. Press, 1995.

Brooker, Joseph. *Flann O'Brien*. Tavistock: Northcote House, 2005.

Cronin, Anthony. *Dead as Doornails. A Chronicle of Life*. Dublin: The Dolmen Press, 1976.

—. *No Laughing Matter. The Life and Times of Flann O'Brien*. 1989. New York: Fromm International, 1998.

Day, Jon. "Cuttings from *Cruiskeen Lawn*: Bibliographical Issues in the Republication of Myles na gCopaleen's Journalism." *"Is It About a Bicycle?": Flann O'Brien in the Twenty-First Century*. Ed. Jennika Baines. Dublin: Four Courts Press, 2011. 35–36.

Ferguson, Charles A. "Diglossia Revisited." *Southwest Journal of Linguistics*. 10.1 (1991): 214–34.

Grice, H. Paul. "Logic and Conversation." *Syntax and Semantics vol. 3: Speech Acts.* Ed. Peter Cole and Jerry Morgan. New York: Academic Press, 1975. 41–58.

Hopper, Keith. *A Portrait of the Artist as a Young Post-modernist.* Cork: Cork Univ. Press, 1995.

Horace. *The Complete Odes and Epodes.* Trans. David West, Oxford: Oxford World's Classics, 1997.

Jakobson, Roman. *Essais de linguistique générale.* Paris: Minuit, 1963.

Kenner, Hugh. *A Colder Eye: The Modern Irish Writers.* Baltimore: The Johns Hopkins Univ. Press, 1983.

Kiberd, Declan. *Inventing Ireland.* London: Jonathan Cape, 1995.

O'Brien, Flann. *At Swim-Two-Birds.* 1939. London: Penguin, 1967; Normal, IL: Dalkey Archive Press, 1993.

—. *The Third Policeman.* 1967. London: Flamingo Sixties Classics, 2001; Normal, IL: Dalkey Archive Press, 1999.

—. *The Poor Mouth.* 1973. Trans. P.C. Power. London: Flamingo Modern Classics, 1993; Normal, IL: Dalkey Archive Press, 1996.

—. *The Best of Myles.* London: Flamingo Modern Classics, 1993; Normal, IL: Dalkey Archive Press, 1999.

—. *Further Cuttings from Cruiskeen Lawn.* London: Paladin, 1989; Normal, IL: Dalkey Archive Press, 2000.

—. *The Various Lives of Keats and Chapman and The Brother.* London: Scribner and Dublin: TownHouse, 2003.

VAL NOLAN

Flann, Fantasy, and Science Fiction: O'Brien's Surprising Synthesis

Providing a locus of collision between Ireland's rich fantasy tradition and the twentieth century's idiom of science and technology, Flann O'Brien's fiction represents a unique—and uniquely *Irish*—form of speculative writing. While Einsteinian readings of O'Brien have been performed before, as have analyses of the author's folkloric satires, it is worth considering O'Brien's writing as a bridge between these two traditions, a synthesis of O'Brien's scientific literacy with the pervasiveness of fantastical notions in the Irish mindset of his day. Central to this is his recurring character de Selby who, through fantastical and technological irresponsibility, embodies both sides of the divide between tradition and modernity and so challenges any clear distinction between the two.[1] Functioning as a forward-looking, fake-scientist counterpart to that backward-looking, real-life mathematician and Ireland's "other de," Éamon de Valera, de Selby personifies O'Brien's tongue-in-cheek combination of atomic theory, relativity, and time travel with parodic representations of spirituality, a project which culminates in *The Dalkey Archive* (1964) with the character's attempts to use an artificially created element to destroy the world in the name of God.

Throughout his career, O'Brien's use of language and reference aimed not to reject the Gaelic tradition but to incorporate aspects of Irish fantasy into a new scientific age. In the aftermath of mass industrialisation, along with the World War and mooted nuclear destruction that characterised the era of *The Third Policeman*'s composition (and, later, the dystopian, post-War condition of Europe, let alone the Iron Curtain years in which *The Dalkey Archive* was written), O'Brien uses de Selby to satirise not only the rampant, destructive pace of change and progress, but also a parochial Irish imagination to which all science is not just science fictional, but, to paraphrase Arthur C. Clarke, "indistinguishable from magic" (Clarke 36).

In an Irish context, this term "magic" is further indistinguishable from that of "fantasy," and is apparent not only in the supernatural strain of traditional Irish culture and literature—the prevalence of fairies, witches and so on in folklore and, subsequently, written forms—but also through the belief in and deference to the various characters and dogmas of the Catholic faith, a facet of Irish social history which constitutes systematised fantasy on a grand scale and little more than the practice of magical rites and rituals by another name. While there is often an ambiguously parodic element in O'Brien's depiction of the latter (who is he *actually* mocking?), I wish to focus instead on his portrayal of the confrontation between the rational and the irrational, a conflict characteristic of much of the Irish fantasy tradition. This tension between logic and lunacy is one of the fundamental aspects of O'Brien's writing, and one which anticipates the contemporary unease with just how increasing technological progress can be squared with our traditional past.

O'Brien, it should be made clear, was not writing to fit any specific genre conventions; nevertheless he has left us with texts such as *The Third Policeman* (written 1939–40, published 1967) and *The Dalkey Archive* which bear the fingerprints of multiple, modern generic subdivisions. Whether these divisions are artistically valid or simply market artefacts is not the issue here; what is important is how O'Brien's writing appeals to, and is often consciously claimed by, a variety of generic categories with markedly distinct reading codes and audiences. For instance, *The Third Policeman* was initially rejected by O'Brien's publishers on the grounds that its imaginative and textual hijinks did not correspond with the expectations of the company's literary readership. The author should "become less fantastic," Longmans said (Cronin 23), while, in the early twenty-first century, this same book is easily read as "an absurd science fiction novel" (quoted in Hopper, 2011). The text itself certainly hasn't changed; the conventions governing generic demarcations, while always fluid to some degree, have not metamorphosed to the extent that the fantastical has flipped into the science-fictional . . . No, these multiple declarations are instead sanctioned by O'Brien's fiction itself, by a breadth of both reference and imagination that transcends cosy delineations of genre the way de Selby evades both professional epistemological specialisation and the gossipy pigeonholing of small town Ireland.

While the influence on O'Brien of the Einsteins and Schrödingers has been investigated in detail by Keith Hopper, Charles Kemnitz, and others, there is also something to be said for Roger Boylan's assertion of Gothic fabulist Sheridan Le Fanu's influence on the author ("We Laughed" 2008). Early reading of Le Fanu, master at "generating an atmosphere of weirdness within an outer shell of everyday banality," shored up the fantasy side of O'Brien's aesthetic as surely as exposure to the great physicists later buttressed the science-fictional. While O'Brien "never wrote of any overtly paranormal phenomena," books such as At Swim-Two-Birds and The Third Policeman are "saturated with the atmospherics of the strange and outré" ("We Laughed" 2008). Are such atmospherics enough to demonstrate O'Brien's debt to the Irish fantasy tradition? Arguably yes, but the contention is bolstered by the manner in which O'Brien's uncanny elements are conditional on the limited scientific or technological imagination of everyman characters who, while not exactly out of time, do appear to be living in a bubble Ireland (literally, in the case of The Third Policeman protagonist), a remote existence wherein which they are detached from the great leaps and bounds of contemporary developments, particularly in the realm of physics. In the year before The Third Policeman was published, the year O'Brien died, the American psychologist Abraham Maslow made a profound and altogether relevant observation which we know today as the Law of the Instrument: "It is tempting, if the only tool you have is a hammer, to treat everything as if it were a nail" (Maslow 15). Equally, if all you have is a ghost story, then, to your imagination, everything is going to look like a ghost.

It is exactly this gulf between the wider world of modern scientific developments and the inner, fantastical world of isolated Irish characters that O'Brien is so gifted at depicting on the page. While the perspective of The Third Policeman is, according to Anne Clissman, "reality viewed through the medium of scientific and philosophical concepts," it is difficult not to envy the masterly and entirely Irish fashion in which this is executed (Clissman 152). O'Brien knew about physics (understanding is another matter entirely); however, he never allows his own knowledge, that tentative grasping towards the shape and structure of reality, to overpower the worldview of his characters.[2] What he does is just the opposite: he obfuscates, he makes the nature of reality all the more mysterious again and, in the process, accurately and effectively mediates Clissman's science and philosophy, what we might term a twentieth-century outlook, through the viewpoint of characters whose imaginative architecture is that of the nineteenth century. As such, the limbo space of *The Third Policeman* reflects not just the protagonist's suspension between physical existence and the hereafter, but the external moment of transition from a superstitious to a scientific culture. Of course, full on replacement of established folkloric or religious mythologies by science or science fiction was never going to occur in the Ireland of the forties, fifties, and sixties. Nonetheless, its effects are not only felt, they underpin the construction of the text as a whole. As Hopper says, "sinister forces of science and technology have conspired to create Noman's hell" (Hopper 196). In *The Third Policeman* and *The Dalkey Archive*, these forces have usurped the narrative machinery of the fantastic that provided forward momentum in many more traditional texts. Consider Hopper's remark again: *technology* has created *hell*; O'Brien has used scientific concepts and terminology to deliver a convincing depiction of a religious—read fantastical—notion.[3]

Simultaneously, O'Brien's characters remain locked in their pre-existing fantastical mindsets. There is an extent to which they can only see the hell and so the technology behind it may as well be magic. The *Policeman*'s protagonist and *Dalkey*'s Mick Shaughnessy display great difficulty in rationalising the semi-scientific improbabilities they encounter against the rigorously codified and delineated boundaries of their mid-century, de Valerian Catholic reality, the most developed and consistent manifestation of the fantasy tradition in the country. Crucially, de Selby himself is in no way immune from this influence. His ideological stance may be "intellectual, philosophic or even mathematical," but his reasoning and his application are fantastical (*Dalkey* 14). He is less an idiot-savant than he is a Hiberno-savant, a genius crippled by the developmental disorder of being Irish, a brilliant man limited by the genetic and geographical, sociological and imaginative constraints of a nation that emerges from O'Brien's texts as one mired in outmoded ways of thinking. Ireland, particularly in the de Selby narratives, is not so much a country as it is a mindset, a point-of-view struggling with the realisation that the world around it has been profoundly shaped and changed by a science and technology it is ill-equipped to imagine, let alone understand.

De Selby provides O'Brien with a lens through which to focus this imaginative disparity. He serves as a bridge between the insular Irish traditions of the past and the seemingly impossible future presented by developments elsewhere in the world. In *The Dalkey Archive*, where de Selby has been elevated from the footnotes of *The Third Policeman* to the high office of the main plot, we find this most unusual man is his "own doctor" (*Dalkey* 9); what's more, he is consistent with the doctorial and professorial "leisured gentleman" mould which Ib Johansen, in his study of the Irish fantastic, traces through Le Fanu's "Green Tea" to the Victorian Gothic, or, as he says, "the fantastic, it might be added" (Johansen 53). Certainly de Selby fulfils what Johansen reads as one of the key aspects of these fantastical "leisured bachelors," the "*destructive* and *self-destructive* character of this easygoing life-style," and that de Selby, in *The Third Policeman*, is able to drive *others* to both destruction and self-destruction only reinforces this reading (Johansen 53). Yet what is key here is the bridging aspect of the character. De Selby does not merely look backwards towards the fantastic: he is a "theologist *and* a physicist" (my emphasis), and he embodies a link between the close reading of religious unreality and the scientific study of how the universe, how reality itself is put together (*Dalkey* 12). Moreover, theology and physics are fields that he sees as extending naturally into "eschatology and astrognosy" along with the maturation of spirits into whiskey, a range of interests through which O'Brien happily mocks both the fantastical and futuristic aspects of the character (*Dalkey* 12). We are told that "his ideas quite transcend this Earth"; that he is a "strange man" with "unusual notions about the world, the universe, time . . ." (*Dalkey* 54). What's more, de Selby, like de Valera, believes he can "suspend time, negate its apparent course," although in his case it is not an effort to inhibit the progress of the nation but to demonstrate that progress itself is in fact an illusionary (if not a downright *delusionary*) notion (*Dalkey* 14). Like de Valera too, the possibility of de Selby being a "foreigner" is raised, and only partially resolved, in the course of *The Dalkey Archive* (though his display of the same fantastical mindset as, say, the incontestably Irish Mick Shaughnessy, might well put to rest questions of his nationality). Yes, he is more than likely a "native of our beloved Ireland," but, regardless, he remains a mysterious, ambiguous outsider and that gives him at least the *potential* to move beyond the accepted State-and-Church sanctioned limitations that regulate the Ireland of his day (*Dalkey* 58).

His investigations in the cave beneath the Dalkey coast are a case in point. Here, de Selby enacts something halfway between a science experiment and "a séance," the use of pseudo-technological means to interact with "a personality who is from heaven" (*Dalkey* 31). The encounter in the cave draws heavily on the nineteenth-century vogue for what might be called investigative occultism or theosophical enquiry. Yet unlike occultism or Catholicism, it is not ritual or invocation, not language but science which our heroes rely upon to generate the link to the other side. Saint Augustine appears to de Selby, Mick, and Hackett only after they don homemade aqualungs and uses the mysterious DMP substance to "annihilate the terrestrial atmosphere and the time illusion" (*Dalkey* 31). Here de Selby, with his mad notions about time and his apparent-through-never-quite-verified ability to contact the spirit world becomes like an electric Yeats, strapping himself into his machinery in the mode of "an Apollo space-man," reaching for the chemicals, and convincing himself that he's talking to the dead, those ever-present figures who haunt—perhaps literally as well as figuratively—the folkloric and religious spaces of the Irish tradition (*Dalkey* 32). Already a self-declared theologist-physicist, de Selby is never more shamanistic, dare it be said, *druidic*, than he is here, altering the perceptive conditions of his immediate environment until he and his drinking companions can interact with the spiritual and supernatural realms.

The role of the shaman is to cross into the other world and bring back vital information for the benefit of the tribe, something which, in an Irish context, again suggests Le Fanu's "Green Tea" and its protagonist Dr. Hesselius, a man who is an expert on "Metaphysical Medicine" (Le Fanu 5). O'Brien's de Selby, though he appears to lack either recognised accreditation or the informal assent of the community, fulfills a similar role. Furthermore the figures he encounters, Francis of Assisi, Ignatius Loyola, and so on are depicted in loaded terms as men who "saw the truth in the course of a dangerous illness," that being the traditional fashion in which shamans are "called" (*Dalkey* 73). The information that de Selby brings back from, for instance, his interview with Augustine, is an energetic challenge to the tribe's status quo, the dominance of Roman Catholicism in Ireland that had been solidified by the complicity of fantasist-in-chief Éamon de Valera. This man, whose vision for Ireland shaped the nation throughout much of O'Brien's life, was a preservationist, adopting a curatorial stance as regards the nation's language and culture. By contrast, O'Brien's de Selby aims "to destroy the whole world" in good faith, a phrase not chosen without cause for, in effect, "good" and "bad" faith is what this is all about. O'Brien's attitude towards religion is complex and teased out only with difficulty; suffice it to say that his hope regarding *The Dalkey Archive* was that the text be read as a parodic joust with fervent believers rather than with belief itself.[4] O'Brien himself saw the novel as a book with "no blasphemy whatever" in it; nonetheless he fully expected (and most likely hoped) for it to be banned on blasphemous grounds (Clissman 295).

Undoubtedly O'Brien had in mind the novel's satirical and sacrilegious depiction of organised Roman Catholicism, which, on the one hand, represented an impressive mechanism of control in its own right, and, on the other, a vast collective fantasy with few enough equivalents in the history of mankind. As ever, the key to unravelling this lies with de Selby. "God had founded his own true Church but contemplated benevolently the cults of even capricious dæmons provided they were intrinsically good," he tells Mick (*Dalkey* 75). Wearing his theologist hat, surely at a jaunty angle, de Selby ascribes a noticeably theosophical outlook to God, an entity for whom all religions have, until now, been "tolerable manifestations" (*Dalkey* 75). Yet, as de Selby says, "every one of those organized religions were in decomposition and atrophy" (*Dalkey* 75). The significant word here is *organized*. Structured and systematized religion, specifically Catholicism, that being what informs the milieus of both O'Brien and de Selby, is a tool created by man, a technology if you will, and one used to perpetuate a fantasy at odds with genuine spirituality. The "Supreme Truth" of God, as O'Brien depicts it, needs to be "protected finally and irrevocably from all the Churches of today" (*Dalkey* 75). Messiah complex firmly in place, de Selby sees himself as just the man to do that, and, naturally enough, intends to do so "by way of complete destruction" (*Dalkey* 75).

O'Brien too—in his na gCopaleenian guise—had already expressed an interest in the terrifying potential of modern explosives technology and the manner in which its effects evoke the nightmares of folklore and the Apocalyptic concerns of religious Eschatology, a subject which, as de Selby says, "has always attracted the minds of men who use reason" (*Dalkey* 75). Take, for instance, the "Cruiskeen Lawn" columns which followed the dropping of the atomic bombs on Japan in 1945: "The dread instrument produced a number of freak effects, the most noteworthy of which was to blow the backs off several human beings, leaving them alive, conscious, and otherwise intact" (*At War* 174). While the destructive power of this "species of atomic bomb" is, on an immediate level, unleashed merely as an excuse for another adventure of recurring clowns Keats and Chapman, it does imply a clear and recognisably sci-fi anxiety: technology dehumanises us, transforms us into something less than the sum of our parts, a loss of some essential aspect of ourselves that is the concurrent payoff for technology's promise of cyborgization (Chapman, able to see Keats's insides, lungs and organs, must fabricate a prosthetic back for him). It is a throwaway sketch but it betrays an authorial disquiet on the subject of scientific advance that draws on the same fantastical well as the narrator's purgatorial journey through *The Third Policeman*. Keats here, rooting through the human offal of the bomb blast, vows "I'm going to get my own back," and, more than a punchline, his declaration stands as a link to the folkloric undead, the walking, *unsatisfied* dead who search for vengeance amongst the byways of oral storytelling and lamp-lit fantasy.

Narrowing in on the de Selbian aspect of all this is Myles's report, in a column from a month later, that a "wise and venerable gentleman" of his acquaintance stated to him that "the atomic bomb was the climax of the growing power of scientists for good or evil" (na gCopaleen, October 1945). How, Myles wonders, "can a cultured and elegant professor possibly imagine that that most limited of men, the scientist, has any power for good or evil that anyone else hasn't got?" (na gCopaleen, October 1945). As far as this satirist was concerned, once the genie was out of the atom it could never be contained again. He predicts that "certain men here in town" will have "a perfectly good bootleg atomic bomb on the market by March next" (na gCopaleen, October 1945). O'Brien's de Selby, particularly the de Selby of *The Dalkey Archive*, could very well be one of those men. Certainly na gCopaleen's solution to the crisis of atomic knowledge (who has it, who wants it, and so on) is de Selbyian in its perverse simplicity: "Make a very big atomic bomb, say 7/8" and just let it off and kill everyone" (na gCopaleen, October 1945). Eschatology indeed! His proposal is a rehash of the ultimate Roman Catholic fantasy, the coming of a fiery, all-destructive Armageddon. For the first time in its history, mankind has the ability to make real the fairytales of scripture; technology can create, if not the hell of *The Third Policeman*, then the Apocalypse of de Selby's imagination and of the most vivid Catholic eschatological impulses. Let us not forget that "the almighty had led de Selby" to his doomsday weapon in the first place, or it at least appears that way to the provincial Mick Shaughnessy (*Dalkey* 75). Then again, the theologian-physicist's verdict on the world is not so far removed from that of na gCopaleen of twenty years before: "It merits destruction," de Selby says. "Its history and prehistory, even its present, is a foul record of pestilence, famine, war, devastation and misery so terrible and multifarious that its depth and horror are unknown to any one man. Rottenness is universally endemic, disease is paramount. The human race is finally debauched and aborted" (*Dalkey* 18).

De Selby is more specific here than he is later and states outright that *people* are the problem (*Dalkey* 105–6). The Church, after all, is a human edifice, something alluded to by what Father Cobble tells Shaughnessy of ecclesiastical organisation: "When it was first proposed that concrete should be used in the construction of churches, there was quite a to-do and the matter had to be referred to Rome" (*Dalkey* 114). It puts the reader in mind of de Selby's interview with Saint Augustine, where the Church itself is shown to have been founded on pomposity and institutional befuddlement. Saint Peter, Augustine says, is "just out to show off his keys, bluster about and make himself a bloody nuisance" (*Dalkey* 37). In Heaven, something of a bawdy drinking den, no one takes the first Pope seriously while fellow Apostles Paul and Luke are little more than a biblical Keats and Chapman. Augustine, of course, thinks of himself as an Irishman, a foul mouthed practitioner of "obscene feats" and the son of "a proper gobshite," an unexpected adjustment to the accepted life of the Saint that cleverly allows O'Brien to bring the conversation back to how the Church represents itself in Ireland. He takes specific issue with the veneration of national oxymoron Saint Patrick, a single, real-life conjurer of miracles who is in fact another fantasy, a conflation of historical figures assembled by the human stewards of a human church and subsequently hitched to the bandwagon of Irish identity: "We have four of the buggers in our place and they'd make you sick with their shamrocks and shenanigans and bullshit," Augustine says of the Patricks (*Dalkey* 37). Something must be done about all this for sure, and de Selby's solution is science fictional in scope and method; he intends to use his DMP substance to "pollute and destroy the whole atmosphere," which, in a nod to Keats, Chapman, and the nuclear arms race during which the novel was composed, was a genuine concern among the scientists who tested the first atomic weapons (*Dalkey* 60).

Nevertheless, there is some evidence with regard to *The Dalkey Archive* that O'Brien feared the double indignity of being dubbed "a writer of science fiction" as well as having the novel received as a parody of religion.[5] That said, and insofar as its plot is contingent on the presence of technology and on scientific or, at worst, pseudo-scientific knowledge, the book *is* a work of science fiction. That the science is mostly nonsense and the technology rudimentary, if not altogether nonsensical, serves not to eject the novel from beneath this particular generic umbrella but to emphasise its connectivity with an antecedent fantasy tradition in which things were not always rigorously explained; and therein lies the fantastic rub, for what could be more science-fictional, more technologically unattainable to the stereotypical Irishman than de Selby's instant whiskey? Equally, the "miraculous" spirit fulfills a fantasy for that same figure, perhaps not in the clichéd trolls and elves fashion of literary fantasy, but certainly in the imposition of the unbelievable on the everyday (*Dalkey* 24). The blurred generic boundaries of O'Brien are almost impossible to resolve and so a novel like *The Dalkey Archive*, "part science fiction, part nod to chaos theory" (itself science fiction as far as most lay people are concerned), can all too easily find itself labelled as a book that's "mainly fantasy" (McKittrick, "The 'Lost' World" 2006).

The classification of Flann O'Brien is a process which has been happily stymied for the last half century by the author's celebrated ability to mean everything and nothing all at once. Claimed by successive generations of readers and critics as comedies, genre fictions, experimental texts, and works of post-modernism in turn, the ramshackle hybridity of Flann's novels have always had a sense of Frankenstein's Monster about them, a sense of stitched-together brilliance which leads us to ascribe to their creator something of the dear Doctor Victor himself, who, as it turns out, was also a dabbler in fantasy—in this case alchemy—before he married that knowledge with his own idiosyncratic take on the sciences. O'Brien's output, fictional as well as journalistic, mines a similarly blended vein. In the case of *The Third Policeman*, for example, it is a short leap from being a "comic novel about the nature of time, death and existence" to being a fictional version of the search for physical and philosophical truths (McKittrick, "The 'Lost' World" 2006).

The question of religion, as we have seen, is somewhat trickier. "The Irish church is very insular," says Father Cobble (*Dalkey* 108). It is a remark bound to raise a chuckle from the native reader, but what, if anything, does it tell us of O'Brien, a man of whom, like de Selby, it could be said that "it is difficult to get to grips with his process of reasoning or to refute his curious conclusions" (*Policeman* 117). The evidence of *The Dalkey Archive* in particular suggests that O'Brien regarded the institution of the Church as another kind of narrative, a fantasy spun—like Saint Patrick—from the fragments of historical record, one that has impaired any possibility of genuine spiritual enlightenment and that must be exploded, atomically if necessary, to reveal the truth and wonder of existence to the masses. Writing in Ireland, in the middle decades of the Twentieth Century, there must have been times when such a possibility surely seemed like science fiction to O'Brien.

NOTES

1   Though the character appears as 'De Selby' in *The Dalkey Archive*, he is always referred to as 'de Selby' in *The Third Policeman*. As this is the best-known appearance of the character, insofar as it creates a pleasing symmetry with Éamon de Valera, 'de Selby' is the preferred usage in this article.

2   On the matter of what O'Brien did and did not know about physics, I direct the reader to "Relative Worlds," chapter six of Keith Hopper's *A Portrait of the Artist as a Young Post-modernist*.

3   For a vividly imagined portrait of just how technology might in fact be used to construct a hell or hells, I recommend Iain M. Banks's novel *Surface Detail* (London: Orbit, 2010).

4   A more detailed discussion of this is to be found in Clissman, Chapter 8: "The DMP and Miracles: *The Dalkey Archive*."

5   A fuller examination of O'Brien's principal intentions (and concerns) as regards *The Dalkey Archive* can again be found in Clissmann, Chapter 8.

WORKS CITED

Boylan, Rodger. "We Laughed, We Cried: Flann O'Brien's Triumph." *The Boston Review* July/August 2008: <http://www.bostonreview.net/BR33.4/boylan.php> Accessed 2 March 2011.

Clarke, Arthur C. "Hazards of Prophecy: The Failure of Imagination." *Profiles of the Future: An Enquiry into the Limits of the Possible*. New York: Harper and Row, 1962, rev. 1973.

Clissman, Anne. *Flann O'Brien: A Critical Introduction to his Writings*. Dublin: Gill and Macmillan, 1975.

Cronin, Anthony. *No Laughing Matter: The Life and Times of Flann O'Brien*. London: Graften, 1989.

Hopper, Keith. *A Portrait of the Artist as a Young Post-modernist*. 2nd ed. Cork: Cork Univ. Press, 2009.

—. "The balm and the bane of the intelligentsia." Review of *"Is It About a Bicycle?": Flann O'Brien in the Twenty-First Century*, edited by Jennika Baines. *The Irish Times* 26 March, 2011: <http://www.irishtimes.com/newspaper/weekend/2011/0326/1224293117975.html> Accessed 26 March 2011.

Johansen, Ib. "Shadows in a Black Mirror: Reflections on the Irish Fantastic from Sheridan Le Fanu to John Banville." *Nordic Irish Studies* Vol. 1 (2002): 51–61.

Le Fanu, Sheridan. "Green Tea." *In a Glass Darkly*. Hertfordshire: Wordsworth Classics, 1995.

Maslow, Abraham. *The Psychology of Science*. New York: Harper and Row, 1966.

McKittrick, David. "The 'Lost' World of Flann O'Brien." *The Independent* 28 February 2006: <http://www.independent.co.uk/arts-entertainment/books/features/the-lost-world-of-Flann-obrien-526271.html> Accessed 14 February 2011.

na gCopaleen, Myles. "Cruiskeen Lawn." *The Irish Times* 11 October 1945: 2.

O'Brien, Flann. *At War*. 1999; Normal, IL: Dalkey Archive Press, 2003.

—. *The Dalkey Archive*. 1964; London: Flamingo, 1993; Normal, IL: Dalkey Archive Press, 1993.

—. *The Third Policeman*. 1967; London: Flamingo, 1993; Normal, IL: Dalkey Archive Press, 1999.

BRIAN Ó CONCHUBHAIR

An Béal Bocht and An tOileánach: Writing on the Margin—Gaelic Glosses or Postmodern Marginalia?

> . . . the sad, ravaging mental attitudes that result from severe physical
> poverty—materialism, opportunism, suspicion, the closed mind, inces-
> tuous stupidity, the lack of definite identity . . . the prevalence of brutality
> and thievery, and the strange, predominant sense of evil and oppression.
> Listening to that list you might think this is a gloomy book, a modern
> anatomy of melancholy and malaise. (Kennelly 93–4)

The publication in the *Irish Times* on 13 December 1941 of a review—possibly
penned by Brian Ó Nualláin—intimately linked the just-published *An Béal
Bocht* with Tomás Ó Criomhthain's *An tOileánach* (1929).[1] The reviewer, F.
Ó. R, advanced the notion that "*An Béal Bocht* pretends to be still another
of the autobiographical sagas we have had from the West; indeed, in certain
aspects of language and style it directly parodies Ó Criomhthain's fine book,
An tOileánach" (Ó Conaire 331).[2] This pronouncement firmly and resolutely
charted its critical trajectory: henceforth *An Béal Bocht* and *An tOileánach*
would be symbiotically linked. *An Béal Bocht*'s debt to the genre of *gaeltacht*
(auto)biographies/memoirs is undeniable (Ó Héalaí; de Paor 1998). Consequently the issue of the most appropriate genre in which to situate *An Béal
Bocht* and its creative, narrative, and structural debt to other texts—primarily
An tOileánach—has dominated and obscured critics' ability to see it as its own
independent text. Awareness of the literary, linguistic, and cultural backdrop
is essential, but it is, nevertheless, an independent work of art (Titley 49–50).
While criticism of his English-language novels has blossomed, positioning
him as an important post-modernist and an unrecognized genius worthy of
his place in the international (post)modernist canon—along with Beckett, as
Ireland's second significant post-Joycean modernist (Deane; Brown)—criti-

cism of *An Béal Bocht* seems anchored down by inevitable comparisons to *An tOileánach*.[3] A reading of the marginalia in Brian Ó Nualláin's personal copy of *An tOileánach* not only explicates the relationship between these two texts, but clarifies his attitude toward Ó Criomhthain's book and sheds critical light on his own work and how we might read it.

Despite Breandán Ó Conaire's immense scholarship in *Myles na Gaeilge*, our understanding of that inspiration is blurry and misconstrued. Ó Conaire asserts: "Tá fianaise thréan ann, idir sheachtrach agus inmheánch, a léireodh go ndeachaigh dírbheathaisnéis Thomáis Uí Chriomhthain go mór i bhfeidhm ar Bhrian Ó Nualláin, agus gur shíolraigh téacs, cáil agus fiúntas an leabhair sin ábhar, friotal agus tinfeadh do An Béal Bocht" [There is strong evidence, both external and internal, to illustrate that Tomás Ó Criomhthain's autobiography greatly influenced Brian Ó Nualláin and that book's text, fame and worth provided subject matter, language and inspiration for *An Béal Bocht*] (ctd. in Ó Conaire 120). Stressing Ó Nualláin's admiration for Ó Criomhthain's text and in particular the islander's rich lexicon, Ó Conaire cites a "Cruiskeen Lawn" article (17 January 1955) where he declared unequivocally that: "One of the finest books I have read in any language is *An tOileánach* by a Blasket islander, now dead . . . every page is a lesson how to write, it is all moving and magnificent" (120). And again "The stranger is advised that it is worthwhile to learn the Irish language to read this work. Against it about 90% of books in English, with their smear of sophistication, fall into the ordained bin of trash" (Myles na gCopaleen, *The Best of Myles*, 389). On varying occasions, Ó Nualláin lauded the text as "magnificent, unique, great, really fine, majestic" (Ó Conaire 120). In his "Cruiskeen Lawn" column (3 January 1957)—four years after the island's evacuation—Myles accentuates his esteem for the 1929 text: "That book, *An tOileánach*, is the superbest of all books I have ever read. Its sheer gauntness is a lesson for all . . . The book was published about 1930 and disturbed myself so much that I put it away, a thing not to be seen or thought about and certainly not to be discussed with strangers. But its impact was explosive. In one week I wrote a parody of it called *An Béal Bocht*" (ctd. Asbee 71).

While Ó Nualláin's respect and admiration for *An tOileánach* is beyond question, the precise aspect of the text that so disturbed him remains a matter of conjecture. What caused the "impact" that led him to "parody" it—if it is indeed parody—in *An Béal Bocht*? Ó Conaire suggests the impact was primarily linguistic and stylistic: ". . . go háirithe ar 'theanga' agus ar 'stíl' an leabhair" [especially on the book's language and style] (122). A possible solution to this persistent question may rest in the Ó Nualláin annotated copy of *An tOileánach* preserved at Boston College. The front piece is signed in black ink "Brian Ó Nualláin 1939" and contains eight annotations. This essay describes these annotations and considers how they may shape our understanding of the scribe's relationship to the text and how readers might reconsider *An Béal Bocht* in their light.

The first annotation occurs on page 13 where the word "lútálaidhe" in the sentence "Lútálaidhe cnuic is guirt dob' eadh é" [He was a fumbler on the hill and in the field] (p. 7) is underlined and in lead pencil appears on the margin the word "cringer." While "lútálaidhe" does not appear as an entry in Dinneen's *Foclóir Gaedhilge agus Béarla / An Irish-English Dictionary* (2nd enlarged edition 1927, reprinted 1934, 1941),[4] "lútáil" is defined as:

> act of saluting, louting or bowing; making up to, fawning, cringing, crouching; handling, fumbling; b'fhearr dhuit gadhair an bhaile ag l. timcheall ort ná aoinne aca ag amhstraigh ort, it were better for you that all the dogs in the village should fawn on you that any of them should bark at you (saying); ag l. ar a chéile, making up to one another. (Dinneen 689)

The next annotation occurs on page 15, where the word "t-árthach" in the sentence, "An bhliain do bhuail an t-árthach so ar an dTráigh Bháin, ní cuimhin liom-sa san, mar ná rabhas ann ná súil go mbeinn" [The year this ship was wrecked on the White Strand I can't remember, for I wasn't born or thought of in those days] (p. 9) is underlined. On the margin, in Irish, appears "long mhór." This annotation recalls 11 January 1941 "Cruiskeen Lawn"— prior to the publication of *An Béal Bocht*—where, considering native speakers' vocabulary, he opined:

> Your paltry English speaker apprehends sea-going craft through the infantile cognition which merely distinguishes the small from the big. If it's small it's a boat, and if it's big it's a ship. In his great book, *An*

tOileánach, however, the uneducated Tomás Ó Criomhthain uses, perhaps a dozen words to convey the varying supermarinity— árthach, long, soitheach, bád, naomhnóg, bád raice, galbhád, púcán and whatever you are having yourself.

The focus on page 37 remains lexical: "Gearrcach"—the first word on page 37— is underlined in the sentence "'Gearrcach sicín iseadh é,' arsa bean an tighe, 'pé riach ruda thug ann é,' ar sise" ["It's a young chicken," said the woman of the house, "whatever the dickens brought it there?"] (p. 28). Directly above the underlined word appears the gloss "nestling," which is the first entry Dineen provides in his dictionary. While the majority of glosses suggest the annotator to be a keen language student focused on new lexical terms, the annotation on page 83 notes an unintended insertion. A redundant preposition—"in"— occurs, and is deleted, in the following sentence: "Má dhein sí an beartú san do chuaidh sí chun cinn leis agus níorbh aon ghnó breallach a dhein sí mar níor cuireadh riamh ~~in~~ iaim ar chóta do bhí chomh dulta síos leis"[5] [When once she had the idea, she carried it out, and it was a complete success, for no colouring matter ever went so deep into a petticoat as that did] (p. 71). This note appears to be the only quibble—grammatical rather than stylistic—the scribe finds. The lack of such corrections in *An tOileánach* stands in contrast to the copy of the *Mo Bhealach Féin* [*My Own Way*] (1940) in the same archival collection. Authored by Seosamh Ó Griannain the 1930s, *Mo Bhealach Féin*, was in part inspired by and a response to *An tOileánach* (de Brún 141– 58). The appearance of the cliché "ar chor ar bith" (whatsoever) three times in the space of five lines on page 15 attracted attention. The implied criticism of such over-zealous use of cliché contrasts with their judicious use and relative scarcity in *An tOileánach* and evokes a "Cruiskeen Lawn" article on 24 February 1942 which proclaimed "*An tOileánach* . . . is not the 'speech of the people' or the 'nice idioms' that confer the nobility of literature on it." Writing on Ó Nualláin's disdain for cliché, Brendan Kennelly has remarked:

> This love of verbal precision is the expression of an essentially moral imagination. Cliché is not only the truth worn dull by repetition; it can also be a form of immoral evasion, a refusal to exercise the mind at a moment when it should be exercised, even to one's own discom-

fort or distress. Cliché is also a form of imaginative fatigue, the un-thinking use of listless formula to fill a blank space. (Kennelly 90–1)
The phrase "lá an ghádhtair" is underlined on page 161 in the sentence: "Do h-innseadh di mar bhí, ach ba bheag uirthi an scéal agus do bhreac sí amach do'n bheirt aosta cad é an oibliogáid a leanfadh an té ná pósfadh duine béal-dorais ach a cheanglochadh le dream eile bhí i bhfad ó bhaile agus ná bheadh cabhair ná congnamh le fagháil uatha lá an ghádhtair" [We told her how things stood, and she didn't like the idea at all; she made it plain to the old couple what a responsibility anyone was taking on himself if he didn't marry near home, but made an alliance with a family that lived a long way off and wouldn't be in a position to lend a hand on a rainy day] (pp 144–5). Alongside the three underlined words appears the hand-written phrase followed by a question mark "H.M. normal act?" "Lá an Ghádhtair, 1941" is the date which Flann O'Brien / An Fear Eagair [The Editor] dated *An Béal Bocht's* pseudo-preface. Appearing on four occasions in *An tOileánach* (Ó Conaire 123), it is synonymous with *An Béal Bocht*, appearing repeatedly to comic effect.

Page 163 is marked by two annotations; the first of which is among the most cryptic marginalia in this book. The phrase "ní ró fhada bhí an t-am" ["the time was not long"] is underlined in the sentence "ní ró fhada bhí an t-am gur tógadh uaim é":

> Do saoluigheadh deichniúr clainne ach níor lean an rath iad san, go bhfóiridh Dia orainn! An chéad duine riamh a baisteadh dom bhí sé a seacht nó a hocht de bhlianaibh nuair a thuit sé le faill agus marbhuigheadh é. As san amach níor thapúla duine orainn na dínn. Dímigh beirt leis an mbrúitínigh agus ní raibh galar dá dtagadh ná beireadh duine éigin uaim. Bádh Domhnall díarraidh an bhean-uasal a thabhairt slán leis ar an dTráigh Bháin. Do bhí buachaill breagh eile agam, ag tarrach chugham. Ní ró fhada bhí an t-am gur tógadh uaim é.

> [Ten children were born to us, but they had no good fortune, God help us! The first of them that we christened was only seven or eight years old when he fell over the cliff and was killed. From that time on

they went as quickly as they came. Two died of measles, and every epidemic that came carried off one or other of them. Donal was drowned trying to save the lady off the White Strand. I had another fine lad helping me. Before I lost him, too.] (p. 147)

On the same page appears an ink line beneath the two words "glaodhadh uirthi" ["she was called/summoned"] in the final sentence on this page: "Bhí naoidhneán beag 'n-a diaidh—ach go raibh cailín beag fásta suas a thug aire di—ní raibh sí ach fásta suas san am gur glaodhadh uirthi chomh maith leo." The entire passage reads:

Do ghoill buairt na neithe sin go léir ar an máthair bhoicht agus tógadh uaim í. Ní rabhas dall ar fad go dtí san. Nár dalladh Dia sinn. Bhí naoidhneán beag 'n-a diaidh—ach go raibh cailín beag fásta suas a thug aire di—ní raibh sí ach fásta suas san am gur glaodhadh uirthi chomh maith leo. An cailín a thóg í sin do phós sí sa Dún Mór. Cailleadh í sin, leis, agus d'fhág seisear leanbh 'n-a diaidh. Buachaill amháin atá fanta faram annso sa bhaile. Buachaill eile i Meirice. Sin é crích d'imigh ar mo chlainn-se. Beannacht Dé leo—a bhfuil san uaigh aca—agus leis an mnaoi bhoicht gur bhris a misneach d'á ndeascaibh.

[All these things were a sore trouble to the poor mother, and she, too, was taken from me. I was never blinded altogether till then. May God spare us the light of our eyes! She left a little babe, only I had a little girl grown up to take care of her; but she, too, was only just grown up when she heard the call like the rest. The girl who had brought her up married in Dunmore. She died, too, leaving seven children. I have only one boy left at home with me now. There is another in America. Such was the fate of my children. May God's blessing be with them—those of them that are in the grave—and with the poor woman whose heart broke for them.] (p. 147)

Beneath this sentence, in English, is the phrase "alas, those waitresses!" Such a phrase appears to be a cold, emotionless response to a passage describing the untimely death of two young children. The pun's humor stems, in part it seems, from the translation of the autonomous form into English (See Hopper 37–8). While in current convention it describes "the elimination of a contract due to the obligation of delivery," for those conversant with contemporary slang of forties Dublin dining rooms and restaurants, it suggests a waitress excusing delays in service by noting that she had been "called away." Recalling his assessment of *An tOileánach* in a "Cruiskeen Lawn" article on 24 February 1942 may help to reconcile Ó Nualláin's respect for Ó Criomhthain's writing in light of this apparently brusque quip:

> *An tOileánach* is literature . . . There is no book (of ours or of any other tribe) in English comparable to it. And it is not the "speech of the people" or the "nice idioms" that confer the nobility of literature on it. The genuine authoritative human stuff is there, it is artistic, it moves the reader to tears or laughter as the author chooses.

Asbee advances the argument that "our ideas of parody have to be adjusted, for it was clearly not O'Brien's intention to denigrate *The Islandman*. He was so deeply affected—'disturbed'—by the book that his comedy is more likely to have been a cathartic exercise for his own feelings . . ." Rather, Asbee contends "the creative energy it inspired had to be 'directed toward other ends'" (Asbee 72). Ó Criomhthain's nonchalant, almost blasé, dismissal of his marriage, and his stoic and remorseless lack of compassion in narrating the death of his wife in addition to the birth and death of several of his children has vexed critics. Yet Asbee tenders:

> The evident emotional restraint in discussing his private life . . . is no indication that these are lacking (by contrast, Defoe's Robinson Crusoe marries, has children, and disposes of them all in one paragraph, without mentioning their names, right at the end of the of the novel) . . . But we never learn his wife's name, or the names of most of his children . . . These are only references, but we do not infer that because they are apparently marginalized, his emotional distress was concomitant. Rather, they assume the status and dignity of private grief not to be exhibited for public examination. (Asbee 78)

At the end of page 187, which concludes the chapter on the seizure of the islanders' boats and their impounding in Dingle, occurs an arrow directing attention to handwritten text at the foot of the page and the following commentary in English: "all the literatures of the world contain nothing so momentously said as that last paragraph." The paragraph in question is that in which Ó Criomhthain narrates his mother's death and funeral preparations. The description is both poignant and pregnant with unstated, yet keenly felt, grief. The final sentence encapsulates his emotional turmoil:

> Sara raibh breacadh an lae ann do bhí glaoidhte aige 'go raibh sí seo ar a' dtaobh thall.' Do dheineas-sa me féin a ghléasadh agus m'aghaidh a thabhairt ar Dhaingean Uí Chúise d'iarraidh ghléas tórraimh. D'fhan an aimsir go breagh nó gur shroich mo mháthair a teampall dúthchais i bhFionntráigh—bóthar fada ó'n mBlascaod mór, idir fhairrge agus thalamh, agus cé go raibh sochraid mhaith ann, cartacha agus capaill cuid mhaith, is ar ghuaille daoine a chuaidh sí go dtí an roilig.
>
> Sin críoch leis an mbeirt do chuir sioladh na teangan so im' chluasa an chéad lá. Beannacht Dé le n-a n-anam.

[Before the dawn came he called out: 'She's in the next world.' I set about getting myself ready to face for Dingle to get the furnishings for the funeral. The weather stayed fine till my mother reached her family churchyard in Ventry—a long journey by sea and land from the Blasket, and, although there was a fine following of many horse-drawn cars, it was on men's shoulders that she went to her grave.

So ended the two who put the sound of the Gaelic language in my ears the first day. The blessing of God be with their souls!] (p. 170)

In an introduction to *The Third Policeman*, Denis Donoghue comments that "it is indeed characteristic of Irish fiction—or at least of Irish anatomies—to stand aside from the common urgencies of feeling and to treat the whole farrago of sensibility as warranting merely speculative attention" (Donoghue xi). Alluding to that novel's murder, Donoghue notes the lack of remorse or moral scruple: "the ethical issue is disposed of in silence. Nature, conventionally a great source of heart-stirring, is not allowed to pour its benisons over the populace. Imagine how a traditionalist novelist, his humanism flowing, would have developed a paragraph that started by taking note of the arrival of the evening" (xi). Such also is the case here. Ó Criomhthain, the Blasket islander, refuses to seek shelter in humanistic warmth. He seeks neither empathy nor compassion. The hand-written gloss not only recognizes but celebrates this refusal to submit to convention; it coolly rejects an opportunity to wallow in standard tropes of loss and clichéd pieties, the chance to connect and form a sympathetic bond with the reader. As Donoghue observes, the refusal of humanistic warmth "is endemic in modern literature, not merely in Irish literature . . . Empathy is humanistic, responsive to the shared travails of human life. Abstraction interposes the artist's mind, puts a distance between that mind and the given world, and consults the artist's desire and its cool, self-propelling forms" (xii). Hence the comment's perspicacity: it recognizes the modern nature of the writing, and more importantly the modern sentiment underpinning it. It is the style of saying or, more precisely, its artistic style of not-saying, which is "momentous" and which presages post-modernist strategies of silence, kinds of silence and non-verbal communication. *An tOileánach*, in discarding the obvious, anticipates the postmodern strategy of rejecting Western aesthetics central to the postmodernist project. The annotation elevates the context in which the scribe reads and considers Ó Criomhthain's work from a minor, regional, Irish literary discourse to a global discourse and should, this essay contends, invite a similar international consideration of *An Béal Bocht*, its strategies, styles, and motifs.

Returning to the lexical level evident in the earlier glosses, the final annotation focuses on an idiom. On page 209 the phrase "ach nár ghnáth-bhéas again dul fé loch" (but it was not our habit to dive) is underlined in the sentence "Do bhí cuid aca nár chuaidh ón tsáile riamh agus cuid eile again go raibh snámh maith again ach nár ghnáth-bhéas again dul fé loch" [That was what should be done; but where were the two to go under water? That was the problem. There were some of them who'd never been in the sea, and others of us who could swim well enough, but we hadn't the habit of going under] (p. 191). Ó Conaire reveals that the phrase "fé loch" occurs frequently in *An Béal*

Bocht (Ó Conaire 153). This idiom appears in *An Béal Bocht* on pages 81–7, 82–31, 83–14, 83–16, 84–29, 85–5, 86–1, 101–16, and particularly in chapter seven where the text caricatures the seal hunt as depicted in *An tOileánach* and the location of the underwater cave where Sitric elects to remain rather than endure the severe austerity and damp deprivations of Corkadoragha.

What, if anything, do these glosses tells us of the annotator's relationship to *An tOileánach* and what guidance do they provide for (re)reading *An Béal Bocht*? If nothing else the marginalia reaffirms Ó Nualláin's deference and admiration for *An tOileánrach*—"all the literatures of the world contain nothing so momentously said as that last paragraph" is as resounding a commendation as one could find not only commending its style but placing it on a global literary stage. It is, however, the troubling and somewhat disturbing response to the girls' deaths that ultimately proves most revealing. Rather than elicit a culturally appropriate or emotionally sensitive response, we find human loss and tragedy educes nothing but black humor—a key postmodernist trope. In a similar vein, the glossing of "lá an ghádhtair" as "H.M. normal act?" adheres to the ironic style associated with postmodernism and adds a political dimension to the context. Is there a case then to reread *An Béal Bocht* in light of these glosses as a proto/early postmodernist text or a late-modernist transitional text (Hopper 158).

Critics generally consider *An Béal Bocht* and Máirtín Ó Cadhain's *Cré na Cille* [*Churchyard Clay* (1948)] to signal the demise of the *gaeltacht* autobiography as the dominant prose form in Irish-language literary discourse, at least in critical circles if not in popular circles (Nic Eoin 211; Titley 50, O'Leary 462–3). These two novels ultimately signaled the end to the uncritical depiction of *gaeltacht* life and the exaltation of a materially poor but spiritually and culturally wealthy lifestyle (Ó Torna). Internecine tensions, pressures, and strife had found delineation in previous authors' work in English and Irish, but Ó Cadhain, as Robert Welch contends, was radically new: ". . . Ó Cadhain differs is in the degree of intense detail he gives. He takes the reader into the interiority of the situation; so that, while the situation is traditional the method is modern" (Welch 189). The privileging of Ó Cadhain's Freudian and Jungian psychological approach (De Paor) all too often relegates Ó Nualláin's work to that of simple parody. Yet as Richard Murphy argues in a recent article: "Since the publication of *At Swim-Two-Birds*, he has been categorized, along with Beckett, as Ireland's second significant post-Joycean modernist (Seamus Deane); a precocious postmodernist (Keith Hopper); a practitioner of Menippean satire (Keith Booker); and the postcolonial exemplar of the Bahktinian dialogic novelist (Kim McMullen)" (Murphy 67). Nevertheless criticism of *An Béal Bocht* remains rooted in debates over influence, literary borrowing, genre, and authorial intent. However, in his exploration of *An Béal Bocht* as a possible naturalist work, Richard Murphy argues convincingly that critics mistakenly associated the text with the modernizing naturalist project, whose genre of choice is the realist bildungsroman of thwarted development. Instead, Murphy argues for a "minor"—in David Lloyd's sense—reading: "O'Brien's critique is different from a corrective naturalism or demystification, nor still is it the voice of the subaltern speaking back to the obscuring and distorting discourse of outsiders, since the novel resists the very claims of authorship required to mount such a reality-based critique." For Murphy then "the episodic structure, the lack of character development, the 'nonoriginal' obedience to conventional setting, idiom and plot" act as "deliberate tools, in a project at once closer to the native satiric tradition in classical Irish literature and to the anti-realism of Beckett and Joyce" (Murphy 70). Contending that Ó Nualláin manipulates the literary cannon to "disrupt, contaminate and rebuke it" while simultaneously drawing on "the tradition of porous generic boundaries, anarchic satire, grotesque fantasy and a nonchalance towards plagiarism," he concludes that Ó Nualláin "infuses the autobiographical frame-tale of origination, development and identity with a healthy dose of mimicry, repetition and identity-theft," and he also argues that, "[e]ven the illustrations and maps recall travel writing and the field-work of the legions engaged in formal or informal anthropology, ethnology and auto-exoticism in the Gaeltacht . . ." (80)

Ignoring the unconventional chronology in terms of literary and cultural history, this essay argues that *An Béal Bocht* (1941) is analogous to *At Swim-Two-Birds* (1939) and anticipates and incorporates many of the stylistics, tropes and techniques that would become fundamental to postmodern aesthetics. If we acknowledge the intertextuality, the spatial distortion, the dismissal of the origin myth and national narratives, it seems logical to prof-fer *An Béal Bocht* not only as the first post-modernist Irish-language novel but to examine it more closely in terms of *At Swim-Two-Birds* and similar postmodernist works as it appears to be closer in style and temperament to Kurt Vonnegut and William Burroughs than Tomás Ó Criomhthain. The use of grotesque distortion to mock received wisdom and approved values; the list of ridiculous pen-names at the Feis; hybrid language; repletion of clichés; metafiction and collage of Free State novels and autobiographies; disparaging of rationality; privileging of the figural over the discursive; and stressing of prescriptive elements of the genre over the interpretation—all point, it seems, toward a postmodern literary sensibility. If the *gaeltacht* au-tobiography was deeply rooted in an anthropological-linguistic discourse, the text that brought about a seismic re-evaluation in how the genre was received and interpreted was less a modernist text concerned with iden-tity, unity and cultural authority, but one which promoted plurality, textu-ality, and skepticism. Ó Cadhain and Ó Nualláin and a handful of others, to paraphrase Philip O'Leary, kept faith with the past in the best possible way, by giving it genuine relevance in the present and meaningful access to the future through challenging creative works (O'Leary 463). The author of *At Swim-Two-Birds*, in reading *An tOileánach*, saw the modernist essence in the midst of the memoir—concreteness, objectivity, and strictness—and through a postmodernist reconfiguration, represents it in his own words from his own mouth in a potent rather than poor fashion. In conclusion, positioning *An Béal Bocht* in a "late-modernist transitional" or early post-modernist context not only broadens our critical horizons but sharpens our critical and cultural perspectives. It challenges us to look beyond the simple context of autobiographies and Free State fiction: clichéd descriptions of *An Béal Bocht* as satire, parody, and/or comedy no longer suffice.

NOTES

1   This essay is predicated on the notion that the Brian Ó Nualláin alone annotated the copy of *An tOileánach* bearing his name and contained in his personal library. The

author thanks the following for discussing various aspects of this topic: Brendan Kane, Richard Murphy, David Horn, and the Burns Library staff.

2   Talbot Press published an English-language translation of *An tOileánach* in 1934 that was followed by an American English-language edition in 1935. Talbot Press and Chatto & Windus republished the translation in 1937. Subsequent editions include: Penguin 1943; Oxford University Press 1951, 1958, 1963, 1967, 1969, 1971 (twice), 1972, 1974, 1977, 1978, 1979 and 1992. *Die Boote fahren nicht mehr aus : Bericht eines irischen* appeared in 1991 and *L'homme des îles* in 2003. All English quotations in this essay are taken from the 1979 Oxford University Press edition.

3   Notable exceptions include Kiberd, McKibben and Wong who offer new interpretations including gendered, postcolonial readings.

4   The well-thumbed *Dinneen* in the O'Nolan archive lacks a title page, but based on the preface and pagination it appears to be the 1934 edition. My thanks to Shelly Barber in ascertaining this information.

5   Ó Coileáin (p. 80) offers "Má dhein, ní raibh a machnamh i vásta, mar níor cuireadh riamh ruaim ar chóta do bhí chuin dulta síos leis."

WORKS CITED

Asbee, Sue. *Flann O'Brien*. Boston: Twayne Publishers. 1991.

Brown, Terence. "Two Post-modern Novelists: Beckett and O'Brien." *The Cambridge Guide to the Irish Novel*. Ed. J. W. Foster. London: Cambridge Univ. Press 2006, 205–22.

De Brún, Fionntán. *Seosamh Mac Grianna: An Mhéin Rúin*. Baile Átha Cliath: An Clóchomhar Tta., 2002.

De Paor, Louis. *Faoin mBlaoisc Bheag Sin: an aigneolaíocht i scéalta Mháirtín Uí Chadhain*. Baile Átha Cliath: Coiscéim, 1991.

—. "Myles na gCopaleen agus Drochshampla na dDealeabhar." *The Irish Review*, 23 (Winter 1998), 24–32.

Dinneen, Patrick S. *Foclóir Gaedhilge agus Béarla / An Irish-English Dictionary*. Dublin: Irish Texts Society, 1927.

Donoghue, Denis. "Introduction." *The Third Policeman*. Dalkey Archive Press, 2006. v–xiii.

Hopper, Keith. *Flann O'Brien: A Portrait of the Artist as a Young Post-modernist*. Cork: Cork Univ. Press, 1995.

Kennelly, Brendan. "Brendan Kennelly on *An Béal Bocht* by Myles na gCopaleen (1911–1966)." *The Pleasures of Gaelic Literature*. Ed. John Jordan. Cork: Mercier Press, 1978. 85–96.

Kiberd, Declan. "*An Béal Bocht* agus an Béarla." *Comhar* 43:4 (1984), 20–27.

McKibben, Sarah E. "The Poor Mouth : A Parody of (Post)Colonial Irish Manhood." *Research in African Literatures*, 34:4 Winter 2003, 96–114.

—. "*An Beal Bocht*: Mouthing Off at National Identity," *Éire-Ireland: Journal of Irish Studies* (Spring/Summer 2003), 6–41.

Murphy, Richard T. "'A Root of the New Sprout'?: Flann O'Brien, Minor Literature and the Modern Gaelic Canon." *"Is It About a Bicycle?": Flann O'Brien in the Twenty-First Century*. Ed. Jennika Baines. Dublin: Four Courts Press, 2011, 67–82.

Nic Eoin, Máirín. *An Litríocht Réigiúnach*. Baile Átha Cliath: An Clóchomhar Tta., 1982.

O'Brien, Flann. *The Best of Myles*. Normal: Dalkey Archive Press, 1999.

Ó Conaire, Breandán. *Myles na Gaeilge*. Baile Átha Cliath: An Clóchomhar Tta., 1986.

O'Leary, Philip. *Irish Interior: Keeping Faith with the Past in Gaelic Prose 1940–1951*. Dublin: Univ. College Dublin Press. 2010.

Ó Torna, Caitríona. *Cruthú na Gaeltachta 1893–1922*. Baile Átha Cliath: Cois Life, 2005.

Titley, Alan. *An tÚrscéal Gaeilge*. Baile Átha Cliath: An Clóchomhar Tta., 1991.

Welch, Robert. *Changing States: Transformations in Modern Irish Writing*. London: Routledge, 1993.

Wong, Donna I. "Following the Law of the Letter: Myles na gCopaleen's *An Béal Bocht*." *New Hibernia Review / Iris Éireannach Nua*, 4: 3 (Autumn, 2000) 93–106.

AMY NEJEZCHLEB

A *Saga* to Remember: Flann O'Brien's Unfinished Novel

Published posthumously in 1967 in the form of seven chapters and seventy pages, the fragment known as *Slattery's Sago Saga* (hereafter *Saga*) is an effort to recast painful historical events in both America and Ireland through rhetorical tactics that Brian O'Nolan polished over the decades. Complicating the novel's execution is O'Nolan's uncertainty as to whether he should write in the mode of Flann O'Brien or Myles na gCopaleen—that is, as a novelist experimenting with formal devices or as a satirical commentator on national events. Documents from the time, including unpublished correspondence, reveal his struggle to resolve the dilemma. The novel plots a narrative that underscores the influx of American culture in Ireland, depicting it as a homogenizing, standardizing process that threatens regional values. At the same time, however, O'Nolan is quick to mock Ireland for its conventional ways. The contradictory impulses in this unfinished work are striking and include O'Nolan's first female character of any depth, who simultaneously functions as a parody of American feminism. On the one hand, O'Nolan writes passages that test the patience of his readers through extensive digressions that reproduce the bureaucratic language of the government pamphlet; on the other hand, his notes (and letters to friends) that develop the plot reveal a journalist's fascination with the recent events of the Kennedy assassination and that Irish-American family in general. If *Saga* is a project left unfinished through O'Nolan's own divided sensibility, these divisions also reveal strains and impulses embedded in his career.

The various elements that complicate the *Saga* fragment have been identified by critics over the years, though these are often dismissed as poor decisions or aberrant behavior. Carol Taaffe attributes O'Brien's "need for financial success" as one factor "anchoring these novels in the kind of bland but marketable comic realism that [is] quite alien to [his] earlier fantasies" (Taaffe 184). Anthony Cronin believes his own novel, *The Life of Riley* (1964), planted the seed for *Saga's* eventual plot, given similarities between their close publication dates and plots closely centered on the potato. Yet Cronin admits that *Saga* singularly interweaves an Irish America, particularly the story of John F. Kennedy (Cronin 241). Sue Asbee recognizes Crawford MacPherson's role in O'Brien's *oeuvre*—most of his females were insignificant, but Crawford is strong and independent (Asbee 110–111). Anne Clissmann first documents the political similarities in the *Saga* plot to the Kennedy family and former Taoiseach Eamon de Valera, who escaped execution for his role in the Easter Rising through his American birth (Clissmann 325–328). The novel's only advocate in the last thirty-four years, Clissmann points out that *Saga* has elements "which would have allowed O'Brien to free his imagination to create, as he had done in *At Swim* and *The Third Policeman*, alternative worlds which were logically consistent within the terms of their own imaginative construction" (Clissmann 334).

What makes *Saga* less typically O'Brienesque is its narrative that positions us in two different locations of the globe, Ireland and America, and that often resembles straightforward naturalist prose. *Saga's* opening scene in Ireland, observes Tim Hartigan, adopted son of Ned Hoolihan, shocked at the thought of receiving a "Bleeding Scotchman" to Poguemahon Hall (Poguemahon means "Kiss My Arse" in Irish) on the orders of his father (O'Brien 23). The arrival of Scottish woman Crawford MacPherson, who we learn later is Ned Hoolihan's American wife, has been announced in Ned's letter from Houston, Texas. The scene's perspective changes abruptly to an omniscient narrator who informs us that Ned's fortune was earned in agriculture, particularly in types of potato crop. Neither Ned's "Earthquake Wonder" or "Faddiman's Fancy" is popular with Irish farmers because "the peasants simply preferred seed of their own domestic procurement," so Ned sets his sights on America, receiving "a citation and praemium from the United States Government" (O'Brien 25). Ned has left Tim as steward of Poguemahon Hall, and settled 7,000 acres in Texas, where oil has made him "unbelievably wealthy" (O'Brien 26). (His front-money was the amassed fortune of his father Constantine Hoolihan B. E., who had been "shamelessly swindled by Henry Ford I" but managed to resourcefully double that which he had lost in "automotive and petrol-engine inventions," thus forming the first-generation link to America's cultural influence and money from products related to oil, or petrol [O'Brien 24].)

Crawford MacPherson's entrance has a two-fold purpose, recalling the disruptive effects of mass-culture's standardization on the Republic of Ireland and embodying America's aggressive impact on the nation. MacPherson, in her role as demonic force—in a letter, O'Nolan calls her "a fearful virago" (29 Oct 1964)[1]—is designed as a stereotype of aggressive American feminists of the 1960s, but the violence she brings appears as a commercializing venture, an economic scheme: her plan is to import sago to Ireland and replace the potato crop. She wishes to completely eradicate the potato from Ireland to rid her "beloved" America of the immoral Irish through taking over "all Irish agricultural land," selling it back to the tenants at "a rent of perhaps a shilling a year," and substituting the hardier sago plant (O'Brien 35–37). Her "object is to protect the United States from the Irish menace," which will be "very costly," but she has "so much money from Texas oil" at her disposal that she fears no difficulty (O'Brien 34). Her detailed plan reveals an analytical mind bent on rescuing a superstitious culture that has walled itself up in tradition (a metaphor to be embodied literally, when Crawford alone can solve the mystery when a local worker turns up missing).

O'Nolan places Crawford at the center of his fragment's most outrageous plot device, summoning the history of the Potato Famine. In extracts on sago from real reference books that take the form of a detailed, factual text, he introduces long passages that critics have denounced as a clumsy narrative device, "tedious to read," and what Sue Asbee asserts are "unworthy of the earlier technical brilliance that O'Brien displayed in *The Third Policeman*" (Asbee 111–112). Yet it is characteristic for O'Nolan to present long stretches of text that test the reader's patience. In *At Swim-Two-Birds*, the tedious recitation has been delivered by Antony Lamont, John Furriskey, and Paul Shanahan, whose dull scientific facts set up the Pooka's disruptive entrance, inaugurating pages that mock the language of the Victorian gentleman's club and merge Irish myth with commonplace dialogue, a joke whose victim is the Anglo-Irish Revival. Though dull and technical the sago extracts may be, these lengthy stretches of text recall nothing less than British pamphlets on preparing maize during the Potato Famine. Excerpts from *The Book of Marco Polo the Venetian* by Col. Sir Henry Yule (a nineteenth-century edition of Polo's thirteenth-century travels) explains that sago flour "is taken and made into *pasta* in strips," which "resembl[e] barley bread and tast[e] much the same" (O'Brien 57). Similarly, A. E. Williams in *Malay Archipelago 1896* tells of producing sago starch through a lengthy process, then forming it into a variety of foods, and like the other texts, Williams's description is nearly agonizing in its lengthy trade-oriented detail: "Sago bread is made . . . by baking it into cakes in a small clay oven containing six or eight slits, side by side, each about three-quarters of an inch wide and six to eight inches square" (O'Brien 58).

On one level, these extracts in *Saga* help familiarize readers with the unfamiliar sago plant even as, on another level, O'Brien's "samplings" from extant texts—blatantly signaled by italicized page numbers in the copy—recall the technical and managerial procedures that were used by Great Britain to validate its presence in Ireland. The historical echoes that O'Nolan rouses begin with the products of the Chairman of the Relief Commission of the 1848 famine, Sir Randolph Routh, who had spent sixteen years familiarizing himself with processes of maize consumption in America, issuing "a pamphlet containing simple recipes for its use, which was sold throughout" Ireland (Kinealy 47). Routh wrote in 1846 to Sir William Trevelyan, the Permanent Secretary at the Treasury during the whole of the Famine period, about the Indian corn preparation process (drying, grinding, and dressing the meal for consumption) with the same care and acute attention as the sago extracts: "First to keep the corn eight hours on the kilns, and turn it twice, so as to be thoroughly dried without parching. It was then allowed to cool for forty-eight hours" (Kinealy 39, 47). American agricultural expert and Editor of *Farmer's Library*, J. S. Skinner, offered an explanation to prepare griddle corn cakes in an 1845 pamphlet that likely circulated England and Ireland: "Be it remembered that the dough, or rather the batter, . . . must be well beat up and prepared directly before being cooked—though it might set an hour . . ." (Bartlett 19). Both descriptions explain ways to use corn because the grain was unfamiliar to the Irish, and they demonstrate that the technical and detailed descriptions in O'Brien's sago excerpts are meant to expose the oppressive policies that are disguised by such official discourse.[2]

Other historical knowledge also informs the inner layers of O'Nolan's rhetoric here. As a Scottish-American, Crawford plays a critical role in the narrative by marking the conflict of Irish and Ulster Scots' emigration from Ireland to America. Such conflict O'Nolan underscores in the character of Doctor the Eustace Baggeley who recalls the Irish rivalry with Scotland as he derides Ned's marriage as generating unnecessary wealth: "*Money?* Pfff! He had more than he could use when he was here, and what use is money to a man who gets himself married to a Scotch hawsie from the fish-gutting sheds of Aberdeen?" (O'Brien 48). That a Scottish woman would engineer a plot to oust the potato from Ireland solely so the Irish will stop immigrating to America would be absurd and ridiculous if the memory of the Famine were not so tragic. Yet O'Nolan must evoke a tragic history that inevitably summons memories of British colonization in Ireland, including absentee landlords, rackrenting, small farm plots, anti-Catholicism, and mass emigration from Ireland to various countries, because he reacts with urgency to an American commercial and cultural colonization that he sees as a twentieth-century parallel.

O'Nolan's assault on feminism thus figures not just as another example of the misogyny threaded through his career but as an added warning about American influence in Ireland. This calculation, however, helps explain why Crawford is regarded with uncharacteristic ambivalence by O'Nolan. To be suitable as allegorizing a serious threat, she must be strong and convincing in her authority, even as her fearfulness must be ferociously mocked. In one sense, given O'Nolan's proclivity for male-centered novels, Crawford's forwardness is almost refreshing. *Saga* distinguishes itself from all other fiction by O'Nolan in that a female character speaks forthrightly, talking back and

taking action, and plays an integral role in the plot. A similar female character appears in O'Brien's television series, *Th'Oul Lad of Kilsalaher* (1964),
where Marie-Thèrése's witty exchanges with her father, Hughie, can be read
as O'Brien's effort (as Myles) in creating more substantial women characters
in his later works.[3] Yet Crawford is also a distinct threat, unlike the young
girl who challenges her father's cautious attitudes. Feminism as a movement
in the 1960s could only threaten Ireland as it calls into question conservative policies that were enacted by the de Valera Constitution and the Catholic
Church. O'Nolan stages confrontations that demonstrate legal issues under
fire. Young Tim addresses Crawford as "ma'am" because he hasn't been introduced to her yet, but Crawford will not allow "ma'am" or "Mrs Hoolihan,"
insisting on "MacPherson" (O'Brien 28–29, 32). O'Nolan has her emphatically single out parallels in legal systems: "I am not compelled by civil or Pres-
byterian canon law to make a laughing-stock of myself with a title the like
of that" (O'Brien 32). Articulate, assertive, and angry, Crawford is to some
extent undermined by O'Nolan's description of her as "an elderly woman clad
in shapeless, hairy tweeds, small red-rimmed eyes glistening in a brownish
lumpy face that looked to Tim like the crust of an apple-pie" (O'Brien 28). Yet
such a description also makes O'Nolan seem anxious and uncertain himself.
He has Crawford continually use the word "weemen" for women: "Have you
no respect for weemen or are you drunk?" (O'Brien 28–29). But such efforts
to reduce Crawford to a laughable figure lack boldness, especially in contrast
to the character's assertive style.

O'Nolan is caught in a bind. If he is to make Crawford convincingly fearful, she must be bold; her boldness may be used to mock her authority, but
if that happens, she loses her capacity to threaten. Crawford is supposed to
model American business practices, their overbearing and adamant form of
problem solving that often disregards other cultural practices. Yet O'Nolan
simultaneously turns Crawford's energetic ways against a slow-moving Irish
culture that, writing as Myles na gCopaleen, he indicted in his newspaper columns (he refers to this segment of Irish society as the Plain People of Ireland).
When the carpenter Billy Colum disappears, Crawford nominates herself as

chief problem-solver. Dr. Baggeley, by contrast, is happy to believe that Billy is not missing but has simply left to see his mother, reminding Crawford that, conventionally, the Irish "don't keep office hours" (O'Brien 62). Crawford demonstrates the fault line between Ireland and America when she unleashes a barrage of questions, pushing aside convention for efficiency: "she seemed to be leading the party, as if she owned the Castle" (O'Brien 64). She wonders whether Billy is sober, eats properly, and whether he has been injected by the Doctor recently for his muscle inflammation before she grabs a stethoscope and places it to the wall where Billy has last been seen working. Crawford builds on knowledge about Baggeley's drug addiction, his "taking doses twice a day now," and it is her method with its persistence that leads to Billy's where-abouts: he has paneled himself into the wall before passing out after receiving an injection (O'Brien 43). After Billy has been given bed rest, all are drinking whiskey, and Crawford drinks "appreciatively, apparently judging that the situation [is] one of some small triumph for her," apologizing "if my manner over this little mystery seemed a bit brusque. But human suffering disturbs me" (O'Brien 68). Ironically, she will be the cause of human suffering when she enacts her potato plot. Though O'Nolan shows her sensing that her ways are disruptive to the Irish people she meets, he also stresses that she does not hold herself accountable nor does she adapt to Irish ways. Crawford's shifting char-acteristics reveal O'Nolan's struggle to portray a character who is at once an allegorical figure of American aggressiveness and a fearful woman who threat-ens conventional ways. While apparently intelligent and strong, she must be undermined as a female, yet her invasive power must be always in play.

Notes that O'Nolan left undeveloped, when work on the novel was inter-rupted by his death, reveal plans that include one character's eventual sojourn, emigration, and election as President. O'Nolan's proposal for *Saga* in a letter to Macgibben & Kee representative Timothy O'Keeffe on October 29, 1964, includes detailed summary for the final plot: Crawford, it will be explained in later passages, will be the source for Hoolihan's financial success from oil in Texas because she "notices black dirt oozing from certain points in the prairie wheatfields" (29 Oct 1964). O'Nolan also meant that the utterly outrageous sago plan would actually be enacted, making this work a venture into a fantasy realm. After twenty-five years, the Irish would be living mostly on sago with sago forests covering the island. Hoolihan will eventually become "a politician, manipulator of votes and money, and a near-hoodlum," later sending for his adopted son, Tim Hartigan, and installing him as Governor of Texas (29 Oct 1964).[4]

In the plot-outline in the proposal, O'Nolan planned to have a conflict develop as Irish men and women arrive in America with complaints of "sago-stomach, sago-leg and dread sagosis, an infectious and lethal disease" (29 Oct 1964). (Of course there is no such disease as "sagosis"; O'Nolan has steered his plot entirely into the realms of the fantastic.) So serious are these ailments that MacIntosh herself dies of sagosis while on return from Ireland in the States. When a Congressional Committee investigates these complaints, the meetings are aborted because sago stomach prevents the members from reaching quorum. Sago is noticeably prevalent on the tiny island, and it "is rumoured to be an ingredient of the hydrogen bomb" (29 Oct 1964)! Rich and powerful in America, Hoolihan buys up radio stations and newspaper chains to enact his plan to elect Tim as President. Doing so provides Tim an opportunity to reinstate the potato in a speech on sago to Congress that would conclude the novel. O'Nolan meant for this narrative to be "straightforward, with no 'literary' complication," yet the narrative includes "literary complications" such as social satire (29 Oct 1964).

Both this proposal as well as items in his correspondence show O'Nolan determined to publish *Saga*, an idea he firmly believed in. Both items also reveal a burgeoning anti-American bias not previously so dramatically evident in O'Nolan's work. O'Nolan alludes to "the Kennedy mud pie" when describing characters in *Saga* that resemble Irish-American President John F. Kennedy and his father Joseph Kennedy. *Saga* characters Ned Hoolihan and adopted son Tim Hartigan lead lives too similar to the story of JFK, his election, and his assassination, to go unnoted. O'Nolan draws connections to the Kennedy dynasty in a letter dated 8 May 1965 to O'Keeffe regarding *Saga*:

> Meditation on the crazy idea behind this book has made it grow
> strange horns and the finished book will turn out to be a comic but

unmistakeable attack on the Kennedy family. Dead President Jack will be let off lightly for undoubtedly he had some fine qualities, but the Pop is a crook and the surviving brothers contemtible [sic] hangers-on. (8 May 1965)

In the surviving pages of *Saga*, we can glimpse Ned Hoolihan as a model for Joseph Kennedy, symbolizing the corrupt nature of Irish-American success stories in American politics. Hoolihan has built an extremely prosperous business in oil (the counterpart to Joseph's liquor enterprise), forming the "Hoolihan Petroleum Corporation ('H. P.')" from "315 oil derricks," and as a result, "the politicians are moving in," but as he writes to Tim, "I think I have their measure" (O'Brien 26). American money, business, and politics are inextricably linked, and Hoolihan's experience is no different, when in a second letter, he tells Tim he "is quietly backing" two New Mexican politicians to aid his interests "because that's the way business goes here" (O'Brien 73). These interests involve grandiose schemes for heightened power and success:

I play the Kennedy R. C. ticket and I'll be just another brave U. S. Catholic as soon as my citizenship comes through—Cactus Mike says I'm perfectly right and that this great State of over seven million souls is entitled to a Cardinal and if he is elected Governor in New Mexico he intends to park some fixers and use money (mine, I presume) in Rome. (O'Brien 73)

There are no limits to Hoolihan's American scheming, and this shows by the letter's end when he plans to advance his business interests by using his connections to a New Mexican politician:

By God, if he wants to serve the Cross that way, why shouldn't he since he serves or used to serve the fiery cross with the K. K. K. outfit—and now with an election next door there's no shortage of those gunboys in nightshirts putting the fear of Jesus into the niggers. (O'Brien 73)

Indeed, where this scheming will ultimately lead, we know from O'Nolan's outline, will be Tim's election as President of the United States after Ned has purchased advertising in radio and newspapers to help elect his son (29 Oct 1964).

From archival material, then, we know Tim Hartigan is modeled on JFK, given his American birth, subsequent adoption by Ned, and eventual sojourn to the United States. Subtle references to Tim's future are registered in the published fragment, as when Doctor Eustace Baggeley, a superstitious landlord well-versed in Irish ways who admires American wealth, is ambitious, and is enterprising, recalls Kennedy's name to Tim—"And do you remember President Kennedy?"—to remind him of the good an Irish immigrant-turned-American has done for Ireland (O'Brien 50). Tim will be the eventual hero for Ireland (and America) when in his speech to American congressmen he succeeds in banning the sago plant (29 Oct 1964). That Baggeley is the character to mention Kennedy by name in the novel seems significant in that he also represents an Irishman influenced by American culture. Baggeley is convinced that Americans "have a lot of money," and he hopes to profit from that wealth by transforming his castle into a casino to draw in the tourists (O'Brien 43). The American colonization of Ireland by way of the sago plant thus will represent, in the novel as finally envisioned, a triumph of those who forget their Irish roots after emigrating. Doctor Baggeley is a man who is open to Crawford's sago scheme, calling it "a thing that will change radically the history of Ireland and later the whole social tilt of Western Europe" (O'Brien 52). Both Doctor Baggeley and Tim Hartigan represent a change from the status quo similar to that by which Kennedy as a young, attractive Catholic candidate in the 1960 election represented change.

The turn to the Kennedys in *Saga's* plot shows the dominance of the Myles persona in the last years: the journalist who is also sharply aware of injustice, ready to point out contradictions, fundamentally angry in many ways at political actions yet insistent on approaching these with a playfulness and a satirical edge rather than just denouncing them. As Myles, O'Nolan would have much to say about the Kennedy clan. His *Cruiskeen Lawn* columns that appeared in *The Irish Times* in 1946 show Myles denouncing Ireland's decision to remain neutral because its civil services such as bus transportation are not as efficient—in fact, chronically tardy—as Córas Iompair Eireann (CIE/Irish Transport Systems) wants to project, which they attempt to do through the use of a modern logo and twenty-five new "checkers."[5] As early as the column dated 27 Oct 1941, Myles was using the American relationship with Ireland as fodder for his critique of Irish concerns. Irish-American greetings on St. Patrick's Day, or "the sea-divided Gael," in "those beshamrocked magazines that appear in America" figure into his biting joke against *The Irish Times* editor R. M. Smyllie (na gCopaleen 27 Oct 1941). America was not the only country Myles undercut in his playful yet biting manner—he also used Great Britain as the starting point for some of his columns. Twenty years later he attacks the British Broadcasting Corporation on 21 April 1961 for various odd inaccuracies: BBC had broadcast, "Adrian was introduced to the name of Oscar Wilde," but Myles points out that one has to be introduced to someone by another individual (na gCopaleen 21 Apr 1961).

O'Nolan pitched the idea for *Saga* a year and eleven days from 22 November 1963, the day of Kennedy's assassination. The perceived role that Dallas police officers played in JFK's assassination was particularly appalling to O'Nolan who believed they should have protected JFK better, as he notes in an angry letter dated three days after JFK's assassination:

> You may well mention the Texas police, and Dallas. That transaction gave a new dimension to Kennedy's courage, for few of us here suspected that apes were so numerous in the U. S. citizenry. There was some sour consolation in having the police and some presidential guards shown up for the awful nincompoops they are. Think of the thousands of films (and books and pulp mags.) which showed them all as invincible supermen. (27 Nov 1963)

The Dallas police officers seem mired in the Catholic versus Protestant antagonisms also present in Ireland. What is noteworthy is the bragging confidence that appears in O'Nolan's own correspondence, a tone that is reproduced in his character Ned's letters to Tim. O'Nolan's correspondent O'Keeffe shows his disdain for Texas police by calling on the only force more violent than Texas Rangers, "your old friends," The Censorship Board, adding "They would have done a better job than those fat bastard Texas police" in protecting JFK (2 Dec 1963). It is the wealthy oil and corrupt politics in Ned Hoolihan and Texas and the Kennedy story in Tim Hartigan that are the themes in *Saga* underscored in O'Nolan's correspondence. They together warn against too much American influence or, at least, influence that leads one to forget where one originally comes from.

Why, then, are these pages from an unfinished novel significant? The sago and potato plot shows that O'Nolan's humor is as ferocious as ever, and undoubtedly complicated: it hits America's influence with its efficient planning and its corporate mindset and its readiness to colonize (all echoing British efforts), but it also is unnervingly close to the nineteenth-century potato dependency and its terrible outcome, thus warning the Irish in the most uncomfortable way imaginable. It is also interesting because O'Nolan was struggling in his later years with characters that he did not imagine earlier, notably women whom he saw often as viragos, as monsters, but whose strengths he found also curious, even interesting. No one wants to mitigate O'Nolan's misogyny, which is a component in his writing that seems to hold back his genius, but he seems able to note the world is changing in some way. Also, O'Nolan's letters and his ambitious outline reveal him to be a shrewd but sometimes inept promoter of his work, wanting to conquer new worlds, hoping for a major breakthrough. Ambitions surround this last work, and they include dreaming of American success such as the Presidency even while admiring its flexibility, its accommodations to the immigrant. Yet it seems also muddled in his mind—he pushed hard for this novel but was never quite galvanized by his theme. Perhaps he was old and tired, perhaps overwhelmed, yet there are glimpses of the old O'Brien and the Mylesian humor in many passages, and the anti-American warning is handled by a striking and dissonant manner, in the potato being reincarnated by the sago plot, by oil being the way to make money in Texas and America, and by the references in his correspondence to the Kennedy family.

NOTES

1   Hereafter all references to correspondence will be identified by the letter's date in the text and are located in the Brian O'Nolan Manuscript Collection (Carbondale, IL).

2   O'Nolan additionally may be saluting eighteenth-century Irish author Jonathan Swift, whose pseudo-rational and pseudo-scientific discourse in his *Modest Proposal* and *Gulliver's Travels* is similar to O'Nolan's tedious, lengthy extracts in *Saga*.

3   See my "O'Dea's Yer Man: Myles, Modernity, and Irish National Television" in *Is It about a Bicycle?: Flann O'Brien in the Twenty-first Century*, edited by Jennika Baines. (Dublin: Four Courts, 2011).

4   Some plot details in the proposal evidently were revised since they change in the written manuscript. The title changed from "Slattery's Sago Saga" to "MacPherson's Sago Saga" to "Sarsfield's Sago Saga" in the correspondence. Tim Hartigan was originally "Tim Clery." Also, it is unlikely that Hartigan could become President, given his orphaned Irish birth in the published portion, but Sarsfield Slattery who could be the likely candidate, since he was orphaned in Chicago, adopted by the Doctor, and brought back to live in Ireland. O'Nolan confuses Hartigan and Sarsfield in the narrative, describing Sarsfield as "another orphan *and* born in Chicago" but obscuring whether Sarsfield and Hartigan were both born in Chicago or whether only Sarsfield was born in America (27 emphasis mine).

5   This series of four columns centers on CIE's "flying snail" logo that the company adopted in 1941 as Myles reworks it to feature different visual designs (na gCopaleen 16, 18, 19, 20 Mar 1946). The series critiques different aspects of bus transportation, be they the logo, merchandizing efforts to promote a modern and efficient image, additions of new checkers despite chronic tardiness, or statements that had "the company's urban policy in 1936" been "directed to having trams rather than buses—there would have been no transport during the late war!" (na gCopaleen 19 Mar 1946).

WORKS CITED

Asbee, Sue. *Flann O'Brien*. Boston: Twayne Publishers, 1991.

Bartlett, John S., M. D. *Maize, or Indian Corn: Its Advantages as a Cheap and Nutritious Article of Food, With Directions for Its Use*. London: Wiley & Putnam, 1846.

Brian O'Nolan Manuscript Collection. Special Collections and Research Center. Morris Library. Southern Illinois University Carbondale. Carbondale, Illinois.

Clissman, Anne. *Flann O'Brien: A Critical Introduction*. Dublin: Gill & MacMillan, 1975.

Cronin, Anthony. *No Laughing Matter: The Life and Times of Flann O'Brien*, 1989. New York: Fromm International Publishing Corporation, 1998.

Kinealy, Christine. *This Great Calamity: The Irish Famine 1845–1852*. Dublin: Gill & Macmillan, 1994.

na Gopaleen, Myles. "Cruiskeen Lawn." *The Irish Times Archive, 4 Oct 1940–1 Apr 1966. Proquest Historical Newspapers The Irish Times, 1859–2007.* Accessed 13 Jan–6 Jun 2009.

O'Brien, Flann. "Slattery's Sago Saga, or From Under the Ground to the Top of the Trees." *Stories and Plays.* Intro. Claud Cockburn. London: Hart-Davis, MacGibbon, 1973. 23–79.

Taaffe, Carol. *Ireland Through the Looking Glass: Flann O'Brien, Myles na gCopaleen and Irish Cultural Debate.* Cork: Cork Univ. Press, 2008.

A FLANN O'BRIEN CHECKLIST

WORKS BY FLANN O'BRIEN / MYLES NA [GCOPALEEN] GOPALEEN / BRIAN [O']NOLAN [Ó NUALLÁIN]:

O'Brien, Flann. *At Swim-Two-Birds*. 1939; London: Penguin, 1980; Normal, IL: Dalkey Archive Press, 1998.

—. *At War*. Ed. John Wyse Jackson. Normal, IL: Dalkey Archive Press, 2003.

—. *An Béal Bocht*. 1941. Trans. Patrick C. Power. *The Poor Mouth*. 1973; London: Grafton, 1986; Normal, IL: Dalkey Archive Press, 1996.

—. *The Dalkey Archive*. 1964; London: Picador, 1976; Normal, IL: Dalkey Archive Press, 1993.

—. *The Hard Life*. 1961; London: Grafton, 1986; Normal, IL: Dalkey Archive Press, 1994.

—. *Rhapsody in Stephen's Green: The Insect Play*. Ed. Robert Tracy. Dublin: Lilliput Press, 1994.

—. *Stories and Plays*. Ed. Claud Cockburn. 1973; London: Grafton, 1986.

—. *The Third Policeman*. 1967; London: Grafton, 1986; Normal, IL: Dalkey Archive Press, 1999.

na gCopaleen, Myles. *Flann O'Brien at War*. Ed. John Wyse Jackson. London: Duckworth, 1999.

na Gopaleen, Myles. *The Best of Myles*. 1968. Ed. Kevin O'Nolan. London: Grafton, 1989; Normal, IL: Dalkey Archive Press, 1999.

—. "Cruiskeen Lawn." *Irish Times*. 4 October 1940–1 April 1966.

—. *Further Cuttings from Cruiskeen Lawn*. Ed. Kevin O'Nolan. London: Hart-Davis MacGibbon, 1976; Normal, IL: Dalkey Archive Press, 2000.

—. *The Hair of the Dogma: A Further Selection from "Cruiskeen Lawn."* 1977. Ed. Kevin O'Nolan. London: Grafton, 1987.

—. *Myles Away From Dublin*. 1985. Ed. Martin Green. London: Grafton, 1987.

—. *Myles Before Myles: A Selection of the Earlier Writings of Brian O'Nolan*. Ed. John Wyse Jackson. London: Grafton, 1983.

—. *The Various Lives of Keats and Chapman and The Brother*. 1976. Ed. Benedict Kiely. London: Grafton, 1988.

Ó Nualláin, Brian. *Mairéad Gillan*. Baile Átha Cliath: Oifig an tSoláthair, 1953. [Translation of stage play *Margaret Gillan* by Brinsley MacNamara (first performed at the Abbey Theatre in 1933). London: Allen & Unwin, 1934].

—. "Nádúir-fhilíocht na Gaedhilge" (Irish Nature Poetry) MA thesis, UCD, 1934.

SPECIAL COLLECTIONS:

Brian O'Nolan Manuscript Collection. Special collections Research Center, Morris Library. Southern Illinois University at Carbondale, Illinois.

Flann O'Brien collection. Archives and Manuscripts, John J. Burns Library. Boston College.

Flann O'Brien Manuscripts and criticism, 1934–1989. Harry Ransom Humanities Research Center. University of Texas at Austin.

MISCELLANEOUS:

Barnabas, Brother [Brian O'Nolan]. "Scenes in a Novel." *Comhthrom Féinne* 8.2 (May 1934). Repr. Clissmann, Anne, and David Powell. Eds. *The Journal of Irish Literature* 3.1 (January 1974). Special Flann O'Brien issue. California: Proscenium, 1974: 14–18.

na Gopaleen, Myles. "Baudelaire and Kavanagh." *Envoy* 3.12 (November 1952): 78–81.

—. "De Me." *New Ireland*. (March 1964): 41–42.

—. "Two in One" [short story]. *The Bell* 19.8 (July 1954): 30–34.

Nolan, Brian. "The Martyr's Crown" [short story]. *Envoy* 1.3 (February 1950): 57–62.

O'Brien, Flann. "The Dance Halls." *The Bell* 1.5 (February 1941): 44–52.

—. "Going to the Dogs." *The Bell* 1.1 (October 1940): 19–24.

—. "John Duffy's Brother" [short story]. *Story* 19.90 (July–August, 1941): 65–68.

—. "The Trade in Dublin." *The Bell* 1.2 (November 1940): 6–15.

O'Nolan, Brian. "A Sheaf of Letters." Ed. Robert Hogan and Gordon Henderson. Repr. Clissmann and Powell: 65–103.

BOOKS, JOURNALS AND THESES ABOUT FLANN O'BRIEN / MYLES NA GCOPALEEN / BRIAN O'NOLAN:

Anderson, Samuel. "Pink Paper and the Composition of Flann O'Brien's *At Swim-Two-Birds*." MA Thesis. Louisiana State University, 2002. Accessed 12 April 2011. <http://etd.lsu.edu/docs/available/etd-0830102-090058/unrestricted/Anderson_thesis.pdf>.

Asbee, Sue. *Flann O'Brien*. Twayne's English Authors series. Boston: Twayne, 1991.

Baines, Jennika. Ed. *"Is It About a Bicycle?": Flann O'Brien in the Twenty-First Century*. Dublin: Four Courts Press, 2011.

Bohman-Kalaja, Kimberly. *Reading Games: An Aesthetics of Play in Flann O'Brien, Samuel Beckett, and Georges Perec*. Illinois: Dalkey Archive Press, 2007.

Booker, M. Keith. *Flann O'Brien, Bakhtin, and Menippean Satire*. Syracuse, New York: Syracuse Univ. Press, 1995.

Brooker, Joseph. *Flann O'Brien*. Writers and their Work series. Tavistock: Northcote House, 2005.

Clissmann, Anne. *Flann O'Brien: A Critical Introduction to his Writings*. Dublin: Gill & Macmillan, 1975.

—, and David Powell. Eds. *The Journal of Irish Literature* 3.1 (January 1974). Special Flann O'Brien issue. California: Proscenium, 1974.

Clune [Clissmann], Anne, and Tess Hurson. Eds. *Conjuring Complexities: Essays on Flann O'Brien*. Belfast: Institute of Irish Studies, 1997.

Costello, Peter, and Peter van de Kamp. *Flann O'Brien: An Illustrated Biography*. London: Bloomsbury, 1987.

Cronin, Anthony. *No Laughing Matter: The Life and Times of Flann O'Brien*. London: Grafton, 1989.

Davis, Victoria. "Restating a Parochial Vision: A Reconsideration of Patrick Kavanagh, Flann O'Brien, and Brendan Behan." PhD Dissertation. The University of Texas at Austin, 2005. Accessed 12 April 2011. <http://repositories.lib.utexas.edu/handle/2152/1532>.

Donohue, Keith. *The Irish Anatomist: A Study of Flann O'Brien*. Bethesda, MD: Academica Press, 2002.

Epp, Michael Henry. "Saving *Cruiskeen Lawn*: Satirical Parody in the Novels and Journalism of Flann O'Brien (Myles na gCopaleen)." MA Thesis. McGill University, Toronto, 1999. Accessed 12 April 2011. <http://www.collectionscanada.ca/obj/s4/f2/dsk1/tape9/PQDD_0023/MQ50512.pdf>.

Foster, Thomas C. Ed. *A Casebook on Flann O'Brien's* At Swim-Two-Birds. Illinois: Dalkey Archive Press, 2004. Accessed 12 April 2011. <http://www.dalkeyarchive.com/book/?GCOI=15647100481040>.

Gillespie, Alana. "Brian O'Nolan's Comic and Critical Reconception of Narratives of the Embellished Past in Independent Ireland, 1938–1966." PhD Dissertation.

Utrecht University, 2010. Accessed 12 April 2011. <http://igitur-archive.library
.uu.nl/dissertations/2010-1022-200216/UUindex.html>.

Imhof, Rüdiger. Ed. *Alive-Alive O!: Flann O'Brien's* At Swim-Two-Birds. Dublin: Wolfhound, 1985.

Jones, Stephen. Ed. *A Flann O'Brien Reader*. New York: Viking Press, 1978.

O'Keeffe, Timothy. Ed. Myles: *Portraits of Brian O'Nolan*. London: Martin Brian &
O'Keeffe, 1973.

Ó Nualláin, Ciarán. *The Early Years of Brian O'Nolan / Flann O'Brien / Myles na gCopaleen.* Trans. from the Irish by Róisín Ní Nualláin. Ed. Niall O'Nolan. Dublin: Lilliput Press, 1998.

Robin, Thierry. *Flann O'Brien: Un Voyageur au bout du langage.* Rennes, France: PU
de Rennes, 2008.

Shea, Thomas F. *Flann O'Brien's Exorbitant Novels.* Lewisburg: Bucknell Univ. Press,
1992; London: Associated University Presses, 1992.

Taaffe, Carol. *Ireland Through the Looking Glass: Flann O'Brien, Myles na gCopaleen
and Irish Cultural Debate.* Cork: Cork Univ. Press, 2008.

Thibodeau, Clay. "Treating the Literary Literally: The Reflexive Structure of
Flann O'Brien's *At Swim-Two-Birds.*" MA Thesis. University of Saskatchewan,
2003. Accessed 12 April 2011. <http://library2.usask.ca/theses/available/
etd-09082003-131223/unrestricted/Thibodeau.pdf>.

Wäppling, Eva. "Four Irish Legendary Figures in *At Swim-Two-Birds*: Flann O'Brien's
Use of Finn, Suibhne, the Pooka and the Good Fairy." Diss. Uppsala University, 1984.

Yurkoski, Chris. "Self-evident Shams: Metafiction and Comedy in Three of Flann
O'Brien's Novels." MA Thesis. University of Western Ontario, 1998. Accessed 12
April 2011. <http://www.collectionscanada.ca/obj/s4/f2/dsk2/tape15/PQDD_0010/
MQ33473.pdf>.

BOOK CHAPTERS AND JOURNAL ARTICLES ABOUT FLANN O'BRIEN / MYLES NA GCO-
PALEEN / BRIAN O'NOLAN:

Anspaugh, Kelly. "Flann O'Brien: Postmodern Judas." *Notes on Modern Irish Literature*
4 (1992): 11–16.

Baines, Jennika. "A Rock and a Hard Place: Sweeny as Sisyphus and Job in Flann
O'Brien's *At Swim-Two-Birds.*" Ed. Edwina Keown and Carol Taaffe. *Irish Mod-*

ernism: Origins, Contexts, Publics. Oxford & New York, NY: Peter Lang, 2010. 145–58.

Benstock, Bernard. "The Three Faces of Brian O'Nolan." *Éire-Ireland* 3.3 (Autumn 1968): 51–65.

Bobotis, Andrea. "Queering Knowledge in Flann O'Brien's *The Third Policeman*." *Irish University Review* 32.2 (Autumn/Winter 2002): 242–58.

Booker, M. Keith. "The Bicycle and Descartes: Epistemology in the Fiction of Beckett and O'Brien." *Éire-Ireland* 26.1 (Spring 1991): 76–94.

—. "Science, Philosophy, and *The Third Policeman*: Flann O'Brien and the Epistemology of Futility." *South Atlantic Review* 56. 4 (November 1991): 37–56.

—. "*The Dalkey Archive*: Flann O'Brien's Critique of Mastery." *Irish University Review* Vol. 23, No. 2 (Autumn–Winter, 1993): 269–285.

Borges, Jorges Luis. "When Fiction Lives in Fiction" (1939) [review of *At Swim-Two-Birds*]. *The Total Library: Non-Fiction: 1922–1986*. Ed. Eliot Weinberger. Trans. Esther Allen, Suzanne Jill Levine, and Eliot Weinberger. London: Allen Lane/Penguin Press, 1999. 160–62.

Breuer, Rolf. "Flann O'Brien and Samuel Beckett." *Irish University Review* 37.2 (Autumn/Winter 2007): 340–51.

Brooker, Joseph. "Estopped By Grand Playsaunce: Flann O'Brien's Post-Colonial Lore." *Journal of Law and Society*, 31: 1 (March 2004), 15–37.

—. "Mind That Crowd : Flann O'Brien's Authors." *Authorship in Context: From the Theoretical to the Material*. Ed. Kyriaki Hadjiafxendi and Polina Mackay. Basingstoke: Palgrave, 2007: 91–110.

—. "Irish Mimes: Flann O'Brien." *The Blackwell Companion to Irish Literature, Volume Two: The Twentieth Century*. Ed. Julia M. Wright. Oxford: Wiley-Blackwell, 2010: 176–191.

—. "Flann O'Brien." *Oxford Encyclopedia of British Literature*. Oxford and New York: Oxford Univ. Press, 2006.

Brown, Terence. "Post-modernists: Samuel Beckett and Flann O'Brien." *The Literature of Ireland: Criticism and Culture*. Cambridge: Cambridge Univ. Press, 2010. 104–121.

Browne, Joseph. "Flann O'Brien: *Post* Joyce or *Propter* Joyce?." *Éire-Ireland* 19.4 (Winter 1984): 148–57.

Burgess, Anthony. "Flann O'Brien: A Note." *Études Irlandaises* 7 (December 1982): 83–86.

Chace, William M. "Joyce and Flann O'Brien." *Éire-Ireland* 22.4 (Winter 1987): 140–52.

Clissmann, Anne. "Brian alias Myles alias Flann." *The Word* (September 1977): 11–13.

Clune, Anne. "Flann O'Brien: Twenty Years On." *The Linen Hall Review* Vol. 3, No. 2 (Summer 1986): 4–7.

Cohen, David. "An Atomy of the Novel: Flann O'Brien's *At Swim-Two-Birds.*" *Twentieth Century Literature* 39.2 (Summer 1993): 208–29.

—. "James Joyce and the Decline of Flann O'Brien." *Éire-Ireland* 22.2 (Summer 1987): 153–60.

Comer, Todd A. "A Mortal Agency: Flann O'Brien's *At Swim-Two- Birds.*" *Journal of Modern Literature* 31.2 (Winter 2008): 104–114.

Conte, Joseph M. "Metaphor and Metonymy in Flann O'Brien's *At Swim-Two-Birds.*" *Review of Contemporary Fiction* 5.1 (1985): 128–34.

Cooper, Stanford Lee. "Eire's Columnist: An Interview with Brian O'Nolan." *Time Magazine* (23 August 1943): 90–92.

Costello, Peter. "Mylesian Mysteries." *Sunday Independent* (6 December 1987).

Coulouma, Flore. "Transgressive and Subversive: Flann O'Brien's Tales of the In-Between." Ed. Ciaran Ross. *Sub-Versions: Trans-National Readings of Modern Irish Literature.* Amsterdam, Netherlands: Rodopi, 2010. 65–85.

Cronin, Anthony. Chapter 6 [on Brian O'Nolan]. *Dead as Doornails.* Oxford and New York: Oxford Univ. Press, 1986.

Curran, Steve. "'No, This is not from *The Bell*': Brian O'Nolan's 1943 *Cruiskeen Lawn* Anthology." *Éire-Ireland* 32.2–3 (Summer–Autumn 1997): 79–92.

Davison, Neil R. "'We are not a doctor for the body': Catholicism, the Female Grotesque, and Flann O'Brien's *The Hard Life.*" *Literature and Psychology: A Journal of Psychoanalytic and Cultural Criticism* 45.4 (1999): 31–57.

Devlin, Joseph. "The Politics of Comedy in *At Swim-Two-Birds.*" *Éire-Ireland* 27.4 (Winter 1992): 91–105.

Dewsnap, Terence. "Flann O'Brien and the Politics of Buffoonery." *Canadian Journal of Irish Studies* 19.1 (July 1993): 22–36.

Dobbins, Gregory. "Constitutional Laziness and the Novel: Idleness, Irish Modernism, and Flann O'Brien's *At Swim-Two-Birds.*" *Novel: A Forum on Fiction* 42.1 (2009): 86–108.

Doherty, Francis. "Flann O'Brien's Existentialist Hell." *Canadian Journal of Irish Studies* 15.2 (December 1989): 51–67.

Donovan, Stewart. "Finn in Shabby Digs: Myth and the Reductionist Process in *At Swim-Two-Birds*. *Antigonish Review* 89 (1992): 147–53.

Downum, Denell. "Citation and Spectrality in Flann O'Brien's *At Swim-Two-Birds*." *Irish University Review* 36.2 (Autumn/Winter 2006): 304–20.

Dotterer, Ronald. L. "Flann O'Brien, James Joyce, and *The Dalkey Archive*," New Hibernia Review 8.2 (Summer 2004): 54–63.

Esty, Joshua. "Flann O'Brien's *At Swim-Two-Birds* and the Post-Post Debate." *ARIEL: A Review of International English Literature* 26.4 (October 1995): 23–46.

Evans, Eibhlin. "'A Lacuna in the Palimpsest': A Reading of Flann O'Brien's *At Swim-Two-Birds*." *Critical Survey* 15.1 (January 2003): 91–107.

Fackler, Herbert V. "Flann O'Brien's *The Third Policeman*: Banjaxing Natural Order," *The South Central Bulletin* 38.4 (Winter, 1978): 142–45.

Gallagher, Monique. "Flann O'Brien: Myles from Dublin." *The Princess Grace Library Lectures*, 7. Gerrards Cross: Colin Smythe, 1991. 7–24.

—. "Flann O'Brien: jeu et double-jeu." *Cycnos* 10.2 (1993): 75–84.

—. "*The Poor Mouth*: Flann O'Brien and the Gaeltacht." *Studies: An Irish Quarterly Review* Vol. 72, No. 287 (Autumn, 1983): 231–241.

—. "Reflecting Mirrors in Flann O'Brien's *At Swim-Two-Birds*." *Journal of Narrative Technique* 22.2 (Spring 1992): 128–35.

Giebus, Jay. "Flann O'Brien's *At Swim-Two-Birds*." *Studies: An Irish Quarterly Review* Vol. 80, No. 317 (Spring, 1991): 65–76.

Harriman, Lucas. "Flann O'Brien's Creative Betrayal of Joyce." *New Hibernia Review* 14:4 (Winter 2010): 90–109.

Hassett, Joseph M. "Flann O'Brien and the Idea of the City." *The Irish Writer and the City*. Ed. Maurice Harmon. New Jersey: Barnes and Noble; Gerrards Cross: Colin Smythe, 1984. 115–24.

Henry, P. L. "The Structure of Flann O'Brien's *At Swim-Two-Birds*." *Irish University Review* 20.1 (1990): 35–40.

Higgins, Aidan. "The Faceless Creator." *The Journal of the American Irish Historical Society* 8.1 (Spring 1995): 30–35.

—. "The Hidden Narrator," *Asylum Arts Review* 1.1 (Autumn 1995): 2–7.

Hogan, Thomas. "Myles na gCopaleen." *The Bell* 13.2 (November 1946): 129–40.

Hopper, Keith. "The balm and the bane of the intelligentsia" [review of *"Is It About a Bicycle?": Flann O'Brien in the Twenty-First Century*, edited by Jennika Baines (Four Courts Press, 2011)], *Irish Times* (26 March 2011), Weekend Review section: 11.

—. "The Dismemberment of Orpheus: Flann O'Brien and the Censorship Code." *Barcelona English Language and Literature Studies* (Proceedings of 1999 IASIL Conference), no. 11 (2000): 119–131. Revised and expanded version in *Literature and Ethics: Questions of Responsibility in Literary Studies*. Eds. Neil Murphy, Brendan Quigley and Tamara Wagner. New York: Cambria Press, 2009. 221–41.

—. "Delighted and Daunted: Reading and Re-reading Flann O'Brien's *The Third Policeman*." *Printed Project 12: Virtual Fictional* (July 2010): 78–87.

Huber, Werner. "Flann O'Brien and the Language of the Grotesque." *Anglo- Irish and Irish Literature: Aspects of Language and Culture*. Eds. Birgit Bramsback & Martin Croghan. Uppsala: Uppsala University, 1988. 123–30.

Hughes, Eamonn. "Flann O'Brien's *At Swim-Two-Birds* in the age of mechanical reproduction." *Irish Modernism: Origins, Contexts, Publics*. Ed. Edwina Keown and Carol Taaffe. Oxford & New York, NY: Peter Lang, 2010. 111–28.

Hunt, Roy L. "Hell Goes Round and Round: Flann O'Brien." *Canadian Journal of Irish Studies* 14.2 (January 1989): 60–73.

Imhof, Rüdiger. "Chinese Box: Flann O'Brien in the Metafiction of Alasdair Gray, John Fowles and Robert Coover." *Éire-Ireland* 25.1 (Spring 1990): 64–79.

—. "Cronin's Miles Inglorious" [review of *No Laughing Matter: The Life and Times of Flann O'Brien* by Anthony Cronin]. *Irish Times* (11 November 1989).

—. "Flann O'Brien: A Checklist." *Etudes Irlandaises* 4 (1979): 125–48.

Ingersoll, Earl G. "Irish Jokes: A Lacanian Reading of Short Stories by James Joyce, Flann O'Brien, and Bryan MacMahon." *Studies in Short Fiction* 27.2 (Spring 1990): 237–45.

Jacek, Eva. "The Conundrum of Clichés: Flann O'Brien's "The Catechism of Cliché" and Jonathan Swift's *A Complete Collection of Genteel and Ingenious Conversation (Polite Conversation)*." *Canadian Journal of Irish Studies* 25.1–2 (July–December 1999): 497–509.

—. "Schemers and Squanderers: Jonathan Swift's *A Modest Proposal* and Flann O'Brien's *Slattery's Sago Saga*." *New Hibernia Review* Vol. 2, No. 2 (Summer, 1998): 100–115.

Jacquin, Danielle. "Never Apply Your Front Breaks First, or Flann O'Brien and the Theme of the Fall." *The Irish Novel in Our Time.* Ed. Patrick Rafroidi and Maurice Harmon. Lille: Publications de l'Université de Lille III, 1976. 187–97.

Janik, Del Ivan. "Flann O'Brien: The Novelist as Critic." *Éire-Ireland* 4.4 (Winter 1969): 64–72.

Johnston, Denis. "Myles na Gopaleen." *Myth and Reality in Irish Literature.* Ed. Joseph Ronsley. Ontario: Wilfred Laurier Univ. Press, 1977. 297–304.

Kemnitz, Charles. "Beyond the Zone of Middle Dimensions: A Relativistic Reading of *The Third Policeman.*" *Irish University Review* 15.1 (Spring 1985): 56–72.

Kennedy, Conan. *Looking for De Selby* (Killala, Mayo: Morrigan, 1998). 31 pp.

Kennedy, Maurice. "*At Swim-Two-Birds.*" *Irish Times* (5 November 1962).

Kennedy, Sighle. "The Devil and Holy Water: Samuel Beckett's *Murphy* and Flann O'Brien's *At Swim-Two-Birds.*" *Modern Irish Literature.* Eds. Raymond A. Porter and James D. Brophy. New York: Iona College Press, 1972. 251–60.

Kenner, Hugh. "The Mocker." *A Colder Eye: The Modern Irish Writers.* New York: Alfred A. Knopf, 1983. 253–61.

Kiberd, Declan. "Flann O'Brien, Myles, and The Poor Mouth." *Inventing Ireland: The Literature of the Modern Nation.* London: Vintage, 1996. 497–512.

Kiely, Benedict. "Bells are Ringing for a Work of High Genius." *Irish Press* (11 November 1961).

—. "Fun After Death." *New York Times Book Review* (12 November 1967).

—. "Rare Roads to Hell." *Irish Times* (2 September 1967).

Kilroy, Thomas. "Tellers of Tales." *Times Literary Supplement* (17 March 1972): 301–02.

—. "The Year in Review." *Irish University Review* 5.1 (Spring 1968): 112–17.

Lanters, José. "Fiction within Fiction: The Role of the Author in Flann O'Brien's *At Swim-Two-Birds* and *The Third Policeman.*" *Dutch Quarterly Review of Anglo-American Letters* 13 (1983): 267–81.

—. "Flann O'Brien (1911–1966)." *Unauthorised Versions: Irish Menippean Satire, 1919–1952.* Washington D.C.: Catholic Univ. of America Press, 2000. 173–234.

—. "'Still Life' Versus Real Life: The English Writings of Brian O'Nolan." *Explorations in the Field of Nonsense.* Ed. Wim Tigges. Amsterdam: Rodopi, 1987. 161–81.

Lee, L.L. "The Dublin Cowboys of Flann O'Brien." *Western American Literature* 4.3 (Fall 1969): 219–25.

MacMahon, Barbara. "The Effects of Word Substitution in Slips of the Tongue: *Finnegans Wake* and *The Third Policeman.*" *English Studies* 82.3 (2001): 231–46.

MacPiarais, Micheál. "Postmodern and Postcolonial Tensions in Flann O'Brien's *At Swim-Two-Birds.*" *New Voices in Irish Literary Criticism: Ireland in Theory.* Eds. Cathy McGlynn & Paula Murphy. New York: Edwin Mellen Press, 2007. 55–68.

Martin, Augustine. "Worlds Within Worlds." *Irish Press* (23 September 1967).

Maslen, R.W. "Flann O'Brien's Bombshells: *At Swim-Two-Birds* and *The Third Policeman.*" *New Hibernia Review* Vol 10, No. 4, (Winter 2006): 84–10

Mathewes, Jeffrey. "The Manichaean Body in The Third Policeman: or Why Joe's Skin Is Scaly." *The Scriptorium: Flann O'Brien.* Accessed 21 January 2008. <http://www.themodernword.com/scriptorium/obrien_mathewes.pdf>.

Mays, J.C.C. "Brian O'Nolan and Joyce on Art and Life." *James Joyce Quarterly* 11.3 (Spring 1974): 238–56.

—. "Flann O'Brien, Beckett and the Undecidable Text of *Ulysses.*" *Irish University Review* Vol. 22, No. 1, Serving the Word: Essays and Poems in Honour of Maurice Harmon (Spring–Summer, 1992): 127–134.

Mazullo, Concetta. "Flann O'Brien's Hellish Otherworld: From *Buile Suibhne* to *The Third Policeman.*" *Irish University Review* 25.2 (Autumn/Winter 1995): 318–27.

McGuire, Jerry L. "Teasing after Death: Metatextuality in *The Third Policeman.*" *Éire-Ireland* 16.2 (Summer 1981): 107–21.

McKibben, Sarah E. "*An Béal Bocht*: Mouthing Off at National Identity." *Éire-Ireland* 38.1–2 (Spring–Summer 2003): 37–53.

—. "The Poor Mouth: A Parody of (Post)Colonial Irish Manhood." *Research in African Literatures* 34.4 (Winter 2003): 96–114.

McLoughlin, Michael. "At Swim Six Characters or Two Birds in Search of an Author: Fiction, Metafiction and Reality in Pirandello and Flann O'Brien." *Yearbook of the Society for Pirandello Studies* 12 (1992): 24–31.

McMullen, Kim. "Culture as Colloquy: Flann O'Brien's Postmodern Dialogue with Irish Tradition," *NOVEL: A Forum on Fiction* 27.1 (Autumn 1993): 62–84.

McWilliams, Brendan. "Winds of a Different Hue." *Irish Times* (11 December 1992).

Mellamphy, Ninian. "Aestho-autogamy and the Anarchy of Imagination: Flann O'Brien's Theory of Fiction in *At Swim-Two-Birds. Canadian Journal of Irish Studies* 4.1 (June 1978): 8–25.

Mercier, Vivian. "*At Swim-Two-Birds.*" *Commonweal* 54.3 (27 April 1951): 68–69.

Merritt, Henry. "Games, Ending and Dying in Flann O'Brien's *At Swim-Two-Birds.*" *Irish University Review* 25 (Autumn/Winter 1995): 308–17.

Mihálycsa, Erika. "Hybridity and Parody in *Ulysses* and Flann O'Brien's *At Swim-Two-Birds.*" *Philologia* 3 (2007): 169–180.

Montgomery, Niall. "An Aristrophanic Sorcerer." *Irish Times* (2 April 1966).

Montresor, Jaye Berman. "Gilbert Sorrentino: At Swim in the Wake of His Gene Pool." *Modern Language Studies* 23.2 (Spring 1993): 4–12.

Murfi, Mikel. Dir. *John Duffy's Brother.* Ireland: Park Films, 2006. 14 mins.

Murphy, Neil. "Flann O'Brien." *The Review of Contemporary Fiction* 25.3 (Fall 2005): 7–41.

—. "Ambiguity, Dissent, and Anxiety: Anti-Realism in the 20th Century Irish Short Story." *Eureka Studies in Teaching Short Fiction.* 9:2: 10–26.

O'Brien, Kate. "Fiction" [includes review of *At Swim-Two-Birds*]. *Spectator* (14 April 1939): 646.

Ó Conaire, Breandán. "Flann O'Brien, *An Béal Bocht* and Other Irish Matters." *Irish University Review* 3.2 (Autumn, 1973): 121–40.

O'Donoghue, Bernard. "Humour and Verbal Logic." *Critical Quarterly* 24.1 (Spring 1982): 33–40.

O'Grady, Thomas B. "*At Swim-Two-Birds* and the Bardic Schools." *Éire-Ireland* 24.3 (Autumn 1989): 65–77.

Ó Háinle, Cathal G. "Fionn and Suibhne in *At Swim-Two-Birds.*" *Hermathena* 142 (1987): 13–49.

O'Hara, Patricia. "Finn MacCool and the Bard's Lament in Flann O'Brien's *At Swim-Two-Birds.*" *Journal of Irish Literature* 15.1 (January 1986): 55–61.

O'Hehir, Brendan P. "Flann O'Brien and the Big World." *Literary Interrelations: Ireland, England and the World.* Studies in English and Comparative Literature, vol. 3: National Images and Stereotypes. Ed. Wolfgang Zach and Heinz Kosok, Tübingen: Gunter Narr Verlag, 1987). 207–16.

Orvell, Miles. "Entirely Fictitious: The Fiction of Flann O'Brien." *Alive-Alive O!: Flann O'Brien's* At Swim-Two-Birds. Ed. Rüdiger Imhof. Dublin: Wolfhound, 1985. 101–06.

—, and David Powell. "Myles na Gopaleen: Mystic, Horse-Doctor, Hackney Journalist and Ideological Catalyst." *Éire-Ireland* 10.2 (Summer 1975): 44–72.

O'Toole, Mary A. "The Theory of Serialism in *The Third Policeman*." *Irish University Review* 18.2 (Autumn 1988): 215–25.

Otoiu, Adrian, "From At Swim-*Two-Birds* to La Doi *Lebădoi*: Translating Flann O'Brien into Romanian." *Internationalist Review of Irish Culture* (Spring 2007): 63–83.

Palm, Kurt. Dir. In Schwimmen-Zwei-Vögel [At Swim-Two-Birds]. Austria: Fischer. Film, 1997. 93 mins.

Pinsker, Sanford. "Flann O'Brien's Uncles and Orphans." *Éire-Ireland* 20.2 (Summer 1985): 133–38.

Powell, David. "An Annotated Bibliography of Myles na gCopaleen's 'Cruiskeen Lawn' Commentaries on James Joyce." *James Joyce Quarterly* 9.1 (Fall 1971): 50–62.

Power, Mary. "Flann O'Brien and Classical Satire: An Exegesis of *The Hard Life*." *Éire-Ireland* 13.1 (Spring 1978): 87–102.

Quintelli-Neary, Marguerite. "Flann O'Brien: *At Swim-Two-Birds*, *The Third Policeman*—Temporal and Spatial Incongruities." *Folklore and the Fantastic in Twelve Modern Irish Novels*. Westport, CT: Greenwood, 1997. 83–97.

Riggs, Pádraigín, and Norman Vance. "Irish Prose Fiction" [includes section on Flann O'Brien]. *The Cambridge Companion to Modern Irish Culture*. Ed. Joe Cleary and Claire Connolly. Cambridge: Cambridge Univ. Press, 2005. 245–66.

Roberts, Ruth. "*At Swim-Two-Birds* as Self-evident Sham." *Éire-Ireland* 6.2 (Summer 1971): 76–97.

Sage, Lorna. "Flann O'Brien." *Two Decades of Irish Writing: A Critical Survey*. Ed. Douglas Dunn. Pennsylvania: Dufour, 1975. 197–206.

Shea, Thomas F. "Flann O'Brien and John Keats: "John Duffy's Brother" and Train Allusions." *Éire-Ireland* 24.2 (Summer 1989): 109–20.

—. "Patrick McGinley's Impressions of Flann O'Brien: *The Devil's Diary* and *At Swim-Two-Birds*." *Twentieth Century Literature* 40.2 (Summer 1994): 272–81.

Sheridan, Niall. "Brian, Flann and Myles." *Irish Times* (2 April 1966).

Silverthorne J. M. "Time, Literature, and Failure: Flann O'Brien's *At Swim-Two-Birds* and *The Third Policeman*." *Éire-Ireland* 11.4 (Winter 1976): 66–83.

Sorrentino, Gilbert. "Reading Flann Brian O'Brien O'Nolan." *Context* 1 (April 2005). Accessed 12 April 2011. <http://www.dalkeyarchive.com/article/show/2>.

Spenser, Andrew. "Many Worlds: The New Physics in Flann O'Brien's *The Third Policeman*." *Éire-Ireland* 30.1 (Spring 1995): 145–58.

Sweeney, Maurice. Dir. *Flann O'Brien: The Lives of Brian* [documentary]. Ireland: RTÉ/ Mint Productions, 2006. 53 mins.

Taaffe, Carol. "The Pathology of Revivalism: An Unpublished Manuscript by Myles na gCopaleen." *Canadian Journal of Irish Studies* 32.2: 27–33.

Throne, Marilyn. "The Provocative Bicycle of Flann O'Brien's *The Third Policeman*." *Éire-Ireland* 21.4 (Winter 1986): 36–44.

Tigges, Wim. "Ireland in Wonderland: Flann O'Brien's *The Third Policeman* as a Nonsense Novel." *The Clash of Ireland: Literary Contrasts and Connections*. Ed. C.C. Barfoot and Theo D'haen. Amsterdam: Rodopi, 1989. 195–208.

Updike, John. "Back Chat, Funny Cracks: The Novels of Flann O'Brien." *New Yorker* (11 and 18 February 2008): 148–52.

Voelker, Joseph C. "'Doublends Jined': The Fiction of Flann O'Brien." *Journal of Irish Literature* 12.1 (January 1983): 87–95.

Wain, John. "To Write for My Own Race: The Fiction of Flann O'Brien." *Encounter* 29 (July 1967): 71–85. Revised and expanded version in John Wain, *A House for the Truth: Critical Essays*. London: Macmillan, 1988. 67–104.

Wall, Mervyn. "A Nightmare of Horror and Humour." *Hibernia* 31.9 (September 1967): 22.

—. "The Man Who Hated Only Cods." *Irish Times* (2 April 1966).

Warner, Alan. "Flann O'Brien." *A Guide to Anglo-Irish Literature*. Dublin: Gill & Macmillan, 1981. 153–65.

White, Michael. "Observations on Flann O'Brien's *At Swim-Two-Birds* in Translation." *Revista Alicantina de Estudios Ingleses* 5 (1992): 155–61.

USEFUL SECONDARY CRITICISM:

Adams, Michael. *Censorship: The Irish Experience*. Dublin: Scepter Books, 1968.

Alter, Robert. *Partial Magic: The Novel as a Self-Conscious Genre*. Berkeley, Los Angeles and London: Univ. of California Press, 1975.

Augustine. *Confessions*. London: Penguin, 1967.

Beckett, Samuel. "Censorship in the Saorstat." *Disjecta: Miscellaneous Writings and a Dramatic Fragment by Samuel Beckett*. Ed. Ruby Cohn. London: John Calder, 1983. 84–88.

Benedict, Julius. *The Lily of Killarney: Opera in Three Acts, Being a Musical Version of the Drama of "The Colleen Bawn."* 1862; Hull: White & Farrell [c.1900].

Benstock, Shari. "At the Margins of Discourse: Footnotes in the Fictional Text." *PMLA* 98.2 (1983): 204–25.

Borges, Jorges Luis. "Time and J.W. Dunne" (1940). *The Total Library: Non-Fiction: 1922–1986*. Ed. Eliot Weinberger. Trans. Esther Allen, Suzanne Jill Levine, and Eliot Weinberger. London: Allen Lane/Penguin Press, 1999. 214–19.

Boucicault, Dion. *The Colleen Bawn; or, The Brides of Garryowen: A Domestic Drama in Three Acts*. 1860; London: Thomas Hailes Lacy, [c.1873].

Brown, Stephen. *Ireland in Fiction: A Guide to Irish Novels, Tales, Romances*. Shannon: Irish Univ. Press, 1969.

Brown, Terence. *Ireland: A Social and Cultural History 1922–1985*. London: Fontana, 1985.

Cabell, James Branch. *The Cream of the Jest*. 1917. New York: The Modern Library, 1927.

Carlson, Julia. *Banned in Ireland: Censorship and the Irish Writer*. London: Routledge, 1991.

Cronin, Anthony. *Heritage Now: Irish Literature in the English Language*. Kerry: Brandon Books, 1982.

Deane, Seamus. *A Short History of Irish Literature*. London: Hutchinson, 1986.

—. Ed. *The Field Day Anthology of Irish Writing*. Derry: Field Day, 1991.

Dunne, J.W. *An Experiment with Time*. 1927. London: Faber, 1934.

—. *Nothing Dies*. London: Faber, 1940.

Dunton, John. *The Athenian Oracle*. London: Andrew Bell, 1703–10.

Genette, Gerard. *Narrative Discourse: An Essay in Method*. Trans. Jane E. Lewin. Ithaca: Cornell Univ. Press, 1980.

Griffin, Gerald. *The Collegians*. 1829; Belfast: Appletree Press, 1992.

Hassan, Ihab. *The Postmodern Turn: Essays in Postmodern Theory and Culture*. Ohio: Ohio State Univ. Press, 1987.

—. *The Dismemberment of Orpheus: Towards a Postmodern Literature*. New York and Oxford: Oxford Univ. Press, 1971.

Hutcheon, Linda. *A Poetics of Postmodernism: History, Theory, Fiction*. London and New York: Routledge, 1988.

—. *The Politics of Postmodernism*. London and New York: Routledge, 1989.

Huxley, Aldous. *Point Counter Point*. 1928. London: Granada, 1978.

Huysmans, J.K. *Against Nature* [*À Rebours*]. 1884. Trans. from the French by Robert Baldrick. London: Penguin, 1959.

Jackson, K.H. *A Celtic Miscellany*. Harmondsworth: Penguin, 1971.

Jeffares, A. Norman. *Anglo-Irish Literature*. Dublin: Macmillan Press, 1982.

Kearney, Richard. *Transitions: Narratives in Modern Irish Culture*. Manchester: Manchester Univ. Press, 1988.

Kenner, Hugh. *Flaubert, Joyce and Beckett: The Stoic Comedians*. London: W.H. Allen, 1964.

Kiberd, Declan. "Irish Literature and Irish History." *The Oxford Illustrated History of Ireland*. Ed. R.F. Foster. Oxford and New York: Oxford Univ. Press, 1989. 275–337.

MacKillop, James. *Fionn Mac Cumhaill: Celtic Myth in English Literature*. Syracuse: Syracuse Univ. Press, 1986.

McHale, Brian. *Post-Modernist Fiction*. New York: Routledge, 1991.

McHugh, Roger, and Maurice Harmon. *A Short History of Anglo-Irish Literature*. Dublin: Wolfhound, 1982.

McMahon, Sean. "The Realist Novel After WWII." *The Genius of Irish Prose*. Ed. Augustine Martin. Dublin: Mercier, 1985.

Mercier, Vivian. *The Irish Comic Tradition*. London: Oxford Univ. Press, 1969.

Murphy, Neil. *Irish Fiction and Postmodern Doubt: An Analysis of the Epistemological Crisis in Modern Irish Fiction*. New York: Edwin Mellen, 2004.

O'Crohan, Tomás. *The Islandman* [*An tOileánach*]. 1937. Trans. from the Irish by Robin Flower. Oxford: Oxford Univ. Press, 1990.

Partridge, A.C. *Language and Society in Anglo-Irish Literature*. New Jersey: Barnes and Noble, 1984.

Rolleston, T.W. *Myths and Legends of the Celtic Race*. 1911. New York: Schocken, 1986.

Ryan, John. *Remembering How We Stood*. Dublin: Lilliput, 1975.

Sterne, Laurence. *The Life and Opinions of Tristram Shandy, Gentleman*. 1759–67; London: McDonald, 1975.

Stewart, Susan. *Nonsense: Aspects of Intertextuality in Folklore and Literature*. Baltimore: John Hopkins UP, 1979.

Swift, Jonathan. *Gulliver's Travels*. 1726. London: Munster Classics, 1968.

Synge, J.M. *The Playboy of the Western World*. 1907. London: Methuen, 1961.

Waugh, Patricia. *Metafiction: The Theory and Practice of Self-Conscious Fiction*. London and New York: Methuen, 1984.

Worton, Michael, and Judith Still. Eds. *Intertextuality: Theories and Practice*. Manchester: Manchester UP, 1991.

CONTRIBUTORS

ANTHONY ADAMS teaches English literature and language at Colby College, Maine. He has written on a variety of literary topics both modern and medieval, and is also a translator and editor of medieval Latin poetry.

JENNIKA BAINES earned her PhD from University College Dublin in 2010. Her thesis was entitled "Flann O'Brien and the Catholic Absurd." She edited the collection *"Is It About a Bicycle?": Flann O'Brien in the 21st Century* (Four Courts, 2011). She is Acquisitions Editor at Syracuse University Press.

JOSEPH BROOKER is Reader in Modern Literature at Birkbeck, University of London. He is the author of *Joyce's Critics: Transitions in Reading and Culture* (Wisconsin University Press, 2004), *Flann O'Brien* (Northcote House, 2005) and *Literature of the 1980s: After the Watershed* (Edinburgh University Press, 2010). He has edited and co-edited special issues of *New Formations* (on the 1990s), the *Journal of Law and Society* (on Law and Literature), and *Textual Practice* (on Martin Amis's novel *Money*).

FLORE COULOUMA is an associate professor in English linguistics at the Université Paris Ouest Nanterre. She wrote her PhD dissertation on the representation of language in the works of Flann O'Brien. Her research interests are pragmatics and linguistics applied to literary analysis, Irish and post-colonial authors, bilingual authors, and diglossia.

CARLOS VILLAR FLOR teaches literature at the University of La Rioja. He is the author of several articles and monographs on 20th century novelists, and has recently completed the critical and annotated editions and translations into Spanish of the Evelyn Waugh trilogy *Sword of Honour*. He is co-editor of *Waugh Without End: New Trends in Evelyn Waugh Studies* (2005), and has published two novels and one collection of short stories.

AIDAN HIGGINS has written short stories, novels, travel pieces, radio plays, and a large body of criticism. His literary reputation rests primarily on the short story collection *Felo De Se* (later re-titled *Asylum and Other Stories*) and the novels *Langrishe Go Down*, *Balcony of Europe*, and *Bornholm Night-Ferry*, and on his trilogy of autobiographies, collectively entitled *A Bestiary*. He has won numerous literary prizes and is frequently considered to be the natural heir of Joyce, O'Brien, and Beckett. His work was recently the subject of a critical collection of essays by Dalkey Archive Press: *Aidan Higgins: The Fragility of Form*.

KEITH HOPPER teaches literature and film studies for Oxford University's Department for Continuing Education. He is the author of *Flann O'Brien: A Portrait of the Artist as a Young Post-modernist* (revised edition 2009), and general editor of the *Ireland into Film* series (2001–7). He is a regular contributor to the *Times Literary Supplement*.

ROBERT LUMSDEN has taught literature at the National University of Singapore and the National Institute of Education in Singapore. He is the author of *Reading Literature after Deconstruction* (Cambria Press, 2009).

NEIL MURPHY has previously taught at the University of Ulster and the American University of Beirut and is currently Associate Professor of contemporary literature at NTU, Singapore. He is the author of *Irish Fiction and Postmodern Doubt* and has edited several essay collections, including *Aidan Higgins: The Fragility of Form*. He has also written numerous articles on Irish writing and contemporary fiction.

AMY NEJEZCHLEB received her doctorate in Irish and British Modernism from Southern Illinois University, Carbondale, in May 2011. She has published an article in *Is It about a Bicycle?: Flann O'Brien in the Twenty-first Century*. She currently resides in southern Illinois where she also teaches.

VAL NOLAN lectures in contemporary literature and creative writing at the National University of Ireland, Galway. Recent publications include "'If It Was Just Th'oul Book . . .': A Brief History of The McGahern Banning Controversy" in *Irish Studies Review* (2011), "The Aesthetics of Space and Time in the Fiction of John Banville and Neil Jordan" in *Nordic Irish Studies* (2010), and a contribution to the "Futures" page of the science journal *Nature* (2010). He is a regular literary critic for the *Irish Examiner* and is currently completing a volume on the work of filmmaker and novelist Neil Jordan.

BRIAN Ó CONCHUBHAIR is Associate Professor in the Department of Irish Language at the University of Notre Dame. His monograph on the intellectual history of the Irish language revival, *Fin de Siècle na Gaeilge: Darwin, An Athbheochan agus Smaointeoireacht na hEorpa* received the 2009 Oireachtas na Gaeilge non-fiction award and the ACIS 2010 award. He has edited *Gearrscéalta Ár Linne* (2006), *WHY IRISH?* (2008), and the four-volume series *Fighting Story 1916–1921* (2009). His critical edition of the *Midnight Court* (Syracuse University Press) appears this September. His current project is a study of Irish-language modernism.

THIERRY ROBIN teaches literature and linguistics at the University of Western Brittany in Brest. He is the author of *Flann O'Brien: Un voyageur au bout du langage* (2008). He co-edited *Political Ideology In Ireland* with Patrick Galliou and Olivier Coquelin (2009). His research mainly focuses on the concepts of reality and representation in history and Irish literature, notably through the works of James Joyce, Samuel Beckett, and John Banville.

MACIEJ RUCZAJ is a PhD student at the Prague's Centre for Irish Studies (Department of Anglophone Literatures and Cultures, Charles University). He is the editor of four selections of contemporary Polish political and social thought in Czech, and the author of several articles dealing with the literary representations of nationalism and Catholicism in Ireland (most recently in *The Politics of Irish Writing*, 2010).

W. MICHELLE WANG is a PhD student in the Department of English at The Ohio State University. She earned her BA (Communications) and MA (English) from Nanyang Technological University, Singapore. Her research interests center on aesthetic theory and the novel, narrative theory, philosophies of art as they relate to literature, and the relationship between literature and the fine arts.

BOOK REVIEWS

Péter Nádas. *Parallel Stories*. Trans. Imre Goldstein. Farrar, Straus and Giroux, 2011. 1152 pp. Cloth: $40.00.

Péter Nádas already enjoys a formidable reputation for *A Book of Memories*, but his extraordinary and staggering *Parallel Stories* places him in a new rank of writers entirely. In describing people and lives in mid-twentieth-century Budapest and Berlin, Nádas operates on the principles of parallelism and chaos in structuring his work; the result is so open-ended in plot and scope that it almost tests readers' mental capacity. Dozens of characters (the most prominent including Gyöngyvér, Döhring, and Kristóf) come, go, and recur in German and Hungarian locales from the 1930s to 1989, connected by the most slender of threads; although several storylines are sustained over larger numbers of chapters, there are no proper beginnings, nor does anything ever quite end. Nothing is treated in a usual manner: the murder that Döhring comes across in the opening pages is almost but not actually solved many chapters later; in a single chapter, Lady Erna experiences both the reality of a cab ride and her memory of nursing her baby simultaneously; and Kristóf's chapters switch from third to first person as he goes from his nighttime sexual activities on Margit Island in Budapest to his daytime journey and meeting with his family. In these disparate places and times, however, the objective author remains a constant, and Nádas is nothing if not a physical writer, from specifying the architecture and history of *Budapesti* buildings to describing genitalia in minute detail during a hundred-page sex scene. The wide canvas, political and historical significance of the novel's events, and thorough attention to both mental and physical states all recall grand nineteenth-century epics. But Péter Nádas's nearly sociological objectivity and gentle refusal to hazard connections and tie up loose strings place him squarely in the contemporary era. Consequently, watching the fine and subtle web of linkages form over the course of reading over one thousand pages of his precise and dense prose is, in a word, breathtaking. [Jeffrey Zuckerman]

Dezső Kosztolányi. *Kornél Esti*. Trans. Bernard Adams. New Directions, 2011. 233 pp. Paper: $16.95.

In this inventive and masterful novel by Dezső Kosztolányi, the reader is treated to a sort of *Thousand and One Nights* of fantastic turn-of-the century Hungary. The first piece in the book frames these tales as episodes in the life of Kornél Esti, the title character, and as joint compositions by the author and Esti together, a collaboration between man and döppelgänger. This opening scenario sets the stage for something special, the book rapidly becoming *by* Kornél Esti as much as it is about him. Esti, of course, exists only in these pages, but he comes alive here as the voice of the author's darker impulses with a dry humor that seems to render Kosztolányi a medium by which Esti's stories are told. These stories vary widely, from the fantastic—an entire town populated only by honest people, a kleptomaniac translator who steals fictional objects from the books he translates, a venerable scholar who can sleep only during lectures—to more commonplace situations. But even in what may be called the commonplace, the author collides with circumstances by turns blackly comic, sinister, hilarious, and bleak: a hopeless widow who cannot hang on even to the living that Esti provides her; a shiftless hero who saved Esti's life but refuses to vacate his apartment; a young man suffering through a sinister first kiss from an insane young girl. Kosztolányi's genius is in his droll presentation. Everything is unbelievable, but neither the author nor the reader ever disbelieves. There is something wonderful in these pages, a European-inflected magic realism that is as old as the fools of Chelm and as contemporary as the work of Michal Ajvaz. As one of Kosztolányi's last works, this book seems full of wry regret at having had but one life to live. [Jeff Waxman]

Steve Weiner. *Sweet England*. New Star Books, 2010. 166 pp. Paper: $19.00.

Unlike Reagan's America, which has been reconstructed into an upbeat theme-park culture-scape redolent with dayspring warmth, Maggie Thatcher's England has darkened into a forbidding nightworld of miasmic unease and emotional drift, of economic alienation and free-floating anxiety blurred into a manageable absurdity only by retreat into alcohol or indifference or pointless rage. For Canadian writer Steve Weiner, love in the time of Thatcher is appropriately desperate and disjointed, a white-noise whir of stochastic event without the politesse of logic. In the beginning of *Sweet England*, an unemployed man whose background, indeed whose name is never certain (we are told only that he is a "mess of wounds") appears, with the thin stability of a conjuration, by a pub in north London. He moves with the inexplicable directness of a dream to an apartment building where he falls (disastrously) in love with Brenda Leigh, a dumpy alcoholic who simply knocks at his door with wonderland imperative (she calls herself his "assignment") and whose death (or perhaps suicide) serves as the central event in Weiner's Escher-esque plot. In a striking visual style that recalls the lacerating imagery of David Lynch, in clipped Beckettian dialogue lashed with non-sequiturs, in a plot suffused with caustic ironies, the two struggle against each other's comfort, a hopeless endeavor that closes appropriately with a hung inquest unable to determine whether Brenda was killed or killed herself. For all the brutal existential absurdities, however, there lingers about Weiner's narrative a persistent spirituality, a haunted sense that this flesh-and-blood masquerade cannot be the endgame it appears to be—religious images recur, characters linger in musty churches, they puzzle out the implications of mortality beyond the cellular holocaust implicit in flesh and blood. They hunger for spiritual investment, and for Weiner that hunger—seductive, even erotic in its ironic intensity—suffices. [Joseph Dewey]

Antonio Ungar. *Tres ataúdes blancos*. Anagrama, 2010. 284 pages. Paper: €18.75.

Winner of the 2010 Herralde Novel Prize, Colombian writer Antonio Ungar's trenchant satirical thriller *Tres ataúdes blancos* (Three White Coffins) is a fresh, disorienting take on the motif of doppelgänger as political impersonator—*The Prince and the Pauper* nightmarishly updated for the decentered twenty-first century. The principal narrator begins as a shiftless souse with an uncanny likeness to one Pedro Akira, leader of the Movimiento Amarillo and sole opposition candidate to Tomás del Pito, diminutive narco-dictator of the hellish tropical republic of Miranda. When Akira is gunned down, the narrator is coerced into a deadly charade of assuming the candidate's identity and carrying on the campaign. Ungar's polyphonic narration masterfully employs a variety of techniques (dreams, radio and TV broadcasts, videotaped sequences, broadsheets, diary entries, blacked-out text), while the anonymous narrator's mordant voice recalls Beckett's *Molloy* and *Watt*. With his love, Ada Neira, and his bodyguard Jairo Calderón, he suffers through a cruel, nightmarish adventure that is by turns hilarious, murderous, and all too benightedly human. His fatalistic account of political tragedy—a possibly posthumous, loose-ended memoir, curiously trapped inside a closed temporal loop—conveys a terrible, visceral sense of enclosure akin to Odysseus in the Cyclops's cave or Arthur Gordon Pym amidships. Capable of subtle lyricism, deep pathos, and macabre realism, the novel spins a web of bravura love, crazy camaraderie, deception, betrayal, hatred, and vengeance, then doubles back to shadow its own episodes and probe its narrative reliability, sorrowfully aware that in Miranda both the executioner's and the narrator's faces are well hidden. *Tres ataúdes blancos* is a political satire that keeps the reader on tenterhooks—laughing in nervous disbelief, cringing in fear—until the last haunted sentence when the telemetric dread is deepened even further by a desire to revisit, replay, and recover control of a story that deftly refuses to give up the ghost or say who, precisely, lies within the three white coffins. [Brendan Riley]

Philippe Jaccottet. *And, Nonetheless: Selected Poetry and Prose 1990–2009*. Trans. John Taylor. Chelsea Editions, 2011. 424 pp. Paper: $20.00.

I had forgotten Philippe Jaccottet was still alive, not because he is old—Jaccottet, born in 1925, is nearing his nineties, but so are many living masters—but because he is so good he is the kind of writer one assumes passed into immortality long ago. Yet this large book is full of very recent work, of the past two decades, all composed after the writer's sixty-fifth birthday. John Taylor, the consummate scholar of contemporary French poetry, translates Jaccottet here, as well as offering a brief and percipient introduction that elucidates how Jaccottet links "style to the frailties and fluctuations and sensibility," which brings him "to the brink of the ineffable." Wandering somewhere between the precision of a Peter Huchel, the spirituality of a St. John Perse, and the linguistic brio of an Edmond Jabès, Jaccottet probes the folds and crevices of experience without seeking either palpable reality or numinous revelation. The subtitle indicates "prose and poetry," but these generic divisions cannot constrain Jaccottet's work, even what in other hands would be diary or commonplace-book entries becoming, in his, poetic meditation. Yet in writing about nature Jaccottet departs from customary lyric perspective. Violets may be "verging on dullness" but connote "an hour in which you cannot speak loudly." Remarkable here is not the exaltation of the humble—a common romantic device—but the recognition of the dull. Similarly, in "As Kingfishers Catch Fire," which takes its title from Gerard Manley Hopkins, a "seemingly unbound bird" draws attention because "no one has ever been required to venerate it." These reality-effects make Jaccottet's musings into parables of life and knowledge, suffused with their persistent subtleties. [Nicholas Birns]

Gérard Bessette. *Not for Every Eye*. Trans. Glen Shortliffe. Intro. and revised trans. Steven Urquhart. Exile Editions, 2010. 111 pp. Paper: $15.95. (Reprint)

Before moving in a more experimental direction with some of his later novels, Gérard Bessette was a chronicler of Quebec's milieu in the late fifties and sixties, a time of social change mirroring that of the U.S. in significance if not in decibels. *Not for Every Eye* (1960), Bessette's slim second novel, documents the Catholic Church's then-considerable influence over a small town in the province and one bookstore's surreptitious attempts at countering censorship. Hervé Jodoin, middle-aged misanthrope and serious drinker, grudgingly takes a job at the bookstore and is soon let in on its secret: it sells books that the Church has forbidden, books by "writers like Gide, Maeterlinck, Renan, Voltaire, Zola." Thus Hervé, sort of a Quebecois proto-slacker, becomes embroiled in a scheme he couldn't care less about and ignites a controversy that at most he finds a little amusing. Presciently, *Not for Every Eye* was published the same year that Quebec's Quiet Revolution began, when the Church's authority gave way to secularization. A modern reader may wonder what the big deal is about a bookstore furtively selling Gide, et al. (aside from the millennial novelty of a bookstore selling them at all), but in an era of Church dominance, the social consequences could be ruinous. Hervé's sardonic attitude toward it all is pretty funny at the same time he telegraphs the changes to come. This edition of *Not for Every Eye* is fleshed out with a substantial introduction, bibliographies and other resources, and questions for discussion, suggesting that Exile has its eye on classroom adoptions. It's not a bad idea—if many Americans' impression of Canada is of a much more progressive country, *Not for Every Eye* is an account from a time when the situation was very much the opposite. [Tim Feeney]

Charles Fourier. *The Hierarchies of Cuckoldry and Bankruptcy*. Trans. Geoffrey Longnecker. Wakefield Press, 2011. 120 pp. Paper: $12.95.

From the vantage point of the twenty-first century, it is difficult to determine whether Charles Fourier was a singular, marvelous crackpot or simply a natural product of a now alien era. The answer probably lies somewhere in the middle: Fourier, who believed that a society properly organized into "phalanxes" of 1,600 workers would result in a universe so harmonious that the Antarctic ice shelf would melt, was distinctly a crackpot of his time. In *The Hierarchies of Cuckoldry and Bankruptcy*, Fourier makes a strict taxonomy of these two social disgraces, which he saw as linked. There are three series of nine categories of thirty-six species ("The Lover's Bankruptcy," "The Atilla Bankruptcy," "The Bankruptcy for The Fun of It") in the hierarchy of bankruptcy and three classes of seventy-two species ("The Cuckold by Quanquam," "The Virtuoso Cuckold," "The Banner-Bearing Cuckold") in the incomplete hierarchy of cuckoldry. To be fair, Fourier is in on the joke, and the description of each "species" is illuminated by his fine dry wit. However, *The Hierarchies* is satire, not farce; the humor forms a thin veneer over Fourier's deeply held and deeply peculiar social concerns (not to mention his obsession with numerology). While modern readers may sympathize with Fourier's disgust for feckless capitalism and unfaithful spouses, his anti-bankruptcy stance is based in a reactionary distrust of all commercial activity, and his specific objections to cuckoldry are as archaic as the word "cuckoldry" itself. Reading a document as removed from modernity as *The Hierarchies* is like viewing a map of a forgotten country, labeled according to an indecipherable legend. Left to wander the foreign landscape, we are freed from the puzzle of the historical Fourier, and left only with the strange, exceptional human being that Fourier undoubtedly was. [Dylan Suher]

Alex Epstein. *Lunar Savings Time*. Trans. Becka Mara McKay. Clockroot Books, 2011. 136 pp. Paper: $15.00.

As I write this, Borders is closing its doors for good, while *The Onion* has composed a mock obituary for the "Last Literate Person On Earth," dead at ninety-eight. Literary writers, it seems, no longer fret over how to capture the kaleidoscopic reality of the new century, but instead wonder why they should bother trying in the first place. In his latest collection, *Lunar Savings Time*, Israeli author Alex Epstein has, if not answered these questions, at least illuminated a new path toward the literary amid the detritus of print and digital culture. The picture that emerges from this mosaic of narratives—many not more than a page in length—is by no means bleak. Epstein's very short fictions delineate the enormous imaginative space that is contained within the book—a virtual reality that encompasses past and present, the obscure and the viral simultaneously within its modest pages. The result is alchemy rather than entropy: "And it was winter. The Zen monk updated his Facebook status: 'In the evening it snowed. In the night I dreamed it was snowing.' And finally, spring: the ghost's water broke." Epstein doesn't bemoan the ephemeral excess of the digital age; his poetic narratives invite the reader to be more attentive for its plentiful (and inevitable) moments of unexpected beauty, as in "On the Writer's Conference": "The writer from the moon has a British accent. He reads a novella set in India. Every time he pronounces the word elephant, the refined audience blushes with pleasure. After him, a Brazilian writer lectures on 'The Nightlife of the Short Story.' In a plaza outside the auditorium, a young woman plump from love is smoking the last cigarette of the evening. In [a] moment she will throw the butt into the sky." [Pedro Ponce]

Joan Aiken. *The Monkey's Wedding and Other Stories*. Intro. Lizza Aiken. Small Beer Press, 2011. 203 pp. Cloth: $24.00.

I intended to read Joan Aiken's retrospective collection methodically, one story at a time, but that's not what happened. The night I picked it up I couldn't sleep because I'd been stung by a bee hours earlier, and so I wound up finishing the whole thing. Worth it, even if it meant suffering a whole swarm of bees—it's wonderful. Aiken started publishing in 1955 and continued as a working writer until her death in 2004. She was part of a storytelling tradition that predates MFA programs and quiet epiphanies, and she concerned herself with a snappier brand of narrative entertainment. The results prove that careful attention to craft raises it to the level of art. Her stories draw on folk and fairy-tale traditions but add a good deal of irony to freshen the taste, similar to the approach of John

Collier. In one, a sailor brings home a mermaid in a jar; in another, a saintly vicar passes away lamenting his wasted life, followed closely by the appearance of a talking black cat who shocks the town with his irreverence. My favorites feature young couples in conflict or love with each other, including "Spur of the Moment," "Red-Hot Favorite," and "Octopi in the Sky." They're exceedingly witty and imaginative, and so lively I couldn't believe how economical they are. The magical elements they share make them quite literally charming. Maybe it was the medicine talking, but I've decided the only proper way to express my appreciation is to open a pub and name it after "The Paper Queen." Not sure how that's going to work out, but I may give it a try. [James Crossley]

Theodor Fontane. *On Tangled Paths: An Everyday Berlin Story.* Trans. and afterword Peter James Bowman. Angel Books, 2010. 192 pp. Cloth: $21.95.
————. *No Way Back.* Trans. Hugh Rorrison and Helen Chambers. Angel Books, 2010. 256 pp. Cloth: $24.95.

Theodore Fontane, the most important German novelist of the years between Goethe and Mann, has enjoyed nowhere near their popularity here in America despite a string of translations beginning in 1964 (*On Tangled Paths—Irrungen, Wirrungen*—is the exception, the first of its five translations into English having appeared in 1917). Set in the mid-1870s and first published in 1888, *On Tangled Paths* possesses a familiar plot (as Fontane was well aware): Lene, a comely young seamstress, falls in love with Baron Botho von Rienäcker, a dashing Prussian lieutenant met by accident during a boating mishap. He returns her love, but his sorry finances may force him to marry his cousin Käthe von Sellenthin, a lovely airhead who happens to be loaded. Will love or money prevail? Well, Fontane writes social realism, so the answer should be obvious. (Not that there aren't surprises: Lene and Botho spend a weekend together, sharing a room at an inn, and neither suffers socially for this escapade.) However, plot is not intended to be the principal attraction here; indeed, Fontane once observed that nothing much ever happened in his novels. As much a psychological as a social realist, the author is interested in the emotional conflicts that arise between individual desire and social conditioning, class expectations and personality—which, as Peter James Bowman observes in his helpful afterword, Fontane limns with a mixture of detached "urbanity, gentle irony, and humanity" that the translation successfully captures.

When Fontane's characters stray too far down tangled paths, they sometimes discover they've reached a point of no return. This is certainly true for Count Holk and his wife Christine in the 1891 novel *No Way Back* (*Unwiederbringlich*). Set in Denmark and the German state of Schleswig-Holstein in the late 1850s, the novel follows the affairs of the Count, an easygoing courtier to a Danish princess. Of his character, his pious and exceedingly solemn wife accurately remarks, "he would be the ideal husband, if only he had some ideals." For his part, Holk has put up with Christine's self-righteousness and relentless reprobation for seventeen years before an extended stay in Copenhagen and acquaintance with the freethinking Fraulein Ebba von Rosenberg push his marital dissatisfactions to a crisis, causing him at one point to explain to Christine her deficiencies: "Of light and sun you have nothing. You lack everything feminine, you are harsh and sullen . . ." Call it a clash between romantic and Moravian sensibilities, or the behavior of a middle-aged man suddenly confronted by what might yet be; the protracted consequences of Holk's flirtation with remaking himself are both tragic and pathetic, although I shan't spoil what is again in many ways a familiar story. What eventuates is, as an early review in the *Kölnische Zeitung* put it, "bitter disaster emerg[ing] from pardonable error," from the "weaknesses and mistakes that everyone is prone to." Again, what interests here is the narrative voice, the deft evocation of period manners, and the probing of perennial concerns: marriage and midlife crisis, the unignorable seductiveness of self-destructive impulses, the can't-get-enough fascination of *chroniques scandaleuses*, the complications of masculinity when its virtues find no outlet. It may be true, Fontane suggests, that "no good can come of lax principles," but it may also be true that "those who have mastered the art of taking things lightly, they are *alive.*" Many readers should be able to sympathize with the "fickle and indecisive" Holk, the well-intentioned but fundamentally lost Christine, both of whom flounder between these competing ways of living. [Brooke Horvath]

Mihail Sebastian. *The Accident.* Trans. Stephen Henighan. Biblioasis, 2011. 257 pp. Paper: $17.95.

In this post-postmodern world of teenybopper angst-pop, maudlin chick flicks, and cheesy reality-show melodrama, love's elegant argument has been largely lost. Indeed, given the narrowed ambitions of minimalism and the astringent ironies of postmodernism, the complicated dynamic of love has been all but ceded to the soft porn of pulp romances. This makes particularly seductive the dignity, the elevation of Romanian writer Mihail Sebastian's dense anatomy of love's compelling illogic, first published in 1940 and available now in a lyrical translation with an afterword by University of Guelph's Stephen Henighan. Known to the English-speaking world largely for his journal, which chronicled fascism in interwar Romania, Sebastian, who died in 1945, here examines the gravitas of attraction—Paul, a classically gloomy intellectual reeling from a tempestuous relationship with a mercurial artist, impulsively assists a stranger, a vibrant French teacher named Nora, when she takes a spill from a Bucharest tram one wintry morning. The metaphor of the fortunate fall becomes Sebastian's most revealing motif—suggesting the redemptive devastation of the reluctant heart. Indeed, Nora sees love as a way to minister to her emotionally disaffected Good Samaritan. She takes Paul on a Christmas ski vacation to the Carpathians. There, against the gathering storm of fascism, the cloaking smother of the sweeping mountains, and a melancholic sense of doom, they meet a young, apparently robust German painter who is doomed by a bad heart. Paul and Nora, like the classic Modernist characters of Proust, Mann, and Pasternak, engage love's Big Questions: the friction between chance and destiny; the terrorism of vulnerability; the struggle with fidelity; the dilemma of obsession; the uncivil war between logic and desire; the tonic pull of nature; and, supremely, the irony of love given the inevitability of mortality. Sebastian's novel is a sumptuous read, a reminder of the unnerving implications of love's dark necessity. [Joseph Dewey]

Mashingaidze Gomo. *A Fine Madness*. Preface by Ngũgĩ wa Thiong'o. Ayebia Clarke Publishing, 2010. 174 pp. Paper: £9.99.

The narrator of Mashingaidze Gomo's first novel is a helicopter gunner, part of the Zimbabwean forces fighting in the Congo during the Great War of Africa of 1998–2003. The story of that war is complex and horrific, but one needn't know it to appreciate *A Fine Madness*, which is interested in the Congolese conflict primarily as a synecdoche for the failures and bloodshed of so-called postcolonial Africa, where the U.S. and the former European colonial powers still sucker the natives with games of economic and ideological three-card monte. Less story than screed, less screed than diary in free verse and prose, *A Fine Madness* obsesses over African capitulations, betrayals, and delusions. It is a "story of designer evil, styled to torment and to take all without moral restraint," of "carrion men massacred" by the "sponsors of neocolonial barbarism." As Gomo's diarist sits watching gunships take off or wanders the shabby streets of Boende, he rehearses the outrages committed against the colonized—from the imposition of a hypocritical Christianity to the loss of one's unsung history and language. Throughout its thirty-four brief chapters, *A Fine Madness* proves compelling not because its analysis of colonialism is particularly original—it is not—but because Gomo made at least this reader believe in his educated but otherwise ordinary soldier's earnest struggle to make sense of his circumstances "in the punishing humid heat of the equatorial sun." As the helicopters beat toward a retreating horizon, Gomo even manages to wrest beauty from a punishing jungle "scroung-

ing around for bits of darkness and tucking them around its gloomy figure . . .
reluctant to be identified" and of those who suffer an impoverishment that
"makes the voice of its victims unreasonable." No wonder Gomo's narrator
feels good to be finally "mad at the whole world." [Brooke Horvath]

Harry Mathews. *The New Tourism*. Sand Paper Press, 2010. 56 pp. Paper:
$15.00.

This first collection of poetry in some twenty years reflects many of Harry
Mathews's concerns in his fiction and also what he has described as his "incompatibility with the world." The volume is divided into three sections. The
first consists of a sequence entitled "Butter and Eggs: A Didactic Poem," which
describes six ways of cooking eggs. Studiedly impersonal, these pieces show
Mathews's respect for his described materials and exploits the double use of
the present tense as a generic narrative or a series of instructions to the reader.
In the second section of fifteen poems, the title piece evokes the physical,
financial, and linguistic estrangement of the self and by so doing it identifies
central themes running through the collection. Mathews repeatedly evokes
states of searching within landscapes that shift constantly between named locations like Tuscany to anonymous seascapes. He engages in a running dialogue with other writers ranging from Henry Vaughan the metaphysical poet
to contemporaries like Kenneth Koch. "Shall I compare thee to a summer's
bay," through a single-letter substitution, playfully diverts Shakespeare's romantic analogy into an extended piece of landscape description wherein the
original human subject is virtually lost. In a similar spirit, "Crème Brûlée"
opens with commentary on Nature and then Mathews humorously focuses
on his own tendency to find puzzles everywhere—in the identification of
trees and in restaurant food. The remainder of *The New Tourism* presents a
sequence of haiku poems, which give glimpses of Mathews's friends and lovers, but also characteristically incorporate reflections on the process of composition, even on individual words. This collection experiments with a range

of poetic modes, where in every case the medium of expression becomes an important part of the subject. [David Seed]

A D Jameson. *Amazing Adult Fantasy*. Mutable Sound, 2011. 168 pp. Paper: $12.95.

The stories in A D Jameson's new collection, *Amazing Adult Fantasy*, are about nonsense. By *nonsense* I mean not just the silly and absurd, although there's plenty of that: terrorist monkeys who seek to conquer the world; mummies who nocturnally roam the Smithsonian, looking for an exit; a talking moon rock who gives questionable advice. But more than that, the belligerent motto of this book might be, "Not Sense!" At every turn and at every level, the stories here seek to explode all our expectations for logic. The logics of narrative sequence, cause and effect, and character motivation are denied as incident piles on incident seemingly haphazardly. The logic of chronology is denied as, in "Oscar the Grouch," two characters meet for the first time over and over and, in "Big Bird and Snuffy," characters die before they are born. The logic of the world/fiction binary is denied when the fictions of TV and film penetrate what purports to be the real world. The very logic of language and grammar is denied as the ends of sentences contradict their beginnings: "Even when eating, the stone never shut up about the Duke, except for long stretches of silence." About halfway through this collection, just when the very lack of structure necessitated by this attack on logic might start to become tedious, a new section, "The Solar Stories," teases the reader with the possibility of connection among characters, incidents, and images. Through these last stories, our desire for structure and meaning are put into conflict with the narrator's insistence that "Our stories, we have to admit, have been the cause of all our problems." Jameson presents here the fantasy of freedom from the many stories that dominate our lives. [Robert L. McLaughlin]

Roberta Allen. *The Dreaming Girl*. Introduction by Luisa Valenzuela. Ellipsis Press, 2011. Paper: $14.00. (Reprint)

The hypnotic prose of *The Dreaming Girl* is effortless to read, especially once the reader gets used to the ways the author flouts convention. Here is a novel almost devoid of dialogue, in which we are not given the names of the two main characters. They are tourists known as "the girl" and "the German," who become lovers in the rain forest in Belize. We are given access to their perspectives, even their dream states, which involve the imagination, fantasy, and visions, as well as actual dreams. This might sound confusing, but the novel is admirably clear as it taps into the individual emotions of these lovers, including regret, longing, and jealousy.

The Dreaming Girl deftly crosses boundaries between reality and dreaming, body and mind, male and female, the jungle and civilization, the present and the past. Perhaps the most important boundary to be crossed is between humanity and nature. In one extended passage, the dreaming girl enters the rain forest in her imagination and sees the animal world in all its disgusting glory. Animals hunt and feed off each other; they act out their violent mating rituals. After immersing her mind in this dark world she concludes, "There's no horror here. Life is beyond horror, nightmare, dream, beauty, wonder. But she can only be in life for a little while." The fate of her relationship with the German could be described similarly. Their passionate need for one another and inability to sustain that need is nothing more or less than lifelike, and Allen renders their experience, as all artists do, with faithful attention to sensation. The story is archetypal, lovely on the surface, and vaguely disturbing on a deeper level. In a word, dreamlike. [D. Quentin Miller]

Steve Katz. *Time's Wallet*. Counterpath Press, 2011. 169 pp. Paper: $15.95.

After novels with titles such as *Swanny's Ways*, *Wier and Pouce*, and *Antonello's Lion*, further allusions to famous novels or painters would not be unexpected for someone like Steve Katz. *Time's Wallet* is no different, as we read in *Troilus and Cressida*, Scene III:

> Time hath, my lord, a wallet at his back,
> Wherein he puts alms for oblivion,
> A great-sized monster of ingratitudes:
> Those scraps are good deeds past; which are devour'd
> As fast as they are made . . .

The exact title is *Time's Wallet, Volume I/54 memoirrhoids of 137*, which, of course, presupposes a Volume II with eighty-three "memoirrhoids" to come. Presumably, these future memoirrhoids will be available without the use of Preparation M. So, what exactly are these memoirrhoids? They are fifty-four snippets of Katz's life here ranging in alphabetical order from *Arunchala in India* and *Galileo & Tot* to *Jewboy* and *My Nabokov* to *Vonneguts* and *Young Artist Finds His Joint* with forty-eight more in between. No memoirrhoid is more than four pages long, but one shouldn't be fooled by the brevity of the pieces. The laconic tales are told with the precision of a writer who has written more than his share. At times, the pieces are written in past tense; at other times, in present. In *Baxter*, Katz writes "Baxter Hathaway was a slim, grey-haired professor, who in his youth had been a pole-vaulter back in Michigan . . ." while in *Belgrade Whoops* he begins "The Aussie couple sitting across from me at a table in Athens's Syntagma Square complains about the pollution in the city." Regardless of the alteration, these reveries offer a resonance that is uniquely "now" whether the author is talking about discovering Berryman's poetry or being in the same room with Williams and Burroughs. [Mark Axelrod]

Yuriy Tarnawsky. *Short Tails*. Civil Coping Mechanisms, 2011. 338 pp. Paper: $17.95.

At the heart of Yuriy Tarnawsky's most recent collection of short prose pieces is a human heart, slowly shrinking into a nugget of dried skin, left behind by what was once a man . . . all this on a perfectly ordinary day in an average city, somewhere. Tarnawsky is a master of the brief, potent, surreal mystery tale. His direct, unadorned prose relates stories whose outer form is that of the absurd—events that seem to arise out of nowhere and unfold beyond the grasp of human reason; but beneath the skin of these stories, Tarnawsky forces his reader to touch the deepest longings, neuroses, fantasies, and terrors of a human being. Many of the stories in *Short Tails* follow a pattern, one that cannot be exhausted by its telling since it is the very pattern of life, beginning with a character plagued by that vague desire to find something, to feel, to "experience." This desire sets a process in motion (a process which, once begun, cannot possibly be reversed), and from there an utter mystery unfolds itself. By the close of the story, hardly a resolution but merely a possible place to end, even if that end is death itself, both the main character (if he even remains) and the reader are left precisely, artfully, and surprisingly smack-dab in the middle of nothing. A single needle drops to the floor of a concert hall after the bodies of the musicians, conductor, and audience have been eaten away by holes, the sound of that single remainder only making the emptiness resound more fully. *Short Tails* puts its reader face to face with the ineffable ambiguity in the center of every mundane afternoon—a breach in the order of things, a tear in the fabric of the real, a doorway we always knew was there, that cathartic scream we've been waiting to release, from a mouth that is gradually disappearing—and the scream, too, will soon be gone. [Michelle Tupko]

Robert Ashley. *Quicksand*. Burning Books, 2011. 152 pp. Paper: $10.00.

New Mexico press Burning Books has blazed back into sight with a most peculiar, and most toothsome, series of "debut novels by seasoned writers." Called "Quadrants," the series does indeed consist of four books (plus one collection of short pieces, *Q+1*) by artists and authors without a novel to their name. Except, of course, that anyone familiar with the operas of Robert Ashley (*Perfect Lives, Atalanta, Improvement*, and many others) knows that long-form narrative has always played a primary role therein: narrative fragmented, narrative deformed, narrative tricked into Poundian culs-de-sac . . . but narrative nonetheless. Nor is it surprising that Ashley—long a vocal fan of John le Carré—would, turning his hand to prose fiction, find himself "composing" a thriller: a tale of international intrigue, dingy hotel rooms, clandestine rendezvous, congee, and murder. ("I called room service and shot the guy." And yet, save for the murder bit, what touring musician doesn't know his or her share about living "on the run"?) *Quicksand*, being neither memoir nor fabrication ("Everything in the novel is true, except for a lot of the facts"), is as full of tiny reveries on the very edge of irrelevance—imagine a cosmopolitan Midwesterner essaying his own version of the work of Jean-Philippe Toussaint—as it is moments of legitimate anxiety or Chandleresque bluff. (The quintessential Ashleyian response to everything from certain death to rudeness: "Oh boy.") One is also reminded of Harry Mathews, particularly his own self-effacing "docufictional" memoir *My Life in CIA*. But how dull to waste one's precious reading time (*Quicksand* is slim) trying to sift the probable from the fantastic, the le Carré from the Ned Rorem: best to accept that Ashley is no more unlikely a continental op than Mathews or Marlowe (Christopher, that is), and immerse oneself in his choppy, twangy, paradoxical sentences and ever-present sense of fun—joy in narrative, joy in the word ("The horizon was suspicious"), joy in cognition, and joy, naturally, in the *gag*: what better cover could an agent ask for than globe-trotting avant-garde composer? Let's hope further adventures are to come. [Jeremy M. Davies]

David Albahari. *Leeches*. Trans. Ellen Elias-Bursać. Houghton Mifflin Harcourt, 2011. 320 pp. Cloth: $24.00.

Leeches begins with its Serbian protagonist startled by the sight of a woman being slapped by a man on a riverbank, an incident he cannot explain or ignore. Witness as well to the larger calamity of the Milosevich regime in Belgrade, this unnamed hack subsists as a columnist for a local paper and generally hangs out with Marko, whose response to all problems is to roll another joint. Pursuing the slapped woman leads the writer to discover a slew of apparent signs that he seeks help to fathom, but his school classmate Dragan's abstruse mathematical hypotheses prove even more baffling. Then, out of the blue, an old manuscript falls into his hands, the tale of Eleazar, a Kabbalistic adept whose successive appearances presage some portentous event. Meanwhile, as tensions rise with a proliferation of skinheads, anti-Semitism threatens the local Jewish community. Disturbed by what he sees happening around him, the writer shares his concerns and the peculiar manuscript with a Jewish artist friend, Jasa, and his companions, whose suggestions leave him fascinated if increasingly bewildered. As his apprehension over these interwoven intrigues is aroused by further developments pointing to an underlying complex order, the writer encounters the slapped woman and, of course, falls for her. Urged on by her allure as well as her developing role in the drama in which he seems fated to star, the writer seizes upon the manuscript itself, a "living document" in which passages move, disappear, or change with a turn of the page, as the key to his self-realization. As these disparate strands knit together, the writer unexpectedly finds himself at the center of the Jewish community's attempts to defend itself against resurgent ethnic hatred. Albahari's seemingly offhand depiction of a mysterious web enveloping an unwitting, susceptible spectator is a subtle, brilliant achievement. [Michael Pinker]

Sigizmund Krzhizanovsky. *Memories of the Future*. Trans. Joanne Turn-bull. New York Review Books, 2009. 256 pp. Paper: $15.95.

Highly regarded in Russia now but almost unknown elsewhere, Krzhizanovsky wrote primarily during the 1920s and 1930s, although nearly all of his work, found in state archives in the 1970s, remained unavailable even to Russian readers until the 1990s. It doesn't take long to see why we should be grateful for its preservation and publication. The seven novellas in this collection, crowned by the masterly title piece, display ingenuity seldom encountered anywhere, even today, attesting to Krzhizanovsky's singular craftsmanship and boldly imaginative style. "Quadraturin," inspired by the cramped quarters in which nearly every Muscovite, including Krzhizanovsky, lived during the early Bolshevik period, concerns a marvelous substance that expands the inner space of an apartment almost infinitely while leaving its outer dimensions intact. "The Bookmark" examines the decline of criticism according to one Saul Straight, a stern, eccentric judge, whose saga continues in "Someone Else's Theme." "The Branch Line" deconstructs the Heavy Industry of Dreams ("Evening Classes for Night Visions"), while "Red Snow" takes a logical conundrum to its ultimate reversal. In "The Thirteenth Category of Reason," an old gravedigger recalls chasing down a corpse that up and walked away. But "Memories of the Future" displays Krzhizanovsky at peak form; appropriately, the translation itself rises to poetic heights. A resolute loner possessed of amazing intellectual prowess, Maximilian Shterer labors to dispel the hold of time by creating a time machine. His single-minded devotion to this pursuit, from before the Great War through the early years of Communism, seeking first materials, then funds sufficient to complete his ever-more-refined device, is as compelling a story of genius as has ever been written, leaving one quite in thrall to the power of Krzhizanovsky's vision. [Michael Pinker]

Bhanu Kapil. *Humanimal: A Project for Future Children*. Kelsey Street Press, 2009. 86 pp. Paper: $17.95.

Kapil prefaces this fiction with relevant nonfictions. In 1920, a missionary, Rev. Joseph Singh, found two girls ("ghosts") living in the jungle among wolves. Singh rescued and recuperated them, changing their diets, breaking limbs to make them walk erect, and teaching them language and morals. One died within a year; the other, named Kamala, survived a little longer. A film crew documented Kapil's visit to Midnapure, where she embarked on a study of hardships that occur in borderlands, where languaged power meets wordless body. Assembling chunks of Singh's diary, the imagined voice of Kamala, and the narrator's interrogation of frontiers (animal/human, feral/moral, un-languaged/syntaxed), Kapil compiles a stunning investigative fiction. Here is Singh, observing a feverish Kamala: "[H]er tongue became active, and she commenced talking in a fashion that amazed us all immensely. Though the words were broken, yet she expressed herself in a wonderful way." Here is the fictive-poetical Kamala: "E. The cook fed us meats of many kinds. I joined my belly to the belly of the next girl. It was pink and we opened our beaks for meat. It was wet and we licked the dictionary off each other's faces." Here is the narrator: "No filming today and so I'm writing. The humanimal document is a machine that produces redness by itself. In Normandy . . . I saw a giant pink moon rise over the brown curves of the field . . . I put it in India. I put it inside the jungle like the light given off by certain animals even in the dark. Self-illuminate. And watched it rise." Kamala's voice ceases with the letter *O* (indeed: the mouth, when there is nothing to say) and the narrator takes over: "O. I've exhausted the alphabet. But I'm not writing this for you." The moral vision of a project for future children "make[s] a body real . . ." This is a text to do that. [Kass Fleisher]

Gary Lutz. *Divorcer*. Calamari Press, 2011. 120 pp. Paper: $13.00.

Gary Lutz, chronicler of unwonderful and morosely moored persons, continues to tickle darkly in *Divorcer* ("Friends don't let friends stay friends"), which concerns the supreme act of breaking off: "Divorce, I kept forgetting, is not the opposite of marriage; it's the opposite of wedding." This collection features four long stories and three shorter, with the titles of the four serving as the perfect settee for his mordant gnosis: "Divorcer," "To Whom Might I Have Concerned?", "I Have to Feel Halved," and "Womanesque." In each of these stories the unnamed narrator is wounded, balling himself into the bland efficiencies he shares with a flighty, sexually etiolated female (in one case male). This murky and meretricious beloved, who comes from a frumpy family ("This sister's kids smelled like pets"), soon finds other ne'er-do-wells of more interest than her huddled husband. These stories don't proceed so much as they grow coral—submerged as they are in the poisoned solvent of aching body odor, unfriendly bodily fluids, and featureless junk food—not arcing but groping themselves underwater before coming up for air at the end. As ever, Lutz's tinkering with and embellishing of language amazes. Who else could squawk a sentence so startling and of such scale: "The first night ran each of us back to people who had milked us for feeling before." And yet, *Divorcer* differs from his earlier collections in that there seems a greater openness here to the pain portrayed, allowing Lutz's considerable humor to spread more evenly. These narrators aren't as bewildered by their station in the skuzzy world. They accept more. They know that by going into others they won't come away conjoined but only again with themselves. What must they do to survive? They must create. [Greg Gerke]

Blake Butler and Lily Hoang, eds. *30 Under 30: An Anthology of Innovative Fiction by Younger Writers.* Dzanc Books, 2011. 304 pp. Paper: $20.00.

The ostensible goal of *30 Under 30* is to bring together, in a coherent way, the work of young writers. Per the subtitle, these writers tend toward "innovative fiction," which here is apt to mean varying degrees of experimentation and departure from conventional narrative. The emphasis on youth and revolution is meant finally, in the publisher's gleeful estimation, to afford readers a glimpse of fiction's future. Reading the resulting collection is a bit like playing Secret Santa: you never quite know what you will get, which is, of course, what makes the project fun. Still, patterns emerge: in the future, there shall be stories about failed stories (as in Devin Gribbons's "A Short Story," which begins, "I wrote a story in which I solved all the problems in the Middle East. But only for a few seconds. Then there was trouble again . . . The story was a failure. It just didn't work."); there shall be parables and allegories aplenty (Joshua Cohen's "Rip Off the Wings of Dragonflies. Virus. On Location. Still Life with

Grapes. Four Art Pieces. Anonymous Anonymous," with its neatly cryptic, insistently profound vignettes, is the most direct stab at the genre, though just about every entry qualifies in some way); and Vonnegut shall be the patron saint (Gribbons again); and typography shall be part of the whole point (Zach Dodson's "I Write to You of This" is rather charmingly hand-scrawled in a reproduction of a Mead Composition notebook). Not every vision of the coming fiction future will be pleasing to all, but that's sort of the point: here are thirty possible destinations, and you pick your own adventure. "Please, follow me," is the last line of Evelyn Hampton's "Mr. Gray," the final inclusion. By all means, do. [Yevgeniya Traps]

Jordan Stump, *The Other Book: Bewilderments of Fiction*. University of Nebraska Press, 2011. 273 pp. Cloth: $30.00.

Stump, one of the most masterful critics working today, has been a longtime, skillful expositor of Raymond Queneau. Thus it is no surprise to see this book lovingly devoted to a thorough examination of Queneau's *Le chiendent* (1933), the writer's first novel. Nor it is startling to see Stump pay detailed attention to the novel's rigorous structure and the playfulness of his language. But Stump is up to far more here. In his examination not just of the printed book but also of its manuscript, its translation into English, and a scholarly critical edition, he widens our view of what a book is. Indeed, Stump's first chapter could be used as a companion to standard accounts of textual criticism as it goes through all the past century's established critical models of a book's material genesis and provides an innovative new take on the subject. Both academic and belletristic readers have fallen into grooves as far as assumptions of what a book is. We think we have a book ready-to-hand when, as Stump insists, we have in any finished form only a phase of its existence. Stump is especially iconoclastic with regard to translation, going into the connotations of both English titles, *The Bark Tree* and *Witch Grass*, and daring to say that the second title is "gloomier, more subterranean," befitting the vexed early twenty-first century, while readers in the sixties' counterculture might have been looking for a more "free-spirited" book. Stump also calls attention to how, in books like Queneau's that have gaps in their language, such gaps also must be transited; they simply cannot pass over into the new tongue wholesale, as they are not whole. Stump's bracing treatise will not only satisfy readers of Queneau but extend the awareness of all who read books. [Nicholas Birns]

George Craig. *Writing Beckett's Letters*. Sylph Editions, 2011. 40 pp. Paper: £10.00.

There have been other intimist accounts of spending revealing lengths of time with Beckett. This one is altogether different, whose author failed to use his letter of introduction to the author and instead grew to know him by privileged access to his words. In this all-too-brief book, George Craig provides a glimpse of the intimate struggle that is translation. It is an especially interesting glimpse, because he is the translator of the informal, unproofed, multilingual, impossibly multicultural letters of Beckett. But this book is not only for those who love Beckett's work. Translation itself is of as much interest here. In a series of short, often coyly inconclusive essays, the author discusses, among much else, the peculiarities of translating something handwritten; of translating something not merely bilingual, but multilingual; of translating letters, as opposed to a settled text; and—for those of us unskilled in it, one of the mystical tricks of the translator's art—of translating culturally specific ideas. How *does* one translate, into a language with no equivalent formality, a witty neologism for the continued use of the formal *vous* after one feels the familiar *tu* has been earned? Such passages, in examining the struggle to translate Beckett's ceaseless, off-hand linguistic inventiveness, also serve witness to the inventiveness required of the translator. In addition to its invaluable content, the book itself is exceptionally produced and pleasing to simply handle, printed on quality paper, with beautiful typesetting, a lovely color scheme, and full-color, full-page plates of postcards and handwritten and typed letters.

How much care Sylph Editions has taken in assembling the Cahiers Series is apparent from cover to cover. In fact, the only possible negative thing to be said about this book is that it is so short. [Stephen Fisk]

Ingeborg Bachmann and Paul Celan. *Correspondence*. Trans. Wieland Hoban. Seagull Books, 2010. 373 pp. Cloth: $24.95.

In spite of, or perhaps because of, the ease of electronic communiqués in to-day's digital age, fascination with the written correspondence between poets continues unabated. Sometimes these letters reveal literary gems, as in Keats's now famous December 1817 letter where he describes negative capability or Dickinson's numerous letters that read more like epistolary poems. Sometimes though, it feels as though we have intruded on something rather intimate and personal that should be, essentially, none of our business. You will find pre-cisely this combination in the letters of Bachmann and Celan. It is interesting, for example, to learn who Celan was translating, say in 1958: Paul Éluard, Osip Mandelstam, and Sergei Yesenin. The letters also provide some insight into the personal context surrounding certain poems, including anecdotes about public readings of Celan's famous "Todesfuge." A smattering of poems and translations (almost exclusively by Celan) are a welcome reprieve from the many bland "missing you" exchanges or unsurprising declarations of love. There are also insights into what was a rather tumultuous relationship, as well as more personal glimpses into the infamous "Goll Affair," when Celan was falsely accused of plagiarism. Martin Heidegger, who loomed rather strangely and paradoxically for both writers, is also discussed—though, unfortunately, only briefly. Celan's struggle with his past and the effects of anti-Semitism is felt in several letters, as is Bachmann's absolute devotion—at least initially—to Celan and his work. The two eventually become rather estranged for reasons that are not made particularly clear in the letters, although it seems Celan's mental and emotional struggles are behind much of the tension; e.g., in an odd but intense moment, Bachman implies that Celan has accused her of murder in the poem "Wolfsbohne" ("Wolfsbane"). The editor's notes are extensive, and the collection will certainly be of interest to scholars of both writers. [Mark Tursi]

David Antin. *Radical Coherency: Selected Essays on Art and Literature, 1966 to 2005*. University of Chicago Press, 2011. 384 pp. Paper: $25.00.

Perhaps the most radical coherency offered by David Antin's book of "essays on art and literature" is his interspersing of talk pieces, edited transcripts of extemporaneous speeches that Antin usually publishes as poetry, with more formal criticism. The juxtaposition suggests the inclusion of either form in each other's category. Poetry, Antin argues, has little to do with formal concerns, rather it describes thinking through language in all art, "prose is a kind of Concrete poetry with justified margins." Though the book is divided into "Art Essays" and "Literary Essays," he generally displays a mistrust of, and a curiosity about, apparently settled categories. Antin's diligent attention to the particulars of his art-encounters points out how often critical response confines itself to hermetic disciplinary conversations. In the art essays, Antin wrestles with the meanings of now established individuals and movements. Early essays on Andy Warhol and video art present nuanced initial understandings of appropriation strategies, while pieces on Marcel Duchamp, Mark Rothko, and Robert Morris offer meticulous reconsideration of artists so well established that many of us no longer bother to look closely at their work. Defending Morris against accusations of a lack of stylistic originality, Antin wonders at the requirement of formal consistency to establish an artist's significance. He carries his defense of eclectic approaches into the lengthy and masterful consideration of modernist and postmodernist poetry that opens the literary section. He proposes a realignment of the modernist canon according to a lineage of collage technique distinct from the ironic formalist traditionalism he detects in many modernist icons. Touching on Oedipus,

Wittgenstein, and John Cage, his literary essays develop a definition of collage as startling intersections between objects from disparate sources, fragments repeated in improvisation, even utterance and its situated instance. Antin argues that art categories are discursive constructs, not as a cold, abstract position, but as modernist collage poetry in action. [Ira S. Murfin]

John Taylor. *Paths to Contemporary French Literature, Volume 3*. Transaction Publishers, 2011. 280 pp. Cloth: $39.95.

John Taylor has been writing about, and translating, French literature for many years. In this third volume of essays and reviews, some published as recently as 2010, his familiarity with trends, issues and writers, and a style absent of jargon, bring out new facets of the work of familiar figures (Aragon, Genet, Pinget) and introduce, to this reader, unknown writers such as Laurence Werner David, Brina Svit, and Marie Étienne. The fifty-odd writers focused upon here are placed in a solid context of present and past French literature, at times extending beyond the borders of the country. A reader will note that class and gender differences are rarely discussed, but that may be due as much to the books and figures Taylor has chosen to review as to his own temperament. However, we are amiably guided through some of the many areas of concern and stylistic choices that constitute twentieth- and twenty-first-century French literature, including post-colonial writing (Jean Haztfeld), Franco-Egyptian works (the neglected Albert Cossery), formal inventors and fabulists (Queneau, Pierre Bettencourt), and prose poets (Pierre-Albert Jourdan). Taylor doesn't hesitate to state when writers fail to measure up to his standards, and among these are practitioners of "autofiction," defined as writing of a "simplistic confessional directness . . ."; the subject of the essay "Two Hesitations about the Recent Fiction of J.M.G. Le Clézio"; and Julien Green, whose "literary essays . . . are uniformly disappointing." He is happiest when describing writers he likes, such as Valery Larbaud, or the novels of Anne Serre. At the back of the book is publishing information on the various pieces, as well as a helpful bibliography that will aid in finding books that John Taylor's encyclopedic knowledge and enthusiasm have indicated are worth finding. *Paths to Contemporary French Literature* is a useful addition to libraries everywhere. [Jeff Bursey]

Akutagawa Ryūnosuke. *A Fool's Life*. Trans. Anthony Barnett and Toraiwa Naoko. Allardyce, Barnett, Publishers, 2007. Paper: $18.00. (F)

Albahari, David. *Leeches*. Trans. Ellen Elias-Bursać. Houghton Mifflin Harcourt, 2011. Cloth: $24.00. (F)

Allen, Roberta. *The Dreaming Girl*. Ellipsis Press, 2011. Paper: $14.00. (F)

Appelfeld, Aharon. *Until the Dawn's Light*. Trans. Jeffrey M. Green. Schocken, 2011. Cloth: $26.00. (F)

Ashley, Robert, Sumner Carnahan, Thomas Fruck, and L. K. Larsen. *Q+1: Short Works from the Quadrants Series Authors*. Burning Books, 2011. Paper: $10.00. (F)

Baldwin, Joshua. *The Wilshire Sun*. Turtle Point Press, 2011. Paper: $12.50. (F)

Barnett, Anthony. *Antonyms & Others*. Allardyce Book, 2012. Paper: $18.00. (F)

—. *Citations Followed on*. Allardyce Book, 2010. Paper: $19.00. (F)

Bingham, Sallie. *Mending: New and Selected Stories*. Sarabande Books, 2011. Paper: $16.95. (F)

Blanco, Alberto. *Afterglow / Tras el rayo*. Bitter Oleander Press, 2011. Paper: $21.00. (P)

Christopher, Lonely. *The Mechanics of Homosexual Intercourse*. Akashic Books, 2011. Paper: $15.95. (F)

Constant, Paule. *Private Property*. Trans. Margot Miller and France Grenaudier-Klijn. Univ. of Nebraska Press, 2011. Paper: $17.95. (F)

Cooper, Dennis. *The Marbled Swarm*. HarperPerennial, 2011. Paper: $14.99. (F)

Craig, George. *Writing Beckett's Letters*. Sylph Editions, 2011. Paper: £10.00. (NF)

Daitch, Susan. *Paper Conspiracies*. City Lights, 2011. Paper: $16.95. (F)

Darwish, Mahmoud. *In the Presence of Absence*. Trans. Sinan Antoon. Archipelago Books, 2011. Paper: $16.00. (NF)

Delaney, Edward J. *Broken Irish*. Turtle Point Press, 2011. Paper: $18.50. (F) de Saussure, Ferdinand. *Course in General Linguistics*. Trans. Wade Baskin. Columbia Univ. Press, 2011. Paper: $27.50. (NF)

Des Forêts, Louis-René. *Poems of Samuel Wood*. Trans. Anthony Barnett. Allardyce Book, 2011. Paper: $18.00. (P)

Dix, Andrew, Brian Jarvis, and Paul Jenner. *The Contemporary American Novel in Context*. Continuum, 2011. Paper: $24.95. (NF)

Doloughan, Fiona J. *Contemporary Narrative: Textual Production, Multimodality, and Multiliteracies*. Continuum, 2011. Paper: $34.95. (NF)

Draeger, Manuela. *In the Time of the Blue Ball*. Trans. Brian Evenson. Dorothy, 2011. Paper: $16.00. (F)

Duchamp, L. Timmel. *Never at Home*. Acqueduct Press, 2011. Paper: $18.00. (F)

Dupin, Jacques. *Of Flies and Monkeys*. Trans. John Taylor. Bitter Oleander Press, 2011. Paper: $24.00. (P)

Fagerholm, Monika. *The Glitter Scene*. Other Press, 2011. Paper: $17.95. (F)

Falkner, Sarah. *Animal Sanctuary*. Starcherone Books, 2011. Paper: $20.00. (F)

Fourier, Charles. *The Hierarchies of Cuckoldry and Bankruptcy*. Trans. Geoffrey Longnecker. Wakefield Press, 2011. Paper: $12.95. (NF)

Freitag, Günther. *Brendel's Fantasy*. Trans. Eugene H. Hayworth. Owl Canyon Press, 2011. Paper: $16.95. (F)

Gerdes, Eckhard. *Hugh Moore*. Civil Coping Mechanisms, 2010. Paper: $16.95. (F)

Gladman, Renee. *The Ravickians*. Dorothy, 2011. Paper: $16.00. (F)

Gregory, Daryl. *Unpossible and Other Stories*. Fairwood Press, 2011. Paper: $17.99. (F)

Henderson, Gretchen E. *Galerie de Difformité*. Lake Forest College Press, 2011. Paper: $15.00. (F)

—. *On Marvellous Things Heard*. Green Lantern Press, 2011. Paper: $12.00. (F)

Jaccottet, Philippe. *And, Nonetheless: Selected Prose and Poetry, 1990–2009*. Trans. John Taylor. Chelsea Editions, 2011. Paper: $20.00. (NF)

Jiménez Mayo, Eduardo and Chris N. Brown, eds. *Three Messages and a Warning: Contemporary Mexican Short Stories of the Fantastic.* Small Beer Press, 2011. Paper: $16.00. (F)

Kaschock, Kirsten. *Sleight.* Coffee House Press, 2011. Paper: $16.00. (F)

Kobek, Jarett. *Atta.* Semiotext(e), 2011. Paper: $12.95. (F)

Kolm, Ron. *The Plastic Factory.* Autonomedia, 2011. Paper: $5.00. (F)

Lentricchia, Frank. *The Sadness of Antonioni.* Excelsior Editions, 2011. Paper: $24.95. (F)

Lerner, Ben. *Leaving the Atocha Station.* Coffee House Press, 2011. Paper: $15.00. (F)

Lutz, Gary. *Divorcer.* Calamari Books, 2011. Paper: $13.00. (F)

Macé, Gérard. *The Last of the Egyptians.* Trans. Brian Evenson. Burning Deck, 2011. Paper: $14.00. (F)

McIlvanney, Liam and Ray Ryan, eds. *The Good of the Novel.* Continuum Books, 2011. Paper: $19.95. (NF)

Mégevand, Martin and Nathalie Piégay-Gros, eds. *Robert Pinget: matériau, marges, écriture.* Presses Universitaires de Vincennes, 2011. Paper: €22.00. (NF)

Melikian, Armen. *Journey to Virginland: Epistle 1.* Two Harbors, 2011. Cloth: $23.95. (F)

Nádas, Péter. *Parallel Stories.* Trans. Imre Goldstein. Farrar, Straus and Giroux, 2011. Cloth: $40.00. (F)

Nadler, Stuart. *The Book of Life.* Reagan Arthur Books, 2011. Paper: $13.99. (F)

Neihardt, John G. *Eagle Voice Remembers: An Authentic Tale of the Old Sioux World.* Univ. of Nebraska Press, 2011. Paper: $18.95. (F)

Pyetsukh, Vyacheslav. *The New Moscow Philosophy.* Trans. Krystyna Anna Steiger. Twisted Spoon, 2011. Paper: $16.00. (F)

Queirós, José Maria de Eça. *The Correspondence of Fradique Mendes.* Trans. Gregory Rabassa. Tagus Press, 2011. Paper: $19.95. (F)

Randall, Martin. *9/11 and the Literature of Terror.* Edinburgh Univ. Press, 2011. Cloth: $100.00. (NF)

Sada, Daniel. *Almost Never.* Trans. Katherine Silver. Greywolf Press, 2012. Paper: $16.00. (F)

Salvatore, Joseph. *To Assume a Pleasing Shape*. BOA Editions, 2011. Paper: $14.00. (F)

Savage, Sam. *Glass*. Coffee House Press, 2011. Paper: $15.00. (F)

Seidlinger, Michael J. *In Great Company*. Enigmatic Ink, 2011. Paper: $12.95. (F)

—. *The Day We Delay*. Civil Coping Mechanisms, 2011. Paper: $13.95. (F)

Selgin, Peter. *Confessions of a Left-Handed Man*. Univ. of Iowa Press, 2011. Paper: $19.95. (F)

Słowacki, Juliusz. *Kordian*. Trans. Gerard T. Kapolka. Green Lantern Press, 2010. Paper: $20.00. (F)

Spatola, Adriano. *The Porthole*. Trans. Beppe Cavatorta and Polly Geller. Otis Books / Seismicity Editions & Agincourt Press, 2011. Paper: $12.95. (F)

Spiegelman, Art. *MetaMaus: A Look Inside a Modern Classic, Maus*. Pantheon, 2011. Cloth: $35.00. (NF)

Spurgeon, Sara L., ed. *Cormac McCarthy: All the Pretty Horses, No Country for Old Men, The Road*. Continuum, 2011. Paper: $29.95. (NF)

Standley, Vincent. *A Mortal Affect*. Calamari Press, 2011. Paper: $18.00. (F)

Stroh, Silke. *Uneasy Subjects: Postcolonialism and Scottish Gaelic Poetry*. Rodopi, 2011. Cloth: $114.00. (NF)

Stump, Jordan. *The Other Book: Bewilderments of Fiction*. Univ. of Nebraska Press, 2011. Cloth: $30.00. (NF)

Tarnawsky, Yuriy. *Short Tails*. Civil Coping Mechanisms, 2011. Paper: $17.95. (F)

Taylor, John. *Paths to Contemporary French Literature, Volume 3*. Transaction Publishers, 2011. Cloth: $39.95. (NF)

Taylor, Keith and Laura Kasische, eds. *Ghost Writers: Us Haunting Them*. Wayne State Univ. Press, 2011. Paper: $18.95. (F)

Tusquets, Esther. *Seven Views of the Same Landscape*. Trans. Barbara F. Ichiishi. Host Publications, 2011. Cloth: $30.00. (F)

Vicari, Justin. *The Professional Weepers*. Pavement Saw Press, 2011. Paper: $14.00. (P)

Wittkopf, Gabrielle. *The Necrophiliac*. Trans. Don Bapst. ECW Press, 2011. Paper: $14.95. (F)

Zambreno, Kate. *Green Girl*. Emergency Press, 2011. Paper: $16.00. (F)

Zlosnik, Sue. *Patrick McGrath*. Univ. of Wales Press, 2011. Paper: $25.00. (NF)

Zweig, Stefan. *Beware of Pity*. Trans. Anthea Bell. Pushkin Press, 2011. Paper: £8.99. (F)

Contributors

Hopper, Keith and Neil Murphy. "A(nother) Bash in the Tunnel," 3: 9–20.

Howard, Gerald. "Gilbert Sorrentino's Bay Ridge: A Guided Tour," 2: 149–158.

Jeppeson, Travis. "Itchy Homo, Or Why Am I So Terrible," 1: 136–145.

Klein, David. "The Five Percent Paradox: Excerpts from an Interview with Gary Indiana," 1: 24–31.

Koestenbaum, Wayne. "Thomas Bernhard's Virtues," 1: 53–55.

Kostelanetz, Richard. "Memoir of my Failures," 1: 20–23.

Krim, Seymour. "For my Brothers and Sisters in the Failure Business," 1: 104–115.

Lethem, Jonathan. "Sorrentino's *Something Said*," 2: 118–121.

Lumsden, Robert. "Voidance in *The Third Policeman*," 3: 49–61.

Miller, Tyrus. "Pitiless Flaws Restored: Satiric Truth in Gilbert Sorrentino's *Flawless Play Restored: The Masque of Fungo*," 2: 40–52.

Murphy, Neil. "Flann O'Brien's *The Hard Life* & the Gaze of the Medusa," 3: 148–161.

Myles, Eileen. "Solo Performance" from *Inferno: A Poet's Novel*, 1: 36–50.

Nejezchleb, Amy. "A *Saga* to Remember: Flann O'Brien's Unfinished Novel," 3: 205–218.

Nolan, Val. "Flann, Fantasy, and Science Fiction: O'Brien's Surprising Synthesis," 3: 178–190.

Ó Conchubhair, Brian. "*An Béal Bocht* and *An tOileánach*: Writing on the Margin—Gaelic Glosses or Postmodern Marginalia?", 3: 191–204.

Perl, Jed. "Connolly's Unquiet," 1: 67–79.

Perloff, Marjorie. "Sorrentino the Reviewer," 2: 113–117.

Robin, Thierry. "Representation as a Hollow Form or the Paradoxical Magic of Idiocy and Skepticism in Flann O'Brien's Works," 3: 33–48.

Ruczaj, Maciej. "Infernal Poetics / Infernal Ethics: *The Third Policeman* Between Medieval and (Post)Modern Netherworlds," 3: 91–105.

Scott, Ramsey. "*Mulligan Stew* and the Political Fantasies of America's Literary Factions," 2: 53–77.

"Selected Bitchery from the Gilbert Sorrentino/Dalkey Archive Press Correspondence," 1: 11, 51–52, 118–119.

Seshadri, Vijay. "Gilbert Sorrentino's Days Off," 2: 122–124.

Sobelle, Stefanie. "*Mulligan Stew* and Gilbert Sorrentino's Aesthetics of Failure," 2: 13–39.

—. Further Reading: A Selected Bibliography, 2: 107–109.

Sorrentino, Gilbert. "What Religion Do the Ants Have?" 2: 169–178.

Taylor, Justin. "Eulogy," 1: 32–35.

Visel, Dan. "The Failing of Americans," 1: 80–103.

Warren, Kenneth. "Mr. Sorrentino's Neighborhood," 2: 131–146.

Wang, W. Michelle. "Lightness of Touch: Subtracting Weight from the Narrative Structure of *At Swim-Two-Birds*," 3: 134–137.

Books Reviewed

Aiken, Joan. *The Monkey's Wedding and Other Stories*, 3: 246–247. (James Crossley)

Albahari, David. *Leeches*, 3: 256–257. (Michael Pinker)

Allen, Roberta. *The Dreaming Girl*, 3: 253. (D. Quentin Miller)

Antin, David. *Radical Coherency: Selected Essays on Art and Literature, 1966 to 2005*, 3: 264–265. (Ira S. Murfin)

Ashley, Robert. *Quicksand*, 3: 255–256. (Jeremy M. Davies)

Bachmann, Ingeborg and Paul Celan. *Correspondence*, 3: 263–264. (Mark Tursi)

Bayard, Pierre. *Et si les oeuvres changeaient d'auteur?*, 1: 173–174. (Warren Motte)

Benedetti, Mario. *The Rest is Jungle and Other Stories*, 1: 181–182. (Jeff Waxman)

Bernheimer, Kate. *Horse, Flower, Bird*, 1: 190. (James Crossley)

Bessette, Gérard. *Not for Every Eye*, 3: 244. (Tim Feeney)

Blasim, Hassan. *The Madman of Freedom Square*, 1: 191–192. (Mark Axelrod)

Bursey, Jeff. *Verbatim: A Novel*, 2: 204–205 (Jeff Dewey)

Burton, Gabrielle. *Impatient with Desire*, 1: 188–189. (David Seed)

Butler, Blake and Lily Hoang, eds. *30 Under 30: An Anthology of Innovative Fiction by Younger Writers*, 3: 260–261. (Yevgeniya Traps)

Castellanos Moya, Horacio. *Tyrant Memory*, 2: 197–198. (Jeffrey Zuckerman)

Cixous, Hélène. *Zero's Neighbour: Sam Beckett*, 1: 175–176. (Lily Hoang)

Craig, George. *Writing Beckett's Letters*, 3: 262–263. (Stephen Fisk)

de la Pava, Sergio. *A Naked Singularity*, 2: 198–199. (Tim Feeney)

Delbanco, Nicholas. *Lastingness: The Art of Old Age*, 2: 206–207. (Tayt Harlin)

Ducornet, Rikki. *Netsuke*, 2: 191–192. (Ralph Clare)

Duvert, Tony. *Diary of an Innocent*, 2: 186–187. (Amanda DeMarco)

Enrigue, Álvaro. *Decencia*, 2: 185–186. (Brendan Riley)

Epstein, Alex. *Lunar Savings Time*, 3: 245–246. (Pedro Ponce)

Federman, Raymond. *Shhh: The Story of a Childhood*, 1: 192–193. (Doug Rice)

Fontane, Theodor. *On Tangled Paths: An Everyday Berlin Story*, 3: 247–249. (Brooke Horvath)

—, *No Way Back*, 3: 247–249. (Brooke Horvath)

Fourier, Charles. *The Hierarchies of Cuckoldry and Bankruptcy*, 3: 244–245. (Dylan Suher)

Garcia, Tristan. *Hate: A Romance*, 1: 180–181. (Jeffrey Zuckerman)

Germanacos, Anne. *In the Time of the Girls*, 1: 183–184. (Ralph Clare)

Gladman, Renee. *Event Factory*, 1: 179. (John Madera)

Gomo, Mashingaidze. *A Fine Madness*, 3: 250–251. (Brooke Horvath)

Gordon, Jaimy. *Lord of Misrule*, 2: 188–189. (John Madera)

Grandbois, Peter. *Nahoonkara*, 2: 202–203. (Cynthia Alicia Smith)

Guyotat, Pierre. *Coma*, 2: 201. (Stephen Fisk)

Hoang, Lily. *The Evolutionary Revolution*, 2: 195–196. (A D Jameson)

Holmes, Julia. *Meeks*, 1: 176–177. (Joseph Dewey)

Indiana, Gary. *Last Seen Entering the Biltmore: Plays, Short Fiction, Poems, 1975–2010*, 2: 194–195. (Stefanie Sobelle)

Iyer, Lars. *Spurious*, 2: 192. (D. Quentin Miller)

Jaccottet, Philippe. *And, Nonetheless: Selected Poetry and Prose 1990-2009*, 3: 243. (Nicholas Birns)

Jaffe, Harold. *Paris 60*, 1: 186–187. (Gary Lain)

Jameson, A D. *Amazing Adult Fantasy*, 3: 252. (Robert L. McLaughlin)

Kafka, Franz. *Amerika: The Missing Person*, 2: 207–209. (John Kulka)

Kalich, Richard. *Penthouse F*, 1: 184–185. (Marc Lowe)

Kapil, Bhanu. *Humanimal: A Project for Future Children*, 3: 258–259. (Kass Fleisher)

Karapanou, Margarita. *The Sleepwalker*, 2: 200. (Scott Esposito)

Kassirer, Norma. *Katzenjammered*, 2: 201–202. (Levi Teal)

Katz, Steve. *Time's Wallet*, 3: 253–254. (Mark Axelrod)

Kelly, Robert. *The Logic of the World*, 1: 180. (Mike Meginnis)

Khoury, Elias. *White Masks*, 1: 177–178. (Brooke Horvath)

Kosztolányi, Dezső. *Kornél Esti*, 3: 240–241. (Jeff Waxman)

Krasznahorkai, László and Max Neumann. *Animalinside*, 2: 187–188. (Michael Pinker)

Krzhizanovsky, Sigizmund. *Memories of the Future*, 3: 257–258. (Michael Pinker)

Kronauer, Brigitte. *Women and Clothes*, 2: 189–190. (Yevgeniya Traps)

Levine, Stacey. *The Girl with Brown Fur*, 2: 193. (Pedro Ponce)

Lutz, Gary. *Divorcer*, 3: 259–260. (Greg Gerke)

Martin, Stephen-Paul. *Changing the Subject*, 1: 178–179. (A D Jameson)

Mathews, Harry. *The New Tourism*, 3: 251–252. (David Seed)

Moore, Stephen. *The Novel: An Alternative History: Beginnings to 1600*, 2: 205–206. (A D Jameson)

Myśliwski, Wieslaw. *Stone Upon Stone*, 1: 185–186. (Michael Pinker)

Nádas, Péter. *Parallel Stories*, 3: 239–240. (Jeffrey Zuckerman)

Novy, Adam. *The Avian Gospels*, 1: 187–188. (Tim Feeney)

Nutting, Alissa. *Unclean Jobs for Women and Girls*, 2: 199–200. (Pedro Ponce)

Olsen, Lance. *Calendar of Regrets*, 1: 182–183. (Mark Tursi)

Ríos, Julián. *Puente de Alma*, 1: 174–175. (Brendan Riley)

Rohe, Oliver. *Vacant Lot*, 2: 191–192. (A D Jameson)

Salvayre, Lydie. *Hymne*, 2: 184–185. (Warren Motte)

Schneiderman, Davis. *Drain: a Novel*, 1: 189–190. (Renée E. D'Aoust)

Scliar, Moacyr. *The War in Bom Fim*, 2: 193–194. (Rhett McNeill)

Sebastian, Mihail. *The Accident*, 3: 249–250. (Joseph Dewey)

Slavnikova, Olga, ed. *Squaring the Circle: Winners of the Debut Prize for Fiction*, 1: 193–194. (Michael Pinker)

Sparling, Ken. *Book*, 2: 196–197. (Amanda DeMarco)

Steiner, Robert. *Negative Space*, 1: 191. (Richard Kalich)

Stump, Jordan. *The Other Book: Bewilderments of Fiction*, 3: 261–262. (Nicholas Birns)

Tarnawsky, Yuriy. *Short Tales*, 3: 254–255. (Michelle Tupko)

Taylor, John. *Paths to Contemporary French Literature*, Volume 3, 3: 265–266. (Jeff Bursey)

Todorov, Vladislav. *Zift: A Noir Novel*, 2: 203–204. (Michael Pinker)

Ungar, Antonio. *Tres ataúdes blancos*, 3: 242–243. (Brendan Riley)

Weiner, Steve. *Sweet England*, 3: 241–242. (Joseph Dewey)

THE ORIGINAL
HANDHELD
DEVICE

SUBSCRIBE ONLINE
AND SAVE WITH SPECIAL
CODE "FICTION"

BOMBSITE.COM / SUBSCRIBE

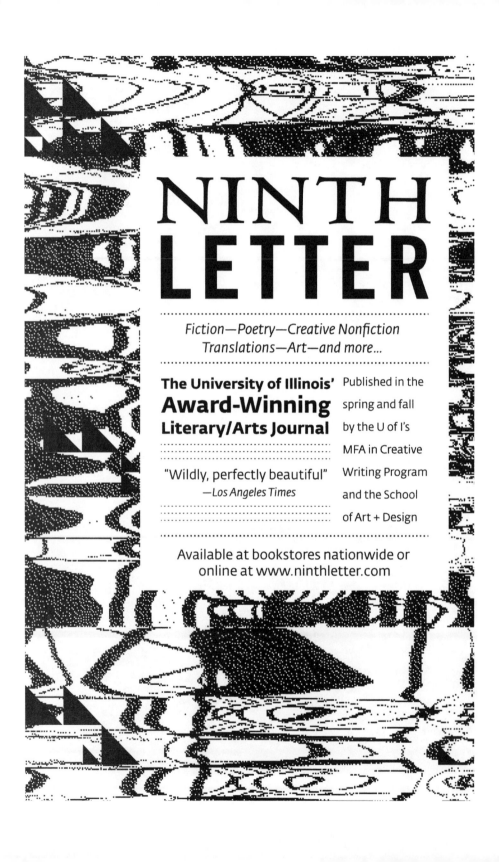

DELILLO FIEDLER GASS PYNCHON
University of Delaware Press
Collections on Contemporary Masters

UNDERWORDS
Perspectives on Don
DeLillo's *Underworld*

**Edited by Joseph Dewey, Steven
G. Kellman, and Irving Malin**

Essays by Jackson R. Bryer,
David Cowart, Kathleen
Fitzpatrick, Joanne Gass, Paul
Gleason, Donald J. Greiner,
Robert McMinn, Thomas Myers,
Ira Nadel, Carl Ostrowski,
Timothy L. Parrish, Marc Singer,
and David Yetter

$39.50

INTO *THE TUNNEL*
Readings of Gass's
Novel

**Edited by Steven G. Kellman
and Irving Malin**

Essays by Rebecca Goldstein,
Donald J. Greiner, Brooke
Horvath, Marcus Klein, Jerome
Klinkowitz, Paul Maliszewski,
James McCourt, Arthur Saltzman,
Susan Stewart, and Heide Ziegler

$35.00

LESLIE FIEDLER
AND AMERICAN
CULTURE

**Edited by Steven G. Kellman
and Irving Malin**

Essays by John Barth, Robert
Boyers, James M. Cox, Joseph
Dewey, R.H.W. Dillard, Geoffrey
Green, Irving Feldman, Leslie
Fiedler, Susan Gubar, Jay L.
Halio, Brooke Horvath, David
Ketterer, R.W.B. Lewis, Sanford
Pinsker, Harold Schechter, Daniel
Schwarz, David R. Slavitt, Daniel
Walden, and Mark Royden
Winchell

$36.50

PYNCHON AND
MASON & DIXON

**Edited by Brooke Horvath and
Irving Malin**

Essays by Jeff Baker, Joseph
Dewey, Bernard Duyfhuizen,
David Foreman, Donald J.
Greiner, Brian McHale, Clifford
S. Mead, Arthur Saltzman,
Thomas H. Schaub, David Seed,
and Victor Strandberg

$39.50

ORDER FROM ASSOCIATED UNIVERSITY PRESSES
2010 Eastpark Blvd., Cranbury, New Jersey 08512
PH 609-655-4770   FAX 609-655-8366   E-mail AUP440@ aol.com

NOON

A LITERARY ANNUAL

1324 LEXINGTON AVENUE   PMB 298   NEW YORK NY 10128

EDITION PRICE $12 DOMESTIC $17 FOREIGN

Dalkey Archive
Scholarly Series

Available Now

Dumitru Tsepeneag and the Canon of
Alternative Literature
LAURA PAVEL

This Is Not a Tragedy:
The Works of David Markson
FRANÇOISE PALLEAU-PAPIN

The Birth of Death and Other Comedies:
The Novels of Russell H. Greenan
TOM WHALEN

When Blackness Rhymes with Blackness
ROWAN RICARDO PHILLIPS

A Community Writing Itself:
Conversations with Vanguard Writers of the Bay Area
SARAH ROSENTHAL, ED.

Aidan Higgins:
The Fragility of Form
NEIL MURPHY, ED.

Nicholas Mosley's Life and Art:
A Biography in Six Interviews
SHIVA RAHBARAN

The Subversive Scribe:
Translating Latin American Fiction
SUZANNE JILL LEVINE

Intersections:
Essays on Richard Powers
STEPHEN J. BURN AND PETER DEMPSEY, EDS.

Phantasms of Matter
in Gogol (and Gombrowicz)
MICHAL OKLOT

Translation in Practice:
A Symposium
GILL PAUL, ED.

Energy of Delusion:
A Book on Plot
VIKTOR SHKLOVSKY

It wasn't until after Dumitru Tsepeneag fled Romania for France in 1971 that he was able to speak frankly about the literary movement that he had helped create. "Oneiricism" wasn't just a new, homegrown form of surrealism, but implicitly a rebuke to the officially mandated socialist and nationalist realism imposed by Ceaușescu on all Romanian authors: here was writing devoted to the logic of dreams, not the grim reality policed by the communist regime. As such, *Dumitru Tsepeneag and the Canon of Alternative Literature* is not just the study of one man's work, but of an entire nation's literary history over the latter half of the twentieth century. The first monograph to appear in English on perhaps the most idiosyncratic and influential Romanian writer working today, *Dumitru Tsepeneag and the Canon of Alternative Literature* places Tsepeneag among the ranks of the great literary innovators—and pranksters—of the twentieth century.

DUMITRU TSEPENEAG AND THE CANON OF
ALTERNATIVE LITERATURE BY LAURA PAVEL

Dumitru Tsepeneag and the Canon of Alternative Literature

LAURA PAVEL
TRANSLATION BY
ALISTAIR IAN BLYTH

Dalkey Archive Scholarly Series
Literary Criticism
$23.95 / paper
ISBN: 978-1-56478-639-5

Laura Pavel is a Romanian essayist and literary critic. She is Associate Professor at the Faculty of Theater and Television of the Babeș-Bolyai University, and Head of the Department of Theater Studies and Media.

The very first book-length study to focus on this seminal American author, *This Is Not a Tragedy* examines David Markson's entire body of work, ranging from his early tongue-in-cheek Western and crime novels to contemporary classics such as *Wittgenstein's Mistress* and *Reader's Block*. Having begun in parody, Markson's writing soon began to fragment, its pieces adding up to a peculiar sort of self-portrait—doubtful and unsteady—and in the process achieving nothing less than a redefinition of the novel form. Written on the verge of silence, David Markson's fiction represents an intimate, unsettling, and unique voice in the cacophony of modern letters, and *This Is Not a Tragedy* charts Markson's attempts to find, in art and language, the solace denied us by life.

This Is Not a Tragedy:
The Works of David Markson

FRANÇOISE PALLEAU-PAPIN

Dalkey Archive Scholarly Series
Literary Criticism
$49.95 / paper
ISBN: 978-1-56478-607-4

THIS IS NOT A TRAGEDY **THE WORKS OF DAVID MARKSON**
FRANÇOISE PALLEAU-PAPIN

Françoise Palleau-Papin teaches American Literature at the Sorbonne Nouvelle University-Paris 3. She has edited a critical study of Patricia Eakins, and published articles on Willa Cather, Carole Maso, John Edgar Wideman, William T. Vollmann, and others.

Russell H. Greenan's *It Happened in Boston?* is one of the most radical narratives to appear in the late 1960s ("this is a book that encompasses everything," as David L. Ulin noted in *Bookforum*). Yet due in large part to the difficulty of classifying Greenan's fiction, many readers are unaware of his other novels. In *The Birth of Death and Other Comedies: The Novels of Russell H. Greenan*, Tom Whalen, drawing widely from the American literary tradition, locates Greenan's lineage in the work of Hawthorne and Poe, "where allegory and dream mingle with and illuminate realism," as well as in the fiction of Twain, West, Hammett, Cain, and Thompson. Examining Greenan's characteristic themes and strategies, Whalen provides perceptive readings of the dark comedies of this criminally neglected American master, and in a coda reflects on Greenan's career and the reception of his work.

The Birth of Death and Other Comedies:
The Novels of Russell H. Greenan

Tom Whalen

Dalkey Archive Scholarly Series
Literary Criticism
$23.95 / paper
ISBN: 978-1-56478-640-1

Tom Whalen is a novelist, poet, translator and author of numerous stories and critical essays. He has written for *Agni, Bookforum, Film Quarterly, The Hopkins Review, The Iowa Review, The Literary Review, Studies in Short Fiction, The Wallace Stevens Journal*, the *Washington Post*, and other publications, and he co-edited the *Review of Contemporary Fiction*'s "Robert Walser Number."

In *When Blackness Rhymes with Blackness*, Rowan Ricardo Phillips pushes African-American poetry to its limits by unraveling "our desire to think of African-American poetry as African-American poetry." Phillips reads African-American poetry as inherently allegorical and thus a successful shorthand for the survival of a poetry but unsuccessful shorthand for the sustenance of its poems. Arguing in favor of the counterintuitive imagination, Phillips demonstrates how these poems tend to refuse their logical insertion into a larger vision and instead dwell indefinitely at the crux between poetry and race, where, when blackness rhymes with blackness, it is left for us to determine whether this juxtaposition contains a vital difference or is just mere repetition.

When Blackness Rhymes with Blackness

Rowan Ricardo Phillips

Dalkey Archive Scholarly Series
Literary Criticism
$25.95 / paper
ISBN: 978-1-56478-583-1

when
blackness
rhymes
with blackness

ROWAN RICARDO PHILLIPS

Rowan Ricardo Phillips's essays, poems, and translations have appeared in numerous publications. He is also the author of *The Ground* (2010). He has taught at Harvard, Columbia, and is currently Associate Professor of English and Director of the Poetry Center at Stony Brook University.

A Community Writing Itself features internationally respected writers Michael Palmer, Nathaniel Mackey, Leslie Scalapino, Brenda Hillman, Kathleen Fraser, Stephen Ratcliffe, Robert Glück, and Barbara Guest, as well as important younger writers Truong Tran, Camille Roy, Juliana Spahr, and Elizabeth Robinson. The book fills a major gap in contemporary poetics, focusing on one of the most vibrant experimental writing communities in the nation. The writers discuss vision and craft, war and peace, race and gender, individuality and collectivity, and the impact of the Bay Area on their work.

A Community Writing Itself Conversations with Vanguard Writers of the Bay Area

Sarah Rosenthal in conversation with:
Michael Palmer **Nathaniel Mackey** Leslie Scalapino
Brenda Hillman Kathleen Fraser **Stephen Ratcliffe**
Robert Glück **Barbara Guest** Truong Tran
Camille Roy Juliana Spahr Elizabeth Robinson

A Community Writing Itself:

Conversations with Vanguard
Writers of the Bay Area

SARAH ROSENTHAL, ED.

Dalkey Archive Scholarly Series
Literature
$29.95 / paper
ISBN: 978-1-56478-584-8

"Sarah Rosenthal's interviews with some of the most engaging and important American poets of the time, all working in the Bay Area, provide vivid commentary on the state of the art and some of the most useful commentary available on the work of each individual writer."

—Charles Bernstein

Drawing together a wide range of focused critical commentary and observation by internationally renowned scholars and writers, this collection of essays offers a major reassessment of Aidan Higgins's body of work almost fifty years after the appearance of his first book, *Felo de Se*. Authors like Annie Proulx, John Banville, Derek Mahon, Dermot Healy, and Higgins himself, represented by a previously uncollected essay, offer a variety of critical and creative commentaries, while scholars such as Keith Hopper, Peter van de Kamp, George O'Brien, and Gerry Dukes contribute exciting new perspectives on all aspects of Higgins's writing. This collection confirms the enduring significance of Aidan Higgins as one of the major writers of our time, and also offers testament that Higgins's work is being rediscovered by a new generation of critics and writers.

Aidan Higgins:
The Fragility of Form

NEIL MURPHY, ED.

Dalkey Archive Scholarly Series
Literary Criticism
$29.95 / paper
ISBN: 978-1-56478-562-6

AIDAN HIGGINS:
THE FRAGILITY
OF FORM

*edited by Neil Murphy
with essays from*

ANNIE PROULX
JOHN BANVILLE
DERMOT HEALY
DEREK MAHON
GERRY DUKES
KEITH HOPPER
GEORGE O'BRIEN
PETER VAN DE KAMP
& AIDAN HIGGINS

Neil Murphy has previously taught at the University of Ulster and the American University of Beirut, and is currently Associate Professor of Contemporary Literature at NTU, Singapore. He is the author of several books on Irish fiction and contemporary literature and has published numerous articles on contemporary Irish fiction, on postmodernism, and on Aidan Higgins. He is currently writing a book on contemporary fiction and aesthetics.

The son of Sir Oswald Mosley, founder of the British Union
of Fascists in the 1930s, and himself the inheritor of a noble
title, Nicholas Mosley nonetheless fought bravely for Britain
during World War II and became a tireless anti-apartheid
campaigner thereafter, finding little sense in living the "hypocritical" life of a British aristocrat . . . and yet his numerous
extramarital affairs came to shake not only the foundations of
his marriage to his first wife, Rosemary, but also his growing
sense of himself as a religious man.

The present biography is written in the form of six interviews, each focusing upon one aspect of Mosley's life—from
his childhood and experiences as a young man, up to his reflections on religion, science, philosophy, and their impact on
the political and ideological developments of our time.

Nicholas Mosley's Life and Art

a biography in six interviews
by shiva rahbaran

Nicholas Mosley's Life and Art:

A Biography in Six Interviews

SHIVA RAHBARAN

Dalkey Archive Scholarly Series
Literary Criticism
$25.95 / paper
ISBN: 978-1-56478-564-0

"Fascinating—Nicholas Mosley is the world's most brilliant con-
versationalist and this book catches the flavour of that."
—A. N. Wilson

To most of us, "subversion" means political subversion, but *The Subversive Scribe* is about collaboration not with an enemy, but with texts and between writers. Though Suzanne Jill Levine is the translator of some of the most inventive and revolutionary Latin American authors of the twentieth century—including Julio Cortázar, G. Cabrera Infante, Manuel Puig, and Severo Sarduy—here she considers the act of translation itself to be a form of subversion. Rather than regret translation's shortcomings, Levine stresses how translation is itself a creative act, unearthing a version lying dormant beneath an original work, and animating it, like some mad scientist, in order to create a text illuminated and motivated by the original. In *The Subversive Scribe*, one of our most versatile and creative translators gives us an intimate and entertaining overview of the tricky relationships lying behind the art of literary translation.

The Subversive Scribe:
Translating Latin American Fiction

SUZANNE JILL LEVINE

Dalkey Archive Scholarly Series
Literary Criticism
$13.95 / paper
ISBN: 978-1-56478-563-3

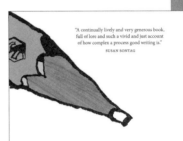

"A continually lively and very generous book, full of lore and such a vivid and just account of how complex a process good writing is."
SUSAN SONTAG

THE SUBVERSIVE SCRIBE
Translating Latin American Fiction
Suzanne Jill Levine

"A fascinating glimpse into the mental gyrations of a first-class literary translator at work."
—Clifford Landers, *Latin American Research Review*

Since his first novel was published in 1985, Richard Powers has assembled a body of work whose intellectual breadth and imaginative energy bears comparison with that of any writer working today. *Intersections: Essays on Richard Powers* pays tribute to that achievement by collecting seventeen essays—by leading literary critics, philosophers, and a novelist—each of which offers important insights into Powers's narrative craft and the intellectual grids that underlie his work. Powers's novels are distinguished by both their multiple narrative forms and their sophisticated synthesis of diverse fields of knowledge; to attempt to adequately address this range, the contributors to this volume mix their study of Powers's narrative innovations with eclectic interdisciplinary perspectives, which range from photography and systems theory to ecocriticism and neuroscience. The volume concludes with an essay by Powers himself.

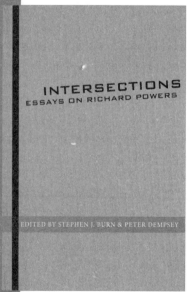

Intersections:
Essays on Richard Powers

STEPHEN J. BURN
& PETER DEMPSEY, EDS.

Dalkey Archive Scholarly Series
Literary Criticism
$29.95 / paper
ISBN: 978-1-56478-508-4

Contributors: Jon Adams, Sven Birkerts, Stephen J. Burn, David Cowart, Anca Cristofovici, Daniel C. Dennett, Joseph Dewey, Charles B. Harris, Scott Hermanson, Jenell Johnson, Bruno Latour, Barry Lewis, Paul Maliszewski, Richard Powers, Carter Scholz, Trey Strecker, Joseph Tabbi, and Patti White.

An investigation into the problem of art and matter in the work of Nikolai Gogol, and, indirectly, into the Neoplatonic tradition in Russian literature, *Phantasms of Matter* constitutes a rigorous examination of Gogol's "image of matter," as well as an attempt to enumerate the rules of its construction. After developing an artistic language corresponding to the Neoplatonic discourse on matter, Gogol subsequently abandoned literature; yet this transposition of the Neoplatonic problem has recurred frequently in Russian and Slavic literature following his death. Oklot therefore extends this investigation into the work of the Polish author Witold Gombrowicz, allowing unique parallels to be drawn between the writings of these two giants of world literature.

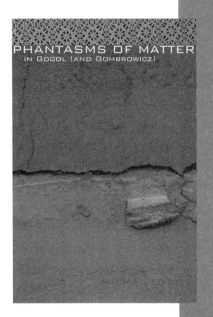

Phantasms of Matter
in Gogol (and Gombrowicz)

MICHAL OKLOT

Dalkey Archive Scholarly Series
Literary Criticism
$34.95 / paper
ISBN: 978-1-56478-494-0

"Combining complex philosophical analysis with uncannily intelligent close readings, Oklot provides strikingly new interpretations of the work of Gogol and Gombrowicz while simultaneously focusing attention on literary manifestations of new–Platonic thought. *Phantasms of Matter* is a tour de force."
—Andrew Wachtel, Northwestern University

Though translation is a vital part of any vibrant literary culture, no practical guide to the process of translating foreign works into English and preparing them for publication has yet been made available to prospective translators, editors, or readers. In February 2008, editors and translators from the US and UK came together at the British Council in London to discuss "best practices" for the translation of literary works into English. This volume comprises the results of that meeting—a collection of summaries, suggestions, and instructions from leading literary translators and publishers. It is intended as an introduction, the first in an ongoing series of documents to be published by Dalkey Archive Press that will address the challenges faced by translators, publishers, reviewers, and readers of literary translations.

Translation in Practice:
A Symposium

GILL PAUL, ED.

Dalkey Archive Scholarly Series
Literary Criticism
$13.95 / paper
ISBN: 978-1-56478-548-0

Contributors: Ros Schwartz (translator, director of the British Translators' Association), Euan Cameron (translator), Rebecca Carter (editor, Random House), Christina Thomas (freelance editor, publisher of *Editing Matters*), Martin Riker (associate director, Dalkey Archive Press), and numerous other translators, editors, and publishers.

One of the greatest literary minds of the twentieth century, Viktor Shklovsky writes the critical equivalent of what Ross Chambers calls "loiterature"—writing that roams, playfully digresses, moving freely between the literary work and the world. In *Energy of Delusion*, a masterpiece that Shklovsky worked on over thirty years, he turns his unique critical sensibility to Tolstoy's life and novels, applying the famous "formalist method" he invented in the 1920s to Tolstoy's massive body of work, and at the same time taking Tolstoy (as well as Boccaccio, Pushkin, Chekhov, Dostoevsky, and Turgenev) as a springboard to consider the devices of literature—how novels work and what they do.

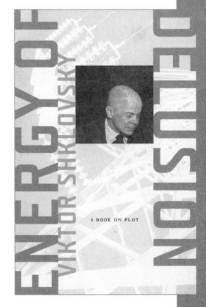

Energy of Delusion:
A Book on Plot

Viktor Shklovsky
Translation by
Shushan Avagyan

Dalkey Archive Scholarly Series
Literary Criticism
$14.95 / paper
ISBN: 978-1-56478-426-1

"A rambling, digressive stylist, Shklovsky throws off brilliant aperçus on every page . . . Like an architect's blueprint, [he] lays bare the joists and studs that hold up the house of fiction."
—Michael Dirda, *Washington Post*

"Perhaps because he is such an unlikely Tolstoyan, Viktor Shklovsky's writing on Tolstoy is always absorbing and often brilliant."
—*Russian Review*

ORDER FORM

Individuals may use this form to subscribe to the *Review of Contemporary Fiction* or to order back issues of the *Review* and Dalkey Archive titles at a discount (see below for details).

Title	ISBN	Quantity	Price

Subtotal _____

Less Discount _____
(10% for one book, 20% for two or more books, and
25% for Scholarly titles advertised in this issue)
Subtotal _____

Plus Postage _____
(U.S. $3 + $1 per book; foreign $7 + $5 per book)

1 Year Individual Subscription to the **Review** _____
($17 U.S.; $22.60 Canada; $32.60 all other countries)

Total _____

Mailing Address _____

_____

_____

_____

xxxi/3

Credit card payment ☐ Visa ☐ Mastercard

Acct. # _____ Exp. date _____

Name on card _____ Phone # _____

Billing zip code _____

Please make checks (in U.S. dollars only) payable to *Dalkey Archive Press.*

mail or fax this form to: Dalkey Archive Press, University of Illinois, 1805 S. Wright Street, MC-011, Champaign, IL 61820
fax: 217.244.9142 tel: 217.244.5700